The Hap
of Thei

The Happiest Days of Their Lives?

*Nineteenth-century education
through the eyes of those who were there*

Marion Aldis and Pam Inder

CHAPLIN BOOKS

www.chaplinbooks.co.uk

Copyright © Marion Aldis and Pam Inder

First published in 2016 by Chaplin Books

ISBN 978-1-911105-01-5

A CIP catalogue record for this book is available from The British Library

Design by Michael Walsh at The Better Book Company

Printed by Imprint Digital

Chaplin Books
1 Eliza Place
Gosport PO12 4UN
Tel: 023 9252 9020
www.chaplinbooks.co.uk

Contents

Acknowledgements

We would like to thank the following people and institutions for their help:

Gavin Beetham (Thurlaston School), Barbara Bender, Birmingham University Special Collections, the Branscombe Project, Mrs June Bruxner-Randall and family, J J Heath Caldwell, Cumbria Record Office, Derbyshire Record Office, Harrow School Archive, Leicestershire Record Office, Mrs I Nicholson, Norfolk Record Office, Jean and Martin Norgate, Norwich Millennium Library, the late Averil Scott Moncrieff, Humphrey and Judy Scott Moncrieff, Colin and Joyce Shenton, John and Sue Sneyd, Staffordshire Record Office, Mark Stephens and the Stephens family, Marjorie and John Taylor and the Wigton Old Scholars Association (WOSA).

Sources of Illustrations

Ancestry.co.uk (p131), Birmingham University Cadbury Research Library Special Collections (p130), the Branscombe Project (pp175, 176, 187), Mrs June Bruxner-Randall and family (p190), Debenham History Society (pp14, 16), Devonia (p171), Harrow School Archive (pp112, 113, 114, 116, 117, 120), Hastings Museum (pxiv), J J Heath Caldwell (pp59, 60, 61, 64, 65, 83, 86), Leicestershire Record Office (pp190, 192, 193, 196), Margaret Maidment History of Handmade Lace (p183), Mrs I Nicholson (pp222, 232), Norfolk Record Office (pp42, 56) Jean and Martin Norgate (p216), Popular Science Monthly 1875-6 (p180a & b), Royal Collection (p183), Mark Stephens and the Stephens family (pp128, 131), WOSA (pp148, 149, 150, 153, 154, 156, 166).

The following images came from Wikimedia Commons and are attributed as follows:

Anemone-projectors (p161), Andim2003/Gallery/France (p134), Jonathan Billingsworth (p170), Ian Calderwood (p236), Sarah Charlesworth (p169), C J DUB (p136), Patrick Clenet 2005 (p137), Richard Dear (p228), Ncadine-commonswiki (p135), Hawobo (p140b), Alan Heardman (p96), Tony Hisgett (p242), David Iliff License: CC-BY-SA 3.0 (p265), Remi Mathis (p238), Nessy (p104), Andrew Smith (p217), Stavros1 (p112), Heilfort Steffen (p140a), Dan Taylor (p248), Pierre Terre (p43), Wellcome Images (pix).

All other images are in private collections or are the authors' own photographs.

Notes on Money

It is never possible to be entirely accurate when converting historical prices to their modern equivalents. The figures below are based on the conversion tables provided by National Archives and give some idea of the changing value of £10 worth of early twenty-first century money at various points in the nineteenth century.

1800	£321.70	1860	£431.60
1810	£339.60	1870	£457.00
1820	£419.20	1880	£483.10
1830	£494.90	1890	£598.90
1840	£441.00	1900	£570.60
1850	£585.30		

Notes on Quotations

The various diarists recorded dates in different ways at different times, as the mood took them – Sep/Sept/September 2/2nd/second and so on. For consistency and ease of reading we have recorded all dates in full (eg September 2nd) and to a standard format. Similarly, punctuation has been added to some entries to make them easier to read.

Introduction

For many people, the words 'nineteenth-century schooling' conjure up memories of *Tom Brown's Schooldays*, Lowood School in *Jane Eyre* or Dotheboys Hall in *Nicholas Nickleby*. They may well also bring to mind sadistic schoolmasters in gowns and mortarboards ever ready to give their charges a vicious caning, little boys in top hats and Eton jackets, uncontrolled bullying, Latin tags and learning-by-heart, little girls in white pinafores meticulously stitching away at samplers, and the smell of chalk and ink. Although there are elements of truth in this jumble of images, there are also many misconceptions.

THE SLOGGER IS THROWN HEAVILY FOR THE THIRD
TIME

Illustration by Louis Rhead from Tom Brown's Schooldays, 1911

v

Our particular interest is in diaries, and for the last twenty years we have been studying the diaries and personal papers of nineteenth-century women. We soon came to realise that original accounts often showed a very different picture to that generally portrayed. In the beginning our interest was sparked by a lady who recorded in her diary in the 1860s that she had just bought some stocks and shares in the newly built Canadian and Indian railways. A married woman buying stocks and shares in the mid-nineteenth century? Surely not? But she did.[1] Until the Married Women's Property Acts of 1870 and 1882, everything a woman owned when she got married, except her clothes and personal belongings, became her husband's. She could own property in her own name but she could not administer it or sell it without her husband's consent. But women were inventive and, like our buyer of railway shares, they found ways to have some say in their lives despite the limitations the law placed on them.

We found that even working women were not completely subordinate to their menfolk. There were, for example, women like Sarah Bromley who worked as a 'paintress' in the Staffordshire potteries; she married in 1812 but abandoned her drunken husband several times, leaving him for good in 1836, and raised her younger children with the money she earned herself – despite the fact that the law said it belonged to him.[2] And such resourceful women were not as unusual as one might suppose.

As social historians we had *thought* we knew a lot about women in the nineteenth century but found a good deal that contradicted accepted wisdom. In the course of our research, we came across some children's letters and diaries – and we wondered whether, on closer examination, they would throw a similar beam of light on to nineteenth century education. So we started looking.

One of our first discoveries was the dubious quality of the education for which apparently intelligent and caring parents were willing to pay good money. '... I believe that water is 2

kinds of air and that there are several kinds of earth those are called elements which cannot be analysed there are 46', wrote Ann Marsh Caldwell in 1805. She was fourteen. Her education at home was a complete rag-bag of anything her tutors came up with on any given day – from how to grow peaches in Kentucky to the arcane workings of the French lottery. [3]

Gerald Upcher, who went to Harrow School, recorded in his diary in 1858, 'This evening I went to a lecture given by Mr J Baker about the Philosophy of Water. It was very interesting … he showed us some pretty experiments.'[4] 'The Philosophy of Water' harks back to Thales of Miletus, a pre-Socratic Greek philosopher, who attempted to explain natural phenomena without reference to mythology. Thales' hypothesis about the nature of matter was that it was all composed of a single substance – water. The theory was obviously still alive and well and being disseminated at Harrow in the 1850s.

A decade later, over in Norwich, little Fred Hibgame, along with twenty or more six- and seven-year-old boys, were having the three Rs beaten into them by 'a woman uneducated and bigoted even beyond her class at that period' – and their parents were paying her for the privilege.[5]

By 1800 most upper- and middle-class families regarded education as important. And they had a wide range of options. Their sons could go to one of the major public schools like Eton or Harrow or Rugby, or to one of their lesser known – but cheaper – imitators. 'Sensitive' children could be home-schooled by tutors or sent to a 'school' that was run in the home of a private individual. Many clergymen augmented their salaries in this way. Early schooling for boys was often in a 'dame' school, frequently run by a spinster or widow in her own home. Girls sometimes went to such schools for the whole of their education, or were taught at home by a governess or by visiting tutors. There was no regulation of the private sector and teachers were not necessarily well-educated or compassionate; for some it was the only job open to them and they disliked and resented the children in their charge. Equally, there were others who were wise and inspirational, loved and fondly remembered by their pupils.

The education of the poor was a different matter and it was largely down to chance as to whether or not there was a school in a particular area, though a range of different types of school did exist for poor children. Some parishes had endowed schools from an early date. Stapleton, in the wilds of Cumbria, was an unlikely case in point with a school founded in the 1770s.[6] Some of the more enlightened mill owners – like the Greggs at Styal or David Dale at New Lanark – made provision for their child employees to attend Sunday School to learn basic reading and writing as well as Bible stories, and many clergymen ran similar Sunday Schools in their own parishes. In areas dominated by a particular craft like lacemaking, embroidery or straw-plaiting there were craft schools which also taught the rudiments of literacy.

In some slum districts in the big cities there were 'ragged schools' – charities where destitute children could be taught and helped for free. The first of these dated from the late eighteenth century but most were established after 1840. On January 15th 1861, Mr Lewis, Secretary to the school in George Yard, Whitechapel, told John Hollingshead:

> We have lately had a number of boys in a most distressing state – homeless, hungry, and almost naked … We have paid for their lodgings, at various lodging-houses, night after night; but now with this severe weather, and the mass of distress it has brought around us, matters have come to such a pass we are compelled to ask the public to lend us a helping hand in our extremity. We have taken a place to shelter them in, and earnestly ask for help to go on. Old boots and shoes, old clothes, old rugs or blankets, rice, potatoes, oatmeal, &c., will be most acceptable. To send these helpless ones adrift is, apart from anything else, to make thieves of them. [7]

These schools were obviously doing a great deal more than simply providing an education.

The National School movement was established by the Church of England in 1811 and the aim was to have a school

The Ragged School, George Yard, St Jude's, Whitechapel. In 1861 the school had 400 boys on its books and - if the image is to be believed – a few girls. There seem to have been at least five classes going on in the same room, and we can see the 'monitorial system' in operation – the teacher taught the older, brighter children who passed on what they had learnt to their peers

in every parish, linked to the local church, teaching Christian values and the three Rs, and basic housewifery to the girls. From 1833 the movement received state support, though in fact many parishes did not acquire a school until towards the end of the century.

Nonetheless, ninteenth-century literacy rates were surprisingly high. We only have to look at the letters ordinary people sent to one another, the diaries they kept or the books they read to realise the high standard many people reached. In 1750 roughly a third of men and two thirds of women had been illiterate. These figures are based on the numbers able to sign their own name in the marriage register – which by any standards is a fairly simplistic measure and takes no account of those individuals who chose never to marry. It also probably gives a false impression. Almost everyone who can write can read – but not everyone who could read was necessarily comfortable writing. Literate wives, for example, may have signed the register with a cross so as not to embarrass their illiterate husbands. People unsure of their own penmanship may have been unwilling to demonstrate their lack of skill in front of an educated authority figure like the local clergyman. On the other hand, some individuals who could write their name could probably not have written much else. There was little apparent change in literacy levels between 1750 and 1820, but by 1870 – a watershed point in the history of British education – 76 percent of the population were capable of signing their own name.[8]

It was in the 1860s that the government began to accept responsibility for education and instituted a series of commissions to produce reports[9]. As a result, reforms of both the public school and grammar school systems were introduced, but it was in the field of elementary education that the greatest changes were seen – even though there were still many wealthy and privileged people who saw the education of all as a threat to their own position. Robert Lowe's laconic statement to Parliament, '… if they are to be our masters I suppose we had better educate them …' probably reflected the attitude of many of his class.[10]

Forster's Elementary Education Act of 1870 established the principle that all children between the ages of five and thirteen should attend school and allowed for the setting up of secular Board Schools in areas where there was no National or charity school provision. However, implementation of the act was patchy and it was difficult to enforce because education was still not free. Families paid a penny a week for the first three children they had in school – the fourth child and any subsequent children were educated free of charge. There were a series of further education acts and in 1880 school attendance was made compulsory. Finally, in 1891 it was made free.[11] This made universal literacy a realisable goal, and by 1900 an estimated 97 percent of the British population could read and write.[12]

The National School movement and the Board schools were excellent in theory. Teachers were trained and certificated, children passed through six carefully regulated 'standards', their progress was externally monitored, textbooks were supplied, schools were inspected regularly, unsatisfactory teachers could be dismissed and there were financial incentives for schools to succeed. But people were the problem. Parents who had themselves received little or no education could not see the value of keeping their older children in school when they could be earning their keep. The reports from parish councils to the National Society for Religious Education show clearly what would-be educators were up against. At West Harling in Norfolk, for example, the local vicar wrote '... the poor are desirous of having their children instructed and parishioners are willing to bear the cost ... they will be kept at school until they can read their Bible if their parents can so long spare them ... and we hope to give many of them at least a little writing if not arithmetic ...'[13]

The problem was that a vast number of working families desperately needed the few pennies children could earn; contributing to the family income mattered more than learning to read and write. And in farming communities, helping to get the harvest in would always be more important than attending school regularly. Some village schoolteachers even re-arranged term times to take account of the agricultural year.

But it was not only the poor whose education was cut short. It is interesting to note that many well-to-do families only sent their children to boarding school for a short period. In the late 1850s, for example, John Sneyd sent his youngest son, Gustavus, to Rugby for a year.[14] Most of the children at Wigton in the 1890s were only there for a couple of years.[15] Living away from home was seen as an integral part of education in these families – but at the end of their stint away, the children would come home to be tutored by the local clergyman for university entrance, for example, or spend a period working on the family estate, in the family business, or for someone else. The time at school was seen as an opportunity for children, particularly boys, to make friends and contacts from their own social or business background who would be useful to them in the future – many families saw this as much more important than the acquisition of a smattering of Latin and Greek.

The education offered to well-to-do girls was very different from that offered to their brothers. Caroline Bingley in *Pride and Prejudice* (first published in 1813) details the education a respectable girl should receive:

> A woman must have a thorough knowledge of music, singing, drawing, dancing, and the modern languages ...; and besides all this, she must possess a certain something in her air and manner of walking, the tone of her voice, her address and expressions ...

– and above all, she must not appear to be more intelligent that the young man she hoped to marry. Ann Marsh Caldwell, born in 1791, railed against this convention.[16] She was clever, keen to learn, and had all the makings of a 'bluestocking', the derogatory term used for women with intellectual interests. But for many more years, society would do all it could to silence and tame young women like Ann. For much of the Victorian period respectable society believed in the doctrine of 'separate spheres' – women were intellectually inferior to men but morally superior; their sphere was domesticity while men dealt with the wider world. But there were always intelligent women who wanted more from their lives than to be the 'angel in the home.'

In 1847 Tennyson wrote a satirical poem – *The Princess, a Medley* – in which he has a young woman called Lilia put the case for women's education, a case he and many like him clearly considered to be totally ridiculous.

> Ah, were I something great! I wish I were
> Some mighty poetess, I would shame you then,
> That love to keep us children! O I wish
> That I were some great princess, I would build
> Far off from men a college like a man's ...

But not all men agreed. A year after this was written, Frederick Denison Maurice, Professor of English Literature and History at King's College, London, founded Queen's College in Harley Street (now an independent girls' school) to provide evening classes for governesses in such 'masculine' subjects as Latin, history, mathematics and moral philosophy. Professor Maurice recognised that one of the problems for girls was that their teachers had themselves often received a fairly inadequate education. If the girls of the future were to fulfil their potential, the people teaching them had to be given the opportunity to fulfil theirs. Queen's was the first college in the world to award academic qualifications to women and five years after it was founded it was given a royal charter. Only a comparatively small number of the great army of British governesses could attend Queen's College – but its alumni included some figures who became highly influential in the field of women's education – notably Sophia Jex-Blake, one of the founders of the London School of Medicine for Women and the UK's first female doctor, Miss Frances Buss, founder of the North London Collegiate School for Ladies, and Miss Dorothea Beale, one of the first principals of Cheltenham Ladies' College.[17] Such dedicated career women were not always respected, even by the girls they taught, for whom marriage was still of paramount importance:

Sophia Jex-Blake (1840-1912). She was one of the first women doctors in the UK and campaigned for women to receive medical training

'Miss Buss and Miss Beale,
Cupid's darts do not feel.
How different from us,
Miss Beale and Miss Buss' [18]

ran a well-known satirical rhyme.

Not until the latter part of the century did attitudes to girls' education really begin to change, partly as a result of the activities of the 'Ladies of Langham Place' (Barbara Leigh Smith, better known by her married name of Barbara Bodichon, Bessie Rayner Parkes and their friends) and the pioneering work of the Association for Promoting the Higher Education of Women (AEW).[19]

Crayon sketch of Barbara Bodichon by Samuel Lawrence, 1880
from a sketch made in 1861

Girton College, Cambridge was established by Barbara Bodichon and Emily Davies in 1869; Newnham College opened three years later, the brain child of Henry Sidgwick and Millicent Garrett Fawcett, another Langham Place lady – though the young lady students all had to live in Hitchin, a safe distance from the male undergraduates and the life of the university proper. The next university to open its doors to women was in London – King's College in 1878 – this was quickly followed by four Oxford colleges: Lady Margaret Hall and Somerville opened in 1879, followed by St Hugh's in 1886 and St Hilda's in 1893. But the women undergraduates were often ridiculed, there were still very few of them and – until 1920 – they were not allowed to take full degrees.

Nineteenth-century women students also faced opposition from the clergy and in particular from the medical profession which warned that excessive study would cause 'menstrual disability' and 'anorexia scholastica'. The girls would become thin, their wombs would shrivel, and they would be unlikely to marry or bear children.[20] Not surprisingly, many fathers were unwilling to let their girls run the risk of such ailments – and many women, even pioneers of women's education, believed at least some of the doctors' propaganda. None of the girls featured in this book would have been immune from these attitudes.

We do not pretend that this book will give you a complete history of education in the nineteenth century – that is not our purpose. What we have tried to do is to give you a snapshot – a brief record – of life in various schools over a period of months or years, from the perspective of the children or teachers who were there at the time. We believe there is value in the detail such accounts provide – though of course the approach also has its limitations.

The schools and individuals we describe are not necessarily typical, but nor are they atypical. Not all clergymen, for example, were as tolerant as Mr Cornish and not all boarding schools were as progressive as Wigton. Dame school teachers could be as vicious as Miss Paraman, or as kind as the Miss

Cranes, or anything in between. Children from well-to-do families were more likely to write diaries than children from homes where reading and writing were seldom practised, and it was only the children at boarding school who wrote letters home. This does mean that many of our subjects came from middle- and upper-class backgrounds – but we have tried to balance that to some extent by using 'official' sources like log books and reports to describe the regime in a lace school and in two National schools. Nonetheless, we acknowledge that there are types of school that we have not covered at all – Sunday schools, grammar schools and industrial schools, for example.

Through this book we hope you will gain a picture of the school life of a number of children, be able to glimpse the backgrounds from which they came and learn what they did with the rest of their lives, because – or in spite – of their education. We hope that you will find our subjects as engaging and alive as we have.

Marion Aldis and Pam Inder

Endnotes

1   Inder, Pam and Aldis, Marion, *Finding Susanna*, Churnet Valley Books, 2002.

2   Inder, Pam and Aldis, Marion, *Nine Staffordshire Women*, History Press, 2010.

3   See chapter 3.

4   See chapter 5.

5   See chapter 2.

6   See chapter 10.

7   Hollingshead, *Ragged London*, 1861 accessed at www.mernick.org.uk/thhol/raglon02.html

8   ourworldindata.org/data/education-knowledge/literacy/

9   The Clarendon Commission investigated the public schools and led to the Public Schools' Act of 1868; the Schools Inquiry Commission under Lord Taunton looked at grammar schools and resulted in the Endowed Schools' Act of 1879; and the reports of the Royal Commission for the state of popular education in England, under the Duke of Newcastle, formed the basis for the Elementary Education Act of 1870.

10 Cassell's *History of England* Vol VI, p.533. Lowe was Chancellor of the Exchequer from 1868 to 1873 and Home Secretary from 1873 to 1874.

11 For an overview see Gillard, Derek, *Education in England, a brief history*, 201. educationengland.org.uk/history/chapter03.html

12 ourworldindata.org/data/education-knowledge/literacy/

13 Norfolk County Record Office, West Harling PD27.

14 *Finding Susanna*, op. cit.

15 See chapter 7.

16 See chapter 3.

17 Wikipedia – Queen's College.

18 www.britannica.com/EBchecked/topic/86327/Frances_Buss

19 Lacey, C A, *Barbara Leigh Smith Bodichon and the Langham Place Group:3* (Women's Source Library), Routledge, 2010

20 A key proponent of this theory was Dr William Acton who published *The Functions and Disorders of the Reproductive Organs* in 1862.

The collector of 'curicsilis'

Boxwood House Leamington February 2nd

My Dear Aunttie,

I aM happy and well at school. I hope you and Papa are quite well and going on well. There are 6 Miss Cranes and more than 20 boys. I must write more next time love to all

I remain

Your affectionate Mephew RDT Sneyd

PS I am sorry my Rabbit is dead

So ran Ralph De Tunstall Sneyd's first letter home from school. The year was 1871, he was eight years old and the school was in Leamington Spa. Boxwood House was in Beauchamp Place and it was a fine, five-storeyed neo-classical building.

Engraving of Beauchamp Square, c.1860. The Miss Cranes' school was in one of the houses on the right

Anyone could set up a school at this date and the Miss Cranes would not have had any sort of training. It would have been a question of luck as to whether or not they were good teachers – but the Cranes do seem to have been kind and fond of the little boys in their care.

Ralph's mother had died of puerperal fever soon after he was born and he had been brought up by Susanna Ingleby, his aunt, who had moved in to look after her widowed brother, John William Sneyd, and little 'Ralphy'. Ralphy called her 'Aunty Susan'. It was not a particularly happy household. John William Sneyd came from a gentry family; he was the eldest son of the Reverend John Sneyd of Ashcombe Park in North Staffordshire (whose diary forms the final chapter of this book), but he and his father had quarrelled violently about money and John William had been disinherited in favour of his younger brother, Dryden. John William was bitterly resentful of this and he and Dryden were no longer on speaking terms. Susanna Ingleby's marriage had been a disaster, she was estranged from her husband and had no children of her own. She and John William were both unhappy, embittered and uncomfortably short of money; 'Ralphy' was the only good thing in their lives and they pampered and indulged him. He grew into a pretty, precocious child with fair curly hair, and through contact with his aunt's friends soon learnt how to charm ladies of a certain age. It was a skill that served him well with the Miss Cranes and his sojourn with them was to be a happy one, despite the fact that the terms were long and he only had two holidays a year – in the summer and at Christmas.

Ralph De Tunstall Sneyd -
'Ralphy' - aged 8

Shortly before he went away to school, Ralph and his aunt made a rather curious pact to keep all the letters each received from the other. The Sneyds had a strong sense of history and a somewhat inflated sense of the importance of their family so, for the edification of posterity – us – year by year, Susanna Ingleby put the surviving letters in sequence and sewed them together in home-made books with brown paper covers.[1] We can therefore trace Ralph's career through four schools over a period of ten years.

March 9th 1871

My dear Aunty,

The rain is fast here today and we cannot go out. I hope you and papa are both well. I have a little cold. I very often draw. Miss Caroline kindly took us to see a stuffed crocodile, it was a very small one. I am glad all my pets are well.

My best love to you and Papa

Before Ralph started school in Leamington, Aunt Susan had been his teacher. She had taught him to read and write and the basics of arithmetic. She had also encouraged him to draw and even as a little boy he showed real talent, though some of the images are quite disturbing – for example, the picture of his childhood home, Armitage Cottage, surrounded by snakes and creepy-crawlies, or the strange dalek-like figure to the left of the picture of a living room. Armitage, where the family lived until 1868, was an industrial village, and Ralph also drew pictures of factories and machinery.

Aunt Susan was also responsible for Ralphy's interest in natural history – they collected leaves and flowers, interesting stones, birds' eggs and butterflies on their walks together. It was something she would come to regret. Many small boys collect things, but collecting became an obsession with Ralph and soon he was also acquiring coins, stamps and all manner of 'curiosities'. His letters home are filled with details of his various acquisitions and extra-curricular activities and tell his family almost nothing about what he is doing in school despite their repeated requests for information. His first holiday lasted

*Drawings by Ralph De Tunstall Sneyd. He had a very strange imagination
– note the picture of his home opposite – Armitage Cottage - surrounded by
snakes and creepy crawlies and the strange creatures in the living room below*

*Armitage was an industrial village and Ralph drew pictures of factory chimneys
and machinery. The Sneyds moved away from Armitage when he was eight so he
was quite young when he drew this. Paper was expensive in the 19th century and
he had obviously given an unwanted publication in which to draw*

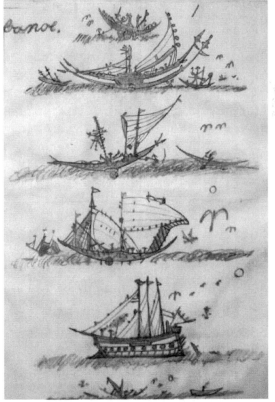

*These ships
are beautifully
detailed*

5

from June 21st to August 3rd, and while his letters home the previous term had often been badly spelt, the first one he sent home after the break reached a new low. He seemed to have forgotten everything he ever knew:

Mrs Susanna Ingleby – Ralph's 'Aunt Susan'

Bonod hose

Orgust [sic] 5th 1871

My dear Aunty,

I have arrived saftly at school. I hope your knee is better today there is a new boy come. Is Papa quite well now I hope the pets are qwite well I am going to slep in the upper room I hope I shall fine you quite well.

I remain yourr

Affectionatlly nephew

R DE T Sneyd

A letter from Ralph in 1871. He was nine

By the next post his father and aunt also had a letter from one of the Miss Cranes expressing concern about Ralph's arithmetic and telling them he was not saying his prayers properly. It was his aunt who wrote a long letter in reply and we get the first example of the 'carrot and stick' technique she would use throughout the rest of his schooldays – a combination of nagging and bribery. It might have been more effective if Ralph had not known he could twist her round his little finger – however much she threatened, he always knew the promised bribe would be his in the end.

Lea Fields [Abbots Bromley]
August 7th 1871
My dearest Ralphy,
    I was very glad to hear you had arrived at school alright. I thought it very kind of the Miss Cranes letting you write so soon ... I hope you will have as pleasant companions in your bedroom as you had last half year ... I hope you will be a good boy and work very hard at your lessons, you know I was very sorry you should have been obliged to be kept to the first 2 rules in sums, because if you pay attention you are not backward at figures and I do hope you will say the church catechism without one mistake, as you can easily do that, and mind you say your prayers slowly, as it is impossible to think of what you are saying when you seem to get them over as soon as possible, do not let Miss Crane have to tell you once about being too quick over them. I was pleased with the way you have got on with nearly all your studies and I think the Miss Cranes have taken great pains with you. If you work hard till Xmas I will give you a book called 'Flowers of the Fields'. I think it is as easy to understand as any book on botany. It has about half as many pictures as there are pages and is a 7 shilling book. Did you remember to tell the Miss Cranes I had made your old suit of clothes large enough for you and that I wished you to wear them until they are too shabby with an old collar buttoned over the jacket as they are not large enough to button on to your shirt. In the two suits that are alike, the set which has been worn the most has a large C on them and the other has B.

Money was tight and Aunt Susan was always embarrassingly frugal when it came to her nephew's clothes. He completely ignored her letter and all the local news she told him and replied:

> They have been putting down new gas pipes and they nearly stopped up the road. We have seen three dragonflies … Miss Crane has given me a book called 'The first steps in General Knowledge, on the Starry Heavens' … We have fine kite flying.

November 16th [1871]

Thank Papa for his kind letter. I should like to have seen the things in the museum [in Lichfield which John William had recently visited] I hope your chilblains are better. I have seen 8 shooting stars … It is just five weeks to the holidays. They are on the 21st December. We had a half-holiday on Tuesday and the boys acted a charade, the word was Portrait it was Frank Barber's birthday. I have bought a telescope for two shillings, it is a very good one …

1872

August 15th

Thank you for your nice letter … Last Monday afternoon Miss M A Crane kindly took us to see Blondin, he did many wonderful things on the tightrope. I like school very much …

September 12th Leamington

Thank Papa for his letter and for the nice account he gave me. I am glad he enjoyed himself. I bought a printed sheet of flags and a sheet of crests of all the Nations, the flags cost one shilling and the crests one shilling and sixpence.

I hope all the pets are quite well, give my rabbits plenty of food please. Last Tuesday evening we all sat up till after ten o'clock to see some beautiful fireworks …

October 3rd

My dear Aunty,

Thank you for your nice letter. Last Michaelmas day
being on Sunday, we went to Warwick on Monday
for our Michaelmas holiday. We went to the castle
and saw all the pictures. There was a table inlaid with
precious stones, worth ten thousand pounds. We saw
a great deal of armour. There was a picture of Charles
the first on horseback ...

If Ralph's letters are to be believed, life with the Miss
Cranes was great fun, a constant round of visits, excursions and
new experiences. There are only very occasional indications
that any work was being done – as, for example, in November
1871 when Ralph wrote home for a Latin primer. He was ten
and still having difficulty writing in English, so we can only
guess how he struggled with Latin. It also seems that before
the Christmas break each year the boys had exams.

November 12th [1872]

The holidays will begin on the 19th of December.
Our examination will be going on next week, so
perhaps I shall not be able to write to you. The
other day we saw two beautiful silver cups in a shop
window. I saw an eclipse of the moon on the morning
of the 15th. Did you see it? I think I shall travel with
Kenny [a school fellow] as far as Armitage ...

At this stage the family were living in Abbots Bromley in
south Staffordshire and the journey to Leamington Spa was
not particularly long. Yet strangely, his father and aunt never
visited Ralph at school though visits were allowed and some
family friends did go to see the little boy. On October 24th he
had written:

... When the Miss Landers came to Leamington they
gave me a book on eggs and nests. They also gave me
a cake and when I left them they filled my pockets
full of apples and pears ...

In May 1872 there had been an outbreak of measles at the school but even then Ralph was not sent home. He does not seem to have been particularly ill and on May 6th his aunt had been able to write 'I was very glad to hear yesterday that you were well enough to sit up. I think it shows you have very good nursing ... I am glad you are being a good boy and that you think it rather jolly to be poorly and to be so attended to; you must give as little trouble as possible ...'

Ralph had got off lightly. Measles could be a serious illness in the days before vaccination – children went blind, some even died. One would have expected Ralph's aunt to have insisted on having him home so she could nurse him herself – but she seems to have been content to let him stay in Leamington. There is no doubt that she loved him dearly – the bond between them was almost unhealthily strong – but it seems to have been seen as part of his education that he should learn to endure long months of separation from his family and pets.

Ralph may have enjoyed his time with the Miss Cranes but in May 1873 he was eleven and it was time to move to a school for older boys. The school the Sneyds chose may well have been recommended by the Miss Cranes for it was only a stone's throw away from their own establishment. It was called Waterloo House and was run by a Mr Walsh. There were thirty-nine boys boarding there in 1871 and they came from as far afield as Ireland, India and the West Indies. A few weeks into term Ralph wrote:

> We get up at ½ past 7 have breakfast at 8 and begin lessons at ½ past and go out at 12, dinner at ½ past 1 and begin work again at ½ past 3 tea at ½ past 5 and lessons at ½ past 6 and have prayers and go to bed at 8. We have for breakfast bacon, ham, brawn, rolled beef and some of the boys have Australian beef which they bring themselves. We have square blocks of bread some of the largest being 4 inches and coffee in mugs – for dinner we generally have mutton, beef, veal, ham, pork and sometimes hash and curry and large treacle or jam tarts. We began our table napkins last Sunday week, at tea we have cups for tea – we play

an hour in between dinner and work, there is a large gymnasium with tan on the ground so if the boys fall from the ladders they may not hurt themselves. I like school very much; the 4th class boys go out with Miss Scott to buy grub every Saturday.

The Sneyds seem to have taken this long, perfectly spelt letter at face value and Aunt Susan replied happily: 'Your Papa and I were very much pleased to receive your long letter and now quite understand how a great part of your time is spent and I am very glad you have so much good food to eat ...'

Waterloo House, Leamington, Mr Walsh's school

However, it would seem that this was a letter Mr Walsh provided for the boys to copy and the reality was rather different. Ralph sent other letters home describing cricket and football matches against Rugby School, a visit to a circus with performing dogs – things he thought might please and interest his family – but towards the end of term things began to deteriorate:

> Leamington
>
> I hope all the pets are quite well. It is only 3 weeks and 6 days to the holodays. I shall be very glad when the holidays come. We have sausiges for dinner every Tuesday, I have soup every second day for lunch, and porridge every other night for supper. The holidays begin on the 18th. We have no examinations hear.
> I send a few crests and a stamp, please to put them with my others ...

It is not known what happened when Ralph returned for the holidays. Maybe he convinced his father that he was miserable at Mr Walsh's; maybe Mr Walsh found him unteachable and didn't want him back – whatever the reason, Ralph did not return to Leamington. After a rather dull Christmas with his father and aunt both unwell and little in the way of festivities, Ralph was packed off to Hockerton in Nottinghamshire, a tiny hamlet deep in the country, fairly near Southwell. The school was run by the Reverend F G Mills who claimed to teach Latin, English, arithmetic and Christian studies – and, most importantly, Mr Mills was a 'gentleman', not just a paid teacher, as Aunt Susan was at pains to point out to Ralph.

Mr Mills had no more success with Ralph than Mr Walsh had had, but if he got a bad report at Easter when he returned home (Mr Mills' school operated on the three-term system with which we are familiar today) his father and aunt were too busy to notice. The Reverend John Sneyd, Ralph's grandfather had died in 1871, and though Ralph's father had been disinherited of Ashcombe Park, the family seat, in 1874 he was able to move into Basford Hall. This was another house on the family estate near Leek in north Staffordshire and was usually reserved for the second son. It was an ignominious return but one Susanna Ingleby and John William Sneyd were determined to make. They found the house in disrepair (it was cold, damp and uncomfortable, conditions which played havoc with Susanna's chilblains); there was the embarrassment of Dryden living just down the road; and their social position in the neighbourhood was precarious, as a son who had been disinherited and a daughter estranged from her husband. But Basford Hall was a Sneyd house, large and prestigious, and they were back on the family lands.

Ralph must have found it lonely. He had not grown up there and had no friends his own age in the neighbourhood. He could visit his Uncle Dryden at Ashcombe Park – the feud between John William and his brother did not extend to Susanna and Ralph – and he saw more of his Aunt Emily, his father and aunt's spinster sister, than he had done when they lived in Abbots Bromley, but neither of them were particularly exciting company for an eleven-year-old boy. The only advantages Basford Hall had for him was that it was huge with lots of rooms and outbuildings in which to house his ever-growing collections, and the land Ralph roamed over in search of specimens mostly belonged to his uncle so he was unlikely ever to be accused of trespassing.

Basford Hall, Ralph's home after 1874

After a rather bleak Easter in the dilapidated, part-furnished house Ralph returned to Hockerton, but after only a few weeks he was back 'very poorly and sick'. He had typhoid fever. Ralph was desperately ill for weeks. His aunts Susan and Emily, the housemaids and family friends took it in turns to nurse the little boy day and night, wiping his fevered body with cool wet cloths to bring his temperature down. The doctors called twice a day and took his pulse which was alarmingly high – his Aunt Susan recorded every reading in her diary. The new-fangled medical thermometers that were just coming into use were cumbersome and inaccurate, so the good doctors of North Staffordshire still relied on the tried-and-tested method of measuring the pulse rate. Gradually Ralph recovered but he was left weak and barely able to walk unaided. He went to Wales in September to convalesce but soon relapsed. It was not until April 1875, almost a year after he had first become ill, that Ralph returned to Mr Mills and Hockerton Rectory.

Hockerton Rectory April 10th 1875

I hope Papa arrived home quite safely. I have got the old day nursery for my bedroom now; my hed is neir the wall, all 3 of the servants are new ones. All the same boys are here. They have not been reeding French History since I have been away so I shall begin again where I left off. My garden is now a wilderness. Have I got any coins yet … I have been working hard getting the plaster off the church. I went up to the frunt dore how are all the pets. Please draw me a sketch of the tadploes. Please tell me if you have got any coins for me …'

Ralph was now less than a month away from his thirteenth birthday and the Sneyds must have been horrified when they read this illiterate letter. They may also have had serious doubts about what was going on in the school – though Aunt Susan's reply does not suggest that she questioned Mr Mills' use of his boys as unpaid labourers in his church:

The getting the plaster off the church must be very dirty work. I should not like to see you in such a mess. Mind you work hard at your lessons and get on with your sums and Latin ...

Nonetheless, in September 1875 John William decided to send his son to yet another school. This time it was to be very much further from home, in Debenham on the Suffolk/Norfolk border, and it was run by the Reverend Cornish who was interested in natural history and archaeology and was himself an avid collector. Perhaps John William thought Ralph would study harder under someone who shared his enthusiasms. Mr Cornish's school, perhaps recommended by the Sneyds' cousins who lived at Holm-next-the-Sea, proved to be an inspired choice.

The Reverend Charles Cornish of Debenham,
Ralph's teacher from 1875-1880

An impression of life at Debenham Vicarage can be gleaned from the memoir written Mr Cornish's eldest son, James:

> Part of the house was old but many rooms had been tacked on so that it was fairly large. Many of the ceilings were very low, and at some of the doors my father had to stoop so as not to knock his head on the lintel. The structure was chiefly a timber frame with intervals filled with lath and plaster – a very flammable method of building and by no means warm in winter. Illumination in winter was difficult. Lamps were little used for colza oil lamps were tiresome to work, and the paraffin lamps invented in the 1860s were ill-made and apt to explode and take fire so candles were generally used ... we spent the winter evenings in semi-darkness ... and our mother used to read aloud ... The Waverley novels, Captain Marryat's First Masterman ready, and the Children of the New Forest ... and poetry too, The Lays of Ancient Rome, the Lay of the Last Minstrel ... Our father would pick up a Livy and translate a passage about Hannibal crossing the Alps, or show us an old atlas on which the marches of Alexander were traced, and tell us of the Persian Wars, of Marathon and Salamis ... Our first interest was in collecting fossils, for Geology was perhaps the most popular science then ... Vaughan [James' brother] had his own special interest which was astronomy. Two large globes stood in our dining room, one terrestrial the other celestial ... night after night he would go star-gazing and learn the constellations and the chief stars.

Having taught his own sons, the Reverend Cornish decided he could probably apply the same methods to other pupils. James continued:

> When I was about ten [so c.1870] my father began to take a few pupils to educate with us, for the income from the living of Debenham was small. Good

preparatory schools then were very scarce, and he
soon had several offers of boys ... now the village
possessed a new interest for we kept things alive with
cricket and football.

The school was therefore quite well established by the time
Ralph arrived in 1875. He was much the same age as the
youngest Cornish, Vaughan, and for a while they shared a
bedroom. Initially Mr Cornish seems to have been rather
shocked by Ralph's lack of ability and his first letter to the
Sneyds was not encouraging.

Debenham Vicarage

Mr Cornish wrote to your Papa last week and said he
found you very backward in everything and that he
thought sums were the thing you could do the best.
I said I always think you did things nearly as well
before you went to any schools ...

Aunt Susan was always ready to remind her nephew of
his shortcomings. Ralph's descriptions of the teaching in
Debenham tally quite closely with James' account. Mrs
Cornish used to read to them in the evenings, they were

encouraged to go out at night and study the stars, and he played cricket and football against boys from the village – but information about what he was actually studying is meagre. There does not seem to have been a fixed timetable and the boys appear to have had a good deal of free time. Ralph seems to have taken to the regime like a duck to water and in Vaughan Cornish he had found a soul-mate.

> Debenham September 26th 1875
>
> My dear aunty,
>
> I hope you will take care of yourself. I hope Papa arrived home quite safely. This is a very nice house … Vaughne has about as good a collection as I have, he has given me 4 sharks teath and 2 coins one of witch is a coin of Constantin the Great. This is a great place for finding fossils. There is a kind of fossil called a sea eye which is very common about here. I hope all the pets are quite well give my love to Papa
>
> Believe me
>
> Your afeconate nephew
>
> Ralph de Tunstale Sneyd

A few days later he asked his aunt to send '…all my best duplicats please put them in a small box and pad them with cotton wool and they will come for 2 pence. I have a very good change with Quaghne he sais he cannot wait till cristmas' – and just to encourage her he sent a present 'a peace of lace bark from Jamaica. It is very prity.' As always, Aunt Susan did as she was asked, stitching the coins into little bags to protect them, but she also reminded him that he should work hard at his lessons.

> Do not think of anything else except them and try to do as well as the other boys, never mind thinking about coins, I am not fond of boys changing things as they know nothing about the value of them and when once that sort of thing is begun they do not know when to stop.

Ralph ignored her.

October 24th 1875

... I [gave] all of them except the Queen anne shilling
and the American cent and the 3 phennings for a
beautiful white sea egg that Vaugn valued at about
18d. I got the other coins changed for a splendid
electrotype of an old great seal. I have bought a
pair of Chinese slippers for 2s ... There are a great
many very old pieces of pipes about here some of
them about the date of Queen Elizabeth I have got
a good many of them. Mr Cornish says the pipes we
find are undoubtedly old ones as they are very thick
and chiney he has seen a good many in the Salsbery
Museom. I am afraid there is not much fur of me
bringing home many colections I cant get foscils for
love or money. The girls produce no more. The men
at the brick kilns do not dig in the summer for clay
and so do not find any & I do not get any on the
stone heaps because the boys who get the stones of
the land when they find foscils ceep them.

It seems that the young gentlemen at Mr Cornish's were
happy to pay local people a few pence for any fossils they
came across in the course of their work.

The boys seem to have spent their free hours wandering
the countryside and shopping in the village. Ralph was thirteen
in 1875 and probably had more pocket money than he had
had in Leamington and Hockerton and he spent it on buying
yet more items for his collection – like the Chinese slippers
and a penknife made 'from a little piece of the Royal George'.

His aunt was worried. She was becoming increasingly
hostile to the whole collecting business but family and friends
continued to supply Ralph with curiosities. In June 1876
Cousin Beatrice Fraser '... was so kind as to bring you ... an
Emu's egg, and a queer shaped piece of wood which is used
for throwing at birds, and three Australian peach stones, they
are so prettily marked that they are often worn as necklaces
...' In desperation the Sneyds offered items as bribes for good

work '... if you get on with your lessons your Papa will let you have a few bones that were found at the Water House in some limestone rocks, the best parts were sent to the Manchester Museum, these your Papa has are quite small, they were a Mammoth and an Irish Elk ...' Ralph's collection was beginning to outstrip that of his friend. In September 1876 he reported smugly 'Vaughan has not got nearly such a lot of nice things as I have' and by Christmas he needed yet another display cabinet – which his aunt bought him.

A letter home when he returned to school after the Christmas holidays unleashed more disapproving responses from Aunt Susan. Ralph had told her that he was now buying coins advertised in *Exchange and Mart*. 'You must not get into debt buying coins or I shall be very angry with you,' she grumbled, then another thought struck her: 'I hope you spell all the words right in your letters about them, I hope Mrs Cornish knows you are getting them and will see all is right.' Ralph was fifteen but his aunt could not allow him to pursue an innocent hobby without nagging. He wrote a sensible letter back saying that the coins were always sent on approval and were very cheap – but his aunt had already fired off a complaint to Mrs Cornish. She had had more than enough of Mrs Ingleby's interference in their management of Ralph and replied that he would not be allowed to buy any more coins by post.

Unabashed, Ralph found another interest, poking around in the bed of the local stream.

> There are a very pleasing varity of creatures in this river here, there are neuts, horse leaches, cadicis, minows and many other things ... When I get home I shall have to look at the natural history of Belmont as I am in a hurry to see them more particularly as Mrs Cornish has put a stop to my reading hir books on the subject, and partly because she thinks some of the things are ugly, in fact I think none of the family care very much for natural history ...

Ralph's drawing of pond life. This probably pre-dates his time in Debenham. Note the hieroglyphs in the top left hand corner – Ralph was fascinated by codes and scripts

The images are beautifully drawn but the subject matter is rather macabre and the juxtaposition of the cow, snake and fish is very odd

It would seem that Mr and Mrs Cornish were beginning to lose patience with their wayward pupil.

Ralph's passion for caddises – caddisfly larvae that cover themselves in a sticky substance and then roll around in the gravel on the river bed so they are encased in a tube coated in grit or tiny pebbles – lasted for several weeks and his aunt was treated to several letters describing the curious items out of which the ones in the local stream had made their shells. 'I do not think these things stop me attending to my lessons as I only get them on half-holidays' he parried when she criticised him, but she was not mollified. A few weeks later she wrote 'I do not care about you bringing any curiosities home as I want your thoughts on your lessons' – but by then Ralph had a new enthusiasm: birds' eggs. He sent a long letter home, complete with diagrams, about the best way to blow and keep eggs. 'The best way to blow eggs is the way they blow them in the shops – with one hole, they do it with an instrument,' he informed her. Aunt Susan was incensed. It was bad enough that she still knew nothing about what Ralph was doing in school – but she had introduced him to collecting birds' eggs when he was a little boy. She had blown them for him – with two holes, one in either end, and laid them out neatly for him on trays of bran. Now he had the effrontery to tell her that it was better to blow them differently and lay them out on cotton wool! Her anger was palpable:

> You know that I do not care at all for eggs & I
> suppose I shall never blow another, but I must say
> those I did for you are nearly as good as any you
> have. I should think it much easier to get them
> really clean when blown from end to end & the best
> collections I have seen are in bran. I am not at all
> fond of wool.

The correspondence troubled Ralph not at all, but it did remind him that he had a collection of birds' eggs back home that might need attention and he asked his aunt to check on them. Birds' eggs were prone to attract mites – it was never possible to ensure that the insides were completely clean – and if mites were found all the eggs in the tray had to be washed carefully and very gently (they became increasingly fragile with age) and replaced on clean bran. This tedious and fiddly job fell to Aunt Susan's lot but on this occasion she could not resist making him feel guilty. 'I will see [the eggs] again when I can walk that far. I have been in bed nearly a week as I have had so much pain ...' She suffered from a whole range of complaints, real and imaginary.

Meanwhile Ralph was still telling her very little about what he was actually learning and his letters were still almost as badly spelt and untidy as they had been when he first went away to school. His aunt was clearly exasperated by his lack of progress – letter after letter began with nagging and criticism.

> You must read your letters over before you send them then you would know that you have written 'nise' for 'nice' and 'ireland' instead of 'Ireland' ...

> You must work very hard at your lessons this term, you are so very backward in everything ...

> I cannot understand how you can be so stupid as not to know the rule of three yet ...

She also spent a lot of time comparing him unfavourably to other boys he knew, which must have been quite hurtful:

> The young Fraser is such a good boy that his master says it is 6 years since he had so good a pupil ...

> The young Bouchers get on so very well Herbert has a 1st class and Charlie has won his 3rd scholarship...

Ralph was not stupid. He read widely and was interested in all sorts of things, but for some reason his spelling and punctuation were always erratic – it seems as if he was too preoccupied with his thoughts to concentrate properly on such mundane matters. His carelessness drove his aunt to distraction and sometimes he really does seem to have gone out of his way to irritate her. His first letter home at the beginning of 1876 described a schoolboy prank:

> Debenham January 23rd 1876
>
> My dear Arty tarts,
>
> I arrived at school all right we got into a gards van for part of the way. I have got all my things safe. Den is not coming to this school again all the others are coming. An organ grinder came here today with a monkey. My stilts at home are twice the weight of these. I have made some very good changes of foscills ...

Susanna Ingleby could never see the world from the perspective of a fourteen-year-old boy and she berated Ralph soundly.

> My dear Ralph,
>
> We were pleased to get your letter yesterday and to hear that you had arrived at school safely, but we were very sorry that you went in the Guard's van as you ought to have known that after your Papa had taken the great trouble in putting you into a comfortable carriage that you ought to have remained there until you arrived at Ipswich, instead of getting out and going to the Guard's van which is not a 'Lawful place' to travel in besides being very draughty and you know what a great deal of money has been spent to try to keep you in better health ... I hope that until you are older and travel alone that you remain where you are placed and all your life travel in the parts of the train that are proper for the passengers and not with the servants of the train ...

Ralph was very fond of his aunt but she comes over as a terrible nag, a fuss-pot and a control freak. Throughout his school career every journey was accompanied by meticulous instructions, how he was to arrange his luggage, what labels he was to put on his cases, how he would recognise each station and so on. In 1877 when he was fifteen she even instructed him to '… be very quiet in the train & do little talking …' Shortly after his eighteenth birthday she was still insisting that he be accompanied as far as London and put on the right train for Debenham – it must have been humiliating. She was also very parsimonious about his clothes. Terms were long and teenage boys go through growth spurts, so poor Ralph frequently found himself in clothes that were too short or too tight and she almost seems to blame him for growing!

> I cannot understand how you have grown so very much in height and width in one term or how your coat can have got wrong in the collar but I hope now your clothes will do until the holidays …

> I think your trousers can be made to do until the holidays. I am sending a piece like them, if the best pair is not worn at the bottom they can be let down there …

Mrs Cornish, who was responsible for ensuring that Ralph was decently clad while he was at school, became increasingly irritated by Mrs Ingleby's demands. She dictated Ralph's reply.

> I have had the older and earlier pair of my trousers that are alike altered by having a piece put on the bottom of the legs to make them longer, & I have also had my jacket let out and lowered at the neck. I have to wear my best trousers because Mrs Cornish thinks both the others are too tight. I will take great cair of them. I neaver climb trees now …

Aunt Susan wrote other letters scolding Ralph roundly for asking their friends, the Hutchinsons, to bring him souvenirs back from a holiday in Egypt – she regarded 'asking for things' as a cardinal sin and was becoming more and more fed up with Ralph's curiosities. But she does not seem to have told any of their friends and relations that Ralph was to be discouraged from collecting, so gifts kept arriving. Over in Norfolk her elderly cousins, Mary and Elizabeth Nelson, gave him boxes of shells, specimens of amber and jet – and a bottle containing two seahorses, a centipede and two scorpions in spirits! This introduced Ralph to a new and particularly unpleasant way of storing specimens and soon there was correspondence about 'putting animals in spirits'. One letter from Aunt Susan conjures up a particularly bizarre image:

> I answered two letters while Mrs Bloor was washing
> the Slow Worm, she cut off the parts you did not like
> & rolled it up & put it in a French Mustard bottle
> & we put the spirits on it, it looks very well, the sore
> part has broken out a little again. Mrs Bloor was very
> kind in doing it so nicely for you … she seems to be
> getting quite fond of such things … I put camphor on
> the things you named and have sealed up the bottles
> with the animals in, because I found the corks very
> damp, you had put the seahorses etc, etc, very badly
> in the spirits, I have made them all hang apart …

Mrs Bloor was the cook. She liked Ralph and seems to have been happy to help his aunt look after his growing collection. On occasion she even boiled up animal corpses for him so he could have the skeletons! 'I saw Mrs Bloor tie down some of your animals with new bladders, I hope you will never get any more of the nasty smelly things …' Aunt Susan wrote in February 1880. But he did, and a year later she was still complaining:

> I hope you have not been buying a lot of rubbish,
> you must remember we cannot have any more things
> here that smell bad, the cupboard your bottles are
> in has to be kept on purpose for them as they cause
> everything to smell bad & that used to be a useful
> cupboard for Elizabeth [the maid] for her sewing …

Ralph's collections were a sore trial to the whole household at Basford Hall. Harrison, the gardener, fancied himself as an amateur taxidermist and sometimes stuffed animals for Ralph.

'I took the squirrel, water wagtail, bat and snake down to the Bath House [Harrison's home] one day last week. Harrison will get a case made for them ...' Aunt Susan reported. Another letter arrived from Ralph requesting that Harrison 'stuff the hedgehog and clean Linda's skull.' Linda was a family pet, a St Bernard dog which had been poisoned. We do not know whether Harrison obeyed the young master's instructions about Linda's skull but he didn't stuff the hedgehog. 'I fancy that animal would be rather a trouble to do,' explained Aunt Susan with uncharacteristic reasonableness.

The collections grew but Ralph's progress at school continued to be unsatisfactory. There were only a handful of pupils at the 'school' – James and Vaughan Cornish, Ralph and his cousin, Richmond Gale, and one or two others, some from excellent families which no doubt pleased Ralph's class-conscious aunt. 'The other [new] boy is called Manners the son of Lord John Manners the Post Master General,' wrote Ralph one term. As the Cornish boys grew up, the age of Mr Cornish's other pupils increased. James and Vaughan and young Manners were being prepared for university and were learning Latin and Greek. Ralph went to the lessons as well, though there was no hope of his passing a university entrance exam. 'Mr Cornish thought I got on very well with my Livy. I shall get on well with my lessons this turm ...' he wrote, but the effect of this promise was rather spoilt by the next sentence – 'I hope I shall get some curicsilis (curiosities) this turm ...'

One might wonder why the Sneyds continued to spend money they could ill afford keeping Ralph at school when it was becoming increasingly clear that he was not benefiting from his education. The answer may well be that he was becoming something of an embarrassment. He was careless and forgetful, he talked too much, he was obsessed with his curiosities and he seemed to have no sense of propriety or any appropriate ambitions. While he was safely at school on the other side of the country he was out of sight, if not quite out of mind.

From time to time he attempted to tell his aunt things that would please her:

I am giving more of my thorts to my leasons I am going to do some more leasons in the mornings I did a page of copeing out before breakfast yesterday. I quite understand that it is very emportant to know French when one goes on the Continent. Do you think I had better learn German next turm. I suppose you could get through Germany with French much better than with English ...

But for the most part he told her about extra-curricular activities – from visiting his Uncle John in Norfolk and going sparrow-shooting to walking on stilts. 'I have lirnt to walk on stilts I have bought a pair for myself for 2 shillings. I went a mile and a half on a pair that was lent me ...'

Then there were outings:

On Tuesday we went to an African panerama chiefly about Doctor Livingstone the pictures were very small, after the panerama we were shown how things looked in different lights. The man dressed up some boys in coloured things and throw some powder on a little fire and they turned different colours.

On Wednesday we all went in a fly to a place called Monelsoan [Mendlesham?] to a Misionary meating there two People spoke one of them very well indeed he told us a great many things about India which I will tell you about when I get home, in the evening we sat down to a large supper party we got home somewhere about 11 o'clock ...

and tales of the boys latest food fads:

The things in the garden are growing very well there are a great many strawberries which Mrs Cornish lets us have for tea, we have them all mushed up on a plate with milk and plenty of sugar, we nearly always now have a dish made of lettice and milk and brown sugar we make it ourselves on our plates I like it very much ...

29

None of this was what Susanna Ingleby and John William Sneyd wanted to hear. They had little money, and though Ralph stood to inherit Basford Hall he would have no income with which to run it. They had probably hoped he would go on to university and perhaps become a clergyman or a solicitor – professions appropriate to the sons of impoverished gentlemen.

John William may have thought that Ralph might join the army – he himself had been a member of the Staffordshire Yeomanry, the volunteer force set up to protect the country from invasion and keep the peace, and had thoroughly enjoyed it. But Ralph was not suited to a military life – indeed it was becoming hard to think of anything that might suit him. He was an oddball, an eccentric who never outgrew his schoolboy hobby of 'collecting curiosities' and in his last year or two at school he was to worry his family even more. The first hint of trouble came just before Christmas 1878 when he was sixteen.

Debenham December 1st 1878

My dear Aunty,

Thank you for your two nice letters. I think nobody was able to see the meteors on the 23rd of last month … on Wednesday last we went to a wild beast show it was a small but good one there was a Gnu, & a Tasmanian devel, a white Yak, a clouded Tiger etc, etc I want very much to go to Cheadle in the holleydays, to see the Catholic Cathedral. I mite take something to eat on the way. I should like to get there on Christmas Eve when something was going on …

Cheadle was some miles from Basford but accessible by train. St Giles' Roman Catholic Church (not Cathedral) was designed by Pugin for the Earl of Shrewsbury and is regarded as his masterpiece. It is a glowing jewel, filled with colour and pattern and wonderful ornate wood and metal ornaments. From a purely architectural point of view it is well worth a visit – but it soon became clear that Ralph was interested in more than the architecture. Over the next year he determined that he wanted to become a Catholic and in the summer of 1879 he announced his intention to his father and aunt.

He made contact with the priests at Alton Catholic Centre, taking the train from Basford in his holidays and climbing the steep wooded path up to the fairy-tale-castle on the hill that was the Catholic centre there. He was wise enough not to tell his family about his visits – but news reached them soon enough. In an isolated country district everyone knew everyone else's business and Ralph was a well-known figure. His father stormed over to Alton and forbade the priests to see Ralph again. Letters flew between the Sneyds and the Cornishes and every letter Ralph received from his aunt contained a tirade of abuse.

Today it is difficult to understand why they were so angry, but in the 1870s and 80s Catholicism was reviled and feared. Within living memory it had been a banned religion – the Catholic Emancipation Act was only passed in 1829 – and like many of her generation Susanna Ingleby regarded Roman Catholicism with deep suspicion bordering on horror. Ralph's grandfather had been a Church of England clergyman and his aunt was a devout and unquestioning Anglican, as were the rest of his family – she regarded Ralph's interest in popery as something evil to be stamped out at all costs.

John William Sneyd, Ralph's father

June 18th 1879

... I am not at all surprised that Mr & Mrs Cornish
do not understand you when all your relations are
so much astonished at your having thought of the
Romanish faith ... I hoped you had given up all that
folly ... you have not the slightest power to change
your religion before you are 21 and I hope that before
that your brains will be able to understand what is
right ...

July 9th

... I hope you will before long know how very wicked
it is to disobey a parent, and it is worse in your case
because of you being an only child and your papa a
widower, & how you could like to follow directions
from a priest who to obey caused you to tell so many
LIES is perfect madness ...

October 8th

... I will not help you forward in anything until I find
you have given up, forever, all your Romanish folly,
and not a penny of mine will help you ...

Seventeen-year-old Ralph had little option but to capitulate:

Debenham September 28th 1879

... I am sorry I went to the Roman Catholic Chapel
in Leek. I wont go there again without you want me
to ...

October 11th

... I hope I shall not cause you any more trouble
again. I will not do anything you do not like me to do
& I will not let my thoughts dwell on any disputed
questions of religion & when I come home will be
able to help you and do good in the place ...

Basford Hall October 20th

... I am glad you are giving up your Romanish
fooleries, of course when you are at home you must
go to Cheddleton Church ... so I hope I shall never
hear any more about Romans, your foolishness has
surprised everyone. Try your very best to attend to
what is said in Church and say your prayers properly
out of the books I gave you & then perhaps you will
get to know what is right. After Easter you will go
somewhere to learn farming or something as an idle
man is a plague to everybody. We cannot let you sit in
the kitchen when you are at home ...

Not only was Ralph flirting with a dangerous religion, he
also had what we would now see as a refreshingly egalitarian
view of the world and was at least as happy sitting in the
kitchen chatting to the cook and the gardener as he was talking
to his aunt and her friends – but now he was growing up his
aunt wanted him to behave as she thought befitted a young
gentleman of his social standing.

November 2nd

... I am very glad to hear that you have at last come
to your senses about the Romans. I cannot think how
you could ever fancy that their teaching which led
to so much lying and deceit could be right, but now
you must pray to be kept in the right way & trust to
your relations & friends to tell you who to make new
friends and not go after strangers who will only get
what little money you have from you. Work very hard
at all your lessons so that you will get knowledge
to be of use in the world, try to please Mr & Mrs
Cornish ... are you cutting your nails properly and
not biting them?

She was still infantilising him. Probably as a punishment for
his interest in the Church of Rome, Ralph was not allowed to
leave school at Easter 1880. His father and aunt decided to
keep him there for another year – perhaps they felt that living
in a clergyman's household was good for him. He, meanwhile,

was re-considering the promises he had made and a few weeks after his eighteenth birthday he wrote a careful letter home.

> Debenham May 30th 1880
>
> My Dear Aunty,
>
> Thank you for your letter. I am very sorry that my wish to become a member of what I believe to be the true church should cause you so much trouble, but do what I may I am unable to believe in some protestants doctrines … and I think you will allow that it is useless to profess to hold opinions which one does not believe in, besides if I did become a member of the Church of Rome, the principle thing I should have to do would be to go to Mass every Sunday and only my nearest relations need know about it. Of course I should never think of joining the Catholic Church without your knowledge … Mrs Cornish wishes me to go to see some friends of hers in Germany this summer …

Whether this had anything to do with his interest in Catholicism we do not know, but in the summer of 1880, Ralph was sent off on a Continental tour with James Cornish who was a couple of years his senior and supposedly a 'good' influence. He enjoyed himself hugely and inevitably added a great many items to his collections, but his aunt could not forgive him for his renewed interest in Catholicism and fired off yet more vitriolic missives. In a letter from Debenham written on July 11th 1880 Ralph pleaded to be allowed to leave school at Christmas but he was out of luck – he was to stay at Debenham until the last possible date – the Easter before his nineteenth birthday.

What happened next? For a while Ralph stayed at home trying hard to please his cantankerous family, taking family prayers, running errands, reading to little old ladies towards whom his aunt was charitably inclined – and at last having time to spend sorting, labelling and displaying his vast collection. For a few weeks he was despatched to Mr Broughton at Wortley to learn farming – as had been mooted two years earlier. Ralph accepted this as the least worst option open to him but he was canny enough to ensure that he did not stay there long. 'Mr Broughton says you seem to take no interest in what is going on only caring for your own pleasures and queer tastes,' wrote Aunt Susan in despair when he had been at Wortley for a few weeks, and soon after that Mr Broughton refused to keep him any longer and sent him home in disgrace.

Ralph was free at last. His aunt paid for him to travel – in Derbyshire, to the Isle of Man, to London, to Norway and finally on a round-the-world voyage to Australia. She seems finally to have accepted that Ralph would never make a financial contribution to the household and though she grumbled constantly and kept him on as short a rein as she could financially, Aunt Susan continued to support Ralph until her death in 1891. She left him all her money and a small farm she owned, up on the Staffordshire Moorlands near Onecote.

In 1883, when he was twenty-one, Ralph converted to Roman Catholicism and though it grieved her deeply and she bitterly resented the contributions he made (with her money) to the Catholic Church in nearby Leek, she eventually came to terms with it. She tolerated the new friends he made, even though they were not people with whom the Sneyds would have expected to socialise. Fortunately she was not still alive when he met the woman who was to be his wife. Ralph was never concerned with social status and Harriet, his bride, was a book-keeper in a local silk mill. It was a step too far for his father, and after the marriage John William Sneyd disinherited his son as, almost four decades earlier, his own father had disinherited him. Ralph never got over the loss of Basford Hall and for the rest of his life on his occasional visits to the Hall he would wander the rooms mournfully, saying 'This should all have been mine.'

Ralph De Tunstall Sneyd with one of his sons. He would have been in his 40s

He and Harriet lived at Fairview, the farm at Onecote that Aunt Susan had left him. It was a happy marriage; Harriet bore him four children, helped him write articles and poems and pamphlets, tolerated his eccentricities and seems to have had no qualms about living in a house in which every surface was covered with 'curiosities' and in which a mummy (minus its case) stood upright on either side of the staircase. A large piece of the Giants' Causeway decorated their lawn, the barn became Ralph's private chapel and then a museum. He toyed with Theosophy and Buddhism, he styled himself a Knight of the Round Table and held Druidical ceremonies of his own invention at Thor's Cave and Arbor Low up on the moors above his home. Aunt Susan would have been mortified, but in fact Ralph is fondly remembered in Leek and the surrounding area as a character, one of the last great eccentrics, but also as a man who was respected and well-liked. In the case of Ralph De Tunstall Sneyd the child really was father to the man.

Endnotes

1   These, and all the other documents on which this chapter is based, are in a private collection belonging to descendants of the Sneyd family.

The sadistic Miss Paraman

If the schooling that Ralph de Tunstall Sneyd received was kind and enriching, this is more than can be said for that of a good many boys, even though parents sent their children to school with the best of intentions and no doubt they chose as carefully as they could. Children hardly ever wrote about ill treatment in letters home – mainly because their letters were written under supervision at special times and were often checked before being sent. It is from the journals or diaries that children kept, and the letters that they wrote much later in life, that the truth comes out.

Caning, as a form of punishment, was widespread and accepted as the norm until well into the twentieth century. Parents beat their children as a form of discipline, 'Spare the rod and spoil the child' as the saying went. Ralph was lucky: the schools he attended did not subscribe to that belief, but many did, as these three short extracts from diaries show. Children at boarding school, not surprisingly, suffered most.

Raleigh Trevelyan was born in 1800, the sixth of the thirteen children of Sir John Trevelyan and his wife Maria. In 1813-14 Raleigh was at school in Brentford and kept a diary in which he recorded regular floggings. One page of entries – for May-June 1813 – is typical and shows what he and his schoolmates endured in the way of beatings and humiliation.

May
Wednesday 26th: Hopkinson flogged – Had to collect fines.

Thursday 27th: Dixon Sr [senior] flogged –
Ascension day. Mr Morris read prayers. Had verses & translations excused. Wrote to Calverly & Lamb.

Friday 28th: Sisson did not come after dinner.

Saturday 29th: Very hot indeed. Bought some oak apples. Henderson came to see us.

Sunday 30th: Price came to see us. The text in the morning was 2d verse of 139 psalm.

Monday 31st: Heard from Mama & Calverly.

Tuesday June 1st: Mitford & Rudge flogged & R had the fools coat on. Heard from Julia.

Wednesday 2nd: Had a half holiday for the Register. Wrote to Calverly.

Thursday 3rd: Sullivan was flogged …

In 1827 John Pocock, aged twelve, was attending a London day school. His diary makes it clear that he was no great scholar and disliked school work, and consequently he was very often in trouble. He left school shortly after his fourteenth birthday and was placed by his father as an under-clerk in a law firm where he copied out legal papers for eight hours a day for no wages. His father then moved him to another firm where he received a small salary. Eventually he emigrated and spent all his working life in South Africa – in Cape Town.

February 23rd: To school in the morning where the usual routine of Spelling, Reading, Writing, Cyphering, Burching and Caneing took place. [1]

George Corrance, who came from a wealthy landed family, had the misfortune to be sent to a school in Brighton owned and run by the Reverend Dr George Proctor. His diary records Dr Proctor as a singularly bad-tempered and violent man. [2] George, like John Pocock, was clearly not a diligent scholar – he does not write about his lessons and seems to have taken no pleasure in any sort of intellectual activity, thus giving the Reverend Dr Proctor abundant excuses for savage chastisement in the name of education. The diary is sparse; sometimes the entries are not more than a word or two long. The weather is described in detail every day – and so are games and other activities. These are just a few entries as many are very repetitive. It is interesting to see the slang words and phrases the boys used. 'In a towering' meant a rage, so did 'a great wax.' 'A great jaw' was a severe telling-off and 'spank' had sexual connotations. But what George recorded most vividly was Dr Proctor's brutality – he seems to have actively enjoyed caning boys.

February 1st: Started lessons.

February 6th: Got a jaw for not doing my holiday task.

February 19th: Dull but fine and cold. Wind changeable. Dr in a towering. Knocked a fellow down and caned lots.

February 20th: …G. Proctor made me stand on a form for 3 hours. Dancing at night. Did not go out.

April 23rd: Dr in great wax. Kept in.

April 24th: Dr gave me a great jaw and compared me to a donkey on a common without a loo.

April 25th: Thick fog. Dull and cold. Wind NW & SE. Rain in evening. Balies would not let us spank them.

'Spank' is underlined with a heavy wavy line and it sounds as if something highly inappropriate was going on.

April 27th: … Balies sneaked to G Proctor.

April 28th: … Did not go out. G Proctor gave me 45.
[presumably lashes] Lost 1 lesson.

April 29th: Played a great game of cricket.

May 1st: Fog. Afterwards fine. Dr flogged 2 and
caned 6 fellows.

May 5th: Fine but some rain. Wind changed to SW.
Went to Latin. Got caned.

June 1st: Fog. Afterwards fine. Dr flogged 2 and
caned 6 fellows.

June 5th: Fine but some rain. Wind changed to SW.
Went to Latin. Got caned.

June 9th: Going to be caned. Put a book up my back.

And so it goes on.

George's brother Henry was also at the same school; he
became very ill and had to go home. Their sister was soon to
die of TB so it is likely that Henry had it as well. During the
summer holidays they must have told their parents what went
on at the school as George did not return to Dr Proctor's, and
on December 31st he wrote:

Had not time to write any more this year – nothing in
particular except that I went to Mr De Haviland as a
day scholar on the 20th of this month and like it very
much. Aunt gave us a magic lantern. She had a tea
party. Thus ends a wretched year.

But it is the letters and memories of a Norwich boy, Frederick Thurlow Hibgame, that shed light on a truly sadistic teacher – Miss Elizabeth Paraman.

Frederick was born in 1856, the youngest child of a retired Indian army officer. His father, Major Edward Thurlow Hibgame, was sixty-four when Frederick was born; too old, perhaps, to cope with having small children in the house. This may explain why little Fred, and at least one of his brothers, were sent to board at Mrs Priest's School which was just a few streets away from their home when they could easily have attended as day boys. Major Hibgame died in 1869 when Frederick was just thirteen. His siblings left home, but in 1881, aged twenty-four, Frederick was still living at home with his mother Augusta and is listed in the census as a 'student'. She died in 1892 and a few years later we find Frederick on the 1897 electoral register in London. He later moved to the West Country. It is not clear what he studied, or where, but he does not ever seem to have earned his own living, though he was a keen historian and antiquarian. In his correspondence he writes of being an invalid and in the portrait of him as an old man he does appear to have a weak spine. Born in Norwich, he was obviously passionate about his city, but it was from Clifton in Bristol in 1904 that he wrote to Mary E Mann – a well-known Norfolk novelist of the period.

In 1903 she had published a novel called *Gran'ma's Jane* which brought to life the Norwich of some fifty years earlier. Frederick must have bought a copy and sent it to her to sign. When it came back he wrote to her again, thanking her, praising her work and saying:

> … [it] affected me so strongly as I feel it must do to everyone who has at least reached middle life. I found so many gaps last time I visited Norwich that I came away quite miserable. Old familiar streets and houses quite seemed to have lost their familiarity when those we have always identified with are no more, and yet I did find quite a few people still living …

Part of a letter from Frederick Hibgame to Mary E Mann

The letter makes it clear that this was not the only time Frederick had written to Mary E Mann. He had obviously sent her some recollections of his school days, perhaps because she had written so much about life in Norwich and the surrounding countryside, and she must have replied that he 'should write a book'. But Frederick Hibgame did not write a book, at least not one about his schooldays; instead he sent her more detailed notes of his recollections and she wrote a novel based on his terrible childhood experiences at school. Referring to his recollections he assured her, '....perhaps you will think them over-drawn but I am quite sure they are not as I have purposefully omitted many things concerning whippings etc ...'

Pottergate in Norwich. Mrs Priest's school was in 'Pottergate Street' but we do not know which house

The school that Frederick Hibgame attended for 'five miserable years' was owned and run by Mrs Maria Priest. Her husband, Henry, was a wine merchant in the city and the school was in their house in Pottergate, Norwich. [3]

One end was the home of the respectable and relatively wealthy – the Rackhams, Mary Mann's birth family, lived there for a time – but we think that Mrs Priest lived at the less salubrious end: her next door neighbour was a travelling salesman, the one after that was a butcher.

At this date anyone could set up a school. There was no training for teachers and schools were not inspected. Mrs

Advertisement for Mrs Priest's School. These advertisements appeared regularly in the Norwich press in the 1850s and 60s

Priest advertised her school in local Norwich newspapers as 'A Preparatory Establishment for Young Gentlemen'

As a child Mary Mann – or 'Polly' Rackham as she was before her marriage – knew Mrs Priest. Her older brother, Willie, was a pupil for a time with Mrs Priest, and so was Mary herself for a little while, 'one little girl in a room full of small boys' so it is not surprising that when she received Hibgame's letters she knew they were true and realised she might have the makings of a novel. That novel was *Memories of Ronald Love* and it was published by Methuen in 1907. After it was published Mary Mann wrote to her nephew, 'I too had the privilege of tuition under the 'tender' rule of Paraman and Priest ... [I remember] the boxes, the stocks, the boys lying under Paraman's chair' and she recalled the abject terror many boys had felt. Both Mary and her brother were only with Mrs Priest for a short time and both went on to other schools; Willie as a boarder to Wymondham Grammar School, Mary to a school for girls in Surrey Street.[4]

Mrs Priest was in her mid-fifties when Mary was at the school, and the description in her novel is probably based on her own memories of her as 'an old lady, fat, pale and intimidating ...' and in a spelling lesson 'encouraging' the boy nearest her with smacks about the head with the lesson book. Miss Paraman too was large and pale but with sandy hair – her bony hands 'encased' in silk gloves. Her treatment was even more vicious. Mary remembered one boy being whacked on the head and on his trembling hands with a gigantic paper-knife that Miss Paraman kept with her. His sin had been failing to write the letter X properly. Frederick Hibgame wrote that 'She was a woman uneducated and bigoted even beyond her class at that period. She knew nothing, and could not even have passed today an examination for the post of infant school-teacher. Little was there that she could teach but a religion of her own, and this she communicated with a cruelty and an ignorance by no means uncommon at that time, yet with a faith and fervour ... at which the present age ... can only wonder.'

She was born in 1827, the eldest daughter of the Norwich city gaoler, Robert Paraman. Her mother, Christiana, was the matron at the prison. Elizabeth, and her brother and sister, were born in the gaol and lived there with their parents – perhaps that had some bearing on her character and later sadistic behaviour. In the 1851 census, aged twenty-three, she was an assistant at Mrs Priest's school. It may be that she had attended the school herself – certainly the 1841 census records her younger sister Ellen being a pupil there, the only girl amongst six little boys. Mrs Priest, unlike most schoolteachers of the time, seemed willing to take pupils of both sexes if their parents were prepared to pay.

Mary Mann was a prolific novelist and short-story writer and we know she relied very heavily on descriptions of real people and events – indeed on one occasion she was nearly sued for libel by a local clergyman.[5] In *Memories of Ronald Love* she barely even troubled to change the teachers' names. Miss Elizabeth Paraman becomes 'Miss Eliza Pergaman' and the headmistress, Mrs Maria Priest, wife of Henry Raven Priest, the wine merchant, becomes 'Mrs Priestly', also married to a wine merchant named Henry. Mary Mann also invents – or describes – an affair between jovial Mr Priestly and Eliza Pergaman, being carried on under his wife's nose, much to the amusement of the boys. This is not beyond the bounds of possibility in that the real Elizabeth Paraman was in her twenties when Mary Mann knew her, and was some thirty years younger than Mr and Mrs Priest.

While Frederick's family were a model of respectability, Mary Mann gives 'Ronald Love' a much more dubious backstory for the titillation of her readers. He is the illegitimate son of Dr Clough and pretty, flirtatious coquette, Nancie Love. The doctor discovers Nancie is two-timing him with Mr Tilly, the market gardener, and abandons her but agrees to pay for Ronnie's schooling. Nancie reluctantly marries Mr Tilly. Ronnie sees very little of his mother thereafter – he has one holiday at home but Mr Tilly finds him a nuisance and the school deems his mother to be an unhealthy influence, so he is doomed to spend all his subsequent holidays at school. In his letter to Mary Mann, Frederick Hibgame vividly recalled being the only child left in the school – perhaps because his father was ill – when the other boys all went home for the holidays. Eventually Nancie has a still-born baby and dies. Mr Priestly has a heart attack and Dr Clough is called in to attend him; Ronnie stows away in the doctor's carriage and is taken to his house where he meets the new Mrs Clough, a kind woman called Eleanor. They take him in and all ends happily. However, most of the book is taken up with descriptions of the school and Mary Mann's main purpose seems to have been to expose Miss Paraman and Mrs Priest (both long dead by the time the book was written) for the monsters they were.

In 1910, after the book was published, Mary Mann had a letter from J D Gooding who had been at school with Fred Hibgame, and he added his own memories of standing in the stocks and having his nose pinched when Miss Paraman administered a dose of senna. He described 'the torture chamber of Miss Paraman's bedroom. In her bedroom, in solitary confinement, I have spent many a miserable day.'

In the novel, little Ronnie is beaten in Miss Pergaman's bedroom with a busk from her corsets and with a hairbrush – the boys never knew which she would choose until the first blow was struck. He is put in the 'stocks', an arrangement of pieces of wood designed to hold the feet in the uncomfortable balletic 'first position'; he stands on his book box with a dunce's cap on his head looking out over the rooftops to the hills beyond, believing the distant country he can see is America (following a description in a letter from Fred Hibgame who also thought the distant hills were America); he is locked in a cupboard on the landing for an entire afternoon, and he is constantly hungry. Ronnie secretly buys 'hollow biscuits' from the nearby shop: they are all he can afford. Like Fred Hibgame's brother, he runs away, is caught, brought back and punished. Ronald's final assessment of his school is Fred Hibgame's own. 'It is more than five and fifty years ago, but he is unforgiving still, and will go down to his grave execrating the memory of a woman who made little children suffer so.'

Mary Mann re-used Mrs Priest/ly's school in a short story, *The Coming of King Ackerman*, published in 1917. Ackerman King is a new boy at the school; his mother has died and his father is away at sea. He is unwilling to knuckle down under the regime – he laughs when he is put in the stocks, he dances a jig on his book box when forced to stand on it wearing a dunce's cap, and he complains about the food. However, the story ends quickly and happily. *Memories of Ronald Love* gives a much more convincing picture of the long drawn-out misery suffered by a child who is unhappy at school for years on end.

Frederick Hibgame must have entered Mrs Priest's school when he was between five and six years old. Mrs Priest's husband died in 1864 and Frederick was certainly there before that as he describes him clearly. He would therefore have started her school in 1862 or 1863 and if he spent 'five miserable years' there he would have left in 1867 or 1868. We know he went on to another school but we do not know which – or whether or not he was happier there.

Below are some extracts from the novel about Ronald's (or Frederick's) first day at school. The level of cruelty is almost unbelievable. How could women treat the little boys in their school as Mrs Priest and Miss Paraman did? How pitiful was not only the savage treatment but the incredibly poor education. For any small child, leaving home for the first time and being thrust – even today – into a completely alien situation is hard to bear, and although most boarding schools were not as savage as this one, for many children in the nineteenth century it was a very painful rite of passage indeed.

The Memories of Ronald Love by Mary E Mann

The servant who had carried his box through the playground and deposited it in the hall, now taking his hand, led him upstairs. Opening the door to the schoolroom, which was on the third floor, she introduced the new-comer to the notice of Mrs Priestly, of her assistant in scholastic duties Miss Eliza Pergaman, and of his school mates.

"Master Love is it? Come and shake hands Master Love," said Mrs Priestly.

Perhaps Mrs Priestly was not a marvel of antiquity; he, later, found reason to believe that Eliza Pergaman, her assistant was far from being the ugliest created thing; yet these two women represented to the child .... the ultimate things in age and hideousness.

To dispassionate eyes there was nothing alarming in the person of an elderly lady of large proportions seated at a desk before which six small boys, in the act of going through a spelling lesson, stood in a semi-circle. To the unseasoned, unreasoning intelligence of Ronald Love she was, in the first instant of his introduction, remaining so to the end of his acquaintance with her, a terrifying figure.

She held out a large white hand encased in a white mitten; her large face was white also; the hair, arranged in flat curls upon her temples was white, quilled net tied beneath her chin with broad white ribbons, over her ample bust white muslin was crossed. Ronald, with one glance at her outstretched hand, flung himself upon the retiring housemaid, and tried to hide in her skirts. With a dexterous whisk of her petticoats the maid freed herself and departed.

At home, when misfortune overtook him .... he flung himself on his back on the floor, ... fight with arms and legs. But already his education was begun; angry and frightened he scowled through his tears, but dared not scream aloud, and he maintained a perpendicular position. In that first instant of his installation his enemy was upon him.

Four little boys were writing copes at an inclined shelf running along the left wall of the room, and serving as a desk. They were under the active supervision of Miss Pergaman; she left them without hesitation, and with ruler, ready for knuckles or head, with which she presided over all lessons in her hand, she bore down upon the new-comer.

"This is Master Love, Eliza," Mrs Priestly explained. "He has refused to shake hands with me."

Miss Pergaman surveyed the newcomer from beneath her sand-coloured lids. "What is your name Sir, your attention if you please, look me in the face and speak out."

He had to proclaim six times that it was Ronnie before he spoke in the exact tone that Miss Pergaman approved. In the end she informed him it was not Ronnie at all but Ronald; by which appellation, turning round upon the school, she proclaimed him to his mates.

"Now put out your hand to Mrs Priestly, sir. Not in that sluggish fashion, if you please, but as if you were proud of the honour of shaking hands with her. You know it is an honour don't you?"

"No," said Ronald, shrinking from the narrow green eyes.

"Say yes, sir."

"Yes Sir," said Ronald.

"Why do you say Sir to me pray? Am I a young gentleman then?"

"I don't know," said Ronald in his bewilderment ...'

Until his box, already ordered for him designed to hold his books and serve him as a seat arrived, he was accommodated on a low form at Mrs Priestly's left hand. A book was given to him to hold; one of the older boys told to teach him his letters. Not much of the alphabet did Ronald acquire that morning. He senselessly repeated the letters after the child who sat beside him, but his sobs kept struggling upwards, and his eyes roamed dejectedly around the space of his captivity. Mistily, through his tears, he saw the hated schoolroom on that first morning as he saw it, frequently, in the time to come.

If anyone had asked him the number of boys assembled that morning he would have said a hundred, that being the figure by which he was accustomed to express any assemblage beyond two. In fact there were twenty-five beside himself: they each sat on their own little box, five deep and five in a line. Those, who were not in the class, sat at the writing shelf, at Mrs Priestly's desk, or under punishment ... one stood on his box, a dunce's cap on his head, round his neck a placard, with which Ronald was to make close acquaintance later, announcing in boldly written characters, "I am a bad boy". Beneath another of the high windows (the school room was in the attic, and all three windows were in the roof) was another piece of *furniture afterwards introduced to the new boy's unwilling notice as "the stocks". This was merely a piece of wood bordered on each side with low walls, arranged for hold the feet in the uncomfortable angle know to dancing academies of the time as "the first position". ... Yet another pupil, undergoing chastisement, lay on his back beneath Miss Pergaman's chair; his narrow body squeezed in between its back and front legs, his arms as in a vice at his sides: his head and feet protruding beyond the lady's skirts, and his eyes fixed on the raftered ceiling. This was her favourite method of enforcing quietude on restless boys. The space beneath the chair was seldom unoccupied. One or other of the children had always fidgeted with his hands or feet in a fashion to qualify him for the painful position ...yet another young gentleman, more culpable than the rest, was led off by Miss Pergaman to her bedroom. In the retirement of that chaste seclusion she was in the habit of administering corporal punishment on the slightest provocation and with no sparing hand. For this ceremonial she had a choice of weapons .... her hairbrush or the busk of her stays ...When Miss Pergaman returned, a little heated from her exertions and unaccompanied – the object of her educational energy having been sent to bed on a diet of bread and water for the rest of the day – she found all in their places.*

Might this passage disguise happenings of a more sexual nature which at the time of writing Mary E Mann felt she could not put into print? Why in the bedroom? If she used a busk – a bone or wooden strip from the front of her stays – had she taken them off? Was she abusing the boys as well as beating them? Were they then sent to bed to be alone all day, the normal sequence, so as not to reveal to the other boys what had happened? And is Mrs Priest aware, but frightened of Miss Paraman herself?

Even Mrs Priestly, who had relaxed vigilance so far as to take a letter out of her pocket ... leaning back in her chair, yawning and rubbing her mittened hands over her great white face, was herself again. She sat erect at her desk, whacking it now and then startlingly with a small cane that she kept beside her for that, and other, purposes; calling an unnecessary "Silence young Gentleman" as her subordinate entered; just to show how alert and vigorous she was.

"*Say A*," *said the boy at Ronnie's side.*

"*A*", *said Ronnie. He was looking vaguely before him, his mind busy at that moment with Hart* [a man servant in his home] *.... that his mother had gone away and that he was shut up in this strange and terrible place ... would he not come instantly to deliver him? He gave a howl at this point because the boy next to him ... had surreptitiously pinched him through the leg of his new trousers ...*

" *Please'm*" *he said addressing Mrs Priestly's assistant, "this little boy won't say B.*"

"*Won't?*" *repeated Miss Pergaman in a tone to make the heart quake. "There is no such word, in this establishment, as 'won't'. Bring him here at once to me.*"

Ronald went, but not docilely, trying to fight off the hand that held him, dragging backwards, struggling; yet, arrived at Miss Pergaman's chair was awed into the outward signs of submission.

"*B*," *said Miss Pergamon, "is for Bad Boy, for the Beating he got, for the Bed he was sent to. Now, sir, will you say B.*"

"*I want my mother*," *said Ronald.* " *I want to go back to her and Sarah, where my home is. I don't wish to be here any more.*"

There was a tittering through the room from the little boys.

"*Silence!*" *commanded Mrs Priestly, and whacked her table.*

"*Say B*" *repeated Miss Pergaman.*

"*I don't want to. I want Sarah.*"

"*Eliza*," *said Mrs Priestly warningly, "Please remember that Master Love is a very little boy.*"

"*B*" *she repeated again in biting tones, "is for Bad Boy, for Beating, for Bed," she paused; in the elucidation of the letter all heard a terrible menace. "Say B sir," she concluded sharply.*

"*B*," *shouted Ronald, "B – B – B!*" *he persisted, in a sudden access of temper, and began to cry out loud.*

"*Go back to your form, take your book, and repeat "B" five hundred times.*"

Before Ronald could compose himself he found Mrs Priestly standing before him...

"*I have said that young gentlemen are not to be punished on their first day of school*," *she pronounced in the direction of Miss Pergaman. "Master Love, put your book down and come with me.*" *It is hardly probable that at Belle Vue Seminary they had, uninterruptedly, the same fare; but as Ronald tries to reconstruct the mid-day meal, there presents itself to his mind's eye invariably mutton, invariably boiled, served with hot water, rice and potatoes; he remembers the plate always swimming in warm water. The dish was preceded by a course of Norfolk Dumplings. Served with treacle or the water in which the mutton was boiled.*

On the occasion of that first dinner three of the young gentleman were cheaply regaled on dry bread and salt tears. One enjoyed the same fare in retirement in his bedroom. Semi-starvation held a high place in the received educational method of that day, and the medical precept to leave the table only partially satisfied was conscientiously obeyed at Belle Vue. Miss Pergaman suffered from bad digestion herself, and was conscientious in her oft repeated dictum that the enjoyment of food was only greediness, that it was far better for the health's sake of young gentlemen, and for their soul's good, to feed as little as possible.

Yet, if conscientious, she was hardly consistent ... she sat on the right hand of Mr Priestly before whom a toothsome dish was always placed, facing his wife, who served the boiled mutton at the other end of the board.

The Master of the house (but not of the school – he was a wine merchant by trade) was a stout, yet spruce and smart looking man, white-haired like his wife ... he always wore a black coat cut in the fashion of those which are now only worn in the evening, tight black trousers ... and a black satin waist-coat. A white cravat about his neck ... Mrs Priestly's husband had a prosperous air about him, was always good-tempered, and being cheerful himself liked to see cheerful faces about him.

"Come, a little sunshine," he would say, rapping his horn-handled knife on the table to command attention, and looking round at the small lugubrious faces on his board.

"Here's a good dinner, and here we are, all well, to eat it. Let me see merry faces."... Perhaps enjoying with good appetite his own savoury meal, he did not realise how uninviting was the fare provided for the children ... perhaps he had never been sent to a boarding school ... had not the means of realising how weary, how dreary, how sick for home were such little hearts ...

Ronald was encouraged by the fat laughter and good humoured face. "I want to go home to my mother," he said, "I hate the old woman, and I hate this one too. I do," he repeated hardily, disregarding the sharp voice of reproof, and gazing into

Mrs Priestly's astounded face. "I hate all the boys, and all of you. I won't stay here. I want Sarah and my Mother: I want to go home."

The fourteen little boarders gazed in delight. Here was a boy who dared to express all they were feeling ... the present was exhilarating with the pleasing certainty of seeing him punished later on! Mrs Priestly and Miss Pergaman were for the moment speechless.

... Mr Priestly rapped the butt of his horn-handled knife on the table.

"Come! Come! This won't do. This is rank subordination. You won't hear the other young gentleman speaking so of their best friends and their happy home, I can assure you. Come" he cried, and turned his encouraging face upon the boarders. "Come boys, you heard what this young gentleman said: now tell us what your feeling is with regard to Mrs Priestly and Miss Pergaman." There was an uncomfortable silence.

"One, two, three, reply," said Miss Pergaman with a smart clap of her hands. Her green eyes roving over the faces fixed upon a small boy pale and narrow faced, and of weed-like growth.

"Percy Green speak up!" she cried.

"We love them," said Percy Green in a thin, wavering voice.

"That's better. And the rest of you? One, two, three – reply!"

"We love them," dropped in a halting chorus from fourteen pairs of perjured lips.

Mr Priestly smiled, but was not altogether satisfied. "Not hearty enough! Give me some heartiness!" he cried, " Now then altogether! What do we think of Mrs Priestly and Miss Pergaman? We love them!"

He led the chorus in stentorian tones. "We love them" was piped by fourteen miserable little boys in unison.

Miss Pergaman turned to him "You hear! Wicked, unfeeling, ungrateful little boy! Aren't you ashamed to be the only one in this school who has no Christian love in your heart for those who only wish to be your benefactors? Don't look at Mr Priestly sir ... look at me, sir. Aren't you ashamed?"

"I hate you," said Ronald.

"Eliza," said Mrs Priestly warningly, " I have asked you to bear in mind that he is only a very little boy."

"I hate you too!" said Ronald. He was desperate now ...

"You are a wicked, rebellious dangerous boy," Miss Pergaman assured him ... She put her face close to his and held his wide frightened blue eyes with her narrow green one. "But do not think, Ronald Love, that I shall not tame you. Why if you were a raging lion, or a wild man from the woods, I should tame you."

A furious row then ensues in the book between Mrs Priestly and Miss Pergaman which again is probably based on fact. Mrs Priest realised that her assistant was dangerously bad-tempered and yet felt that she could not control her, and not many years after this Miss Paraman left Mrs Priest's school and set up one of her own with her sister Ellen. One dreads to imagine what that establishment was like.

Of further occurrences of his first day at school Ronald Love remembers nothing. One day in that establishment was hopelessly like the rest; to distinguish one afternoon from the interminable desert of afternoons that followed would be an impossible task. An interview that he had with Miss Pergaman before he went to bed that night fixed itself on his memory.

Alternating during many hours, between the fiery state of rebellious raging and despairing tears he was so worn out with his emotions that when she led him to her bedroom had she taken him in her arms he would have let his head rest on gratefully even on that hard breast ... But Miss Pergaman was not capable of conceiving such treatment to be her duty. She was a Christian of the rigid school, in too high repute at that time, and believed she had duties to fulfil that she would have scorned to shirk. The petting and consoling of helpless children she could not imagine to be one of these ... she [just] constantly repeated in his ears that he must pray – pray hard for forgiveness so that God in his mercy should cease to hate him.

"Pray. Pray."'

There were, the occasions, unhappily few and far between, when Miss Pergaman suffered from toothache and had to absent herself from class. To be sure Mrs Priestly, doing her best to fill her teacher's place, dispensed punishments with liberal hand, but they were punishments compared with the ingenious tortures of Eliza ... An application of bitter aloes on the fingers of a boy who sucked them, the infliction of an hour and a half in the stocks to him whose toes turned in. What were such inconveniences as these to the methods of the younger woman? The shameful whippings, the pressing of little restless bodies into a cramped and unnatural position to be maintained for hours, the lonely imprisonment in a black cupboard.

There was one boy who, having the bad habit of biting his nails, Miss Pergaman cut hers and put the parings in front of him … "If you enjoy yours Master Pratt you can't possibly object to eating mine – they are at least clean and wholesome, which yours, young gentleman, are often not."

When he was asked afterwards by the other boys what they tasted like he replied that anything to eat was better than nothing in this establishment.

Eventually, unable to take any more, Ronald Love runs away from the school and makes for the coast where he hopes he might find a ship to take him far away. This part of the novel is again based on fact, for Frederick Hibgame's elder brother had done just that. A search is put out for him, he is found and eventually dragged back to school by Miss Pergaman who then questions him relentlessly about why he ran away – trying to twist every answer he gives and assuring him that everything she does is to make him a purer boy and one who will not suffer the everlasting wrath of God. At the end of one particularly long punishing session she demands of Ronald:

"Do I punish you for my pleasure?"
"Yes," replied Ronald.

He had identified Miss Pergaman for what she was, a sadist, who lived for the thrill of inflicting pain on others for her own satisfaction – albeit in the name of Christianity.

Despite his introduction to education, Frederick Hibgame developed a love of learning. He did not follow Mary Mann's advice and write about his schooldays – but he did write two books, *A Curious Norwich Story Book* (undated) and *Recollections of Norwich 50 Years Ago* in 1919. He converted to

Catholicism in 1877, as did his elder sister Emily a few years later. She became a Dominican nun, while he was involved with the building of St John's Roman Catholic Church in Norwich (now St John's Cathedral). He contributed a lengthy description of the inauguration to *The Great Gothic Fane*, published in 1913, which was a vast tome describing the history of Catholicism in Norwich and celebrating the building of St John's. As an old man he had returned to his beloved Norwich, and he died there in 1922.

Portrait of Frederick Thurlow Hibgame as an old man

Endnotes

1 *The Diary of a London Schoolboy 1826 – 1830* by John Thomas Pocock. Camden History Society, 1980.

2 Corrance Papers, Suffolk County Record Office.

3 Mrs Priest called it 'Pottergate Street' in her advertisement but today it is just 'Pottergate'.

4 Aldis, M and Inder, P, *MEM, a biography of Mary E Mann,* Larks Press, Dereham, 2013.

5 Ibid. chapter 8. In October-November 1904 'old Dr B' was threatening to take her to court for libel. Mary Mann was especially critical of clergymen in her novels and short stories and 'Dr B' thought one of her characters was based on him. We think 'Dr B' was Reverend Frederick William Bussell DD, vicar of Mundford in Norfolk.

The making of a bluestocking

Girls got an even worse deal than their brothers. Ann[1] Marsh Caldwell was born with a silver spoon in her mouth – though it was not always dipped in honey, as a memoir to her daughters in later life indicates. Memory can play tricks, but there must be an element of truth in this: 'There was little caressing and kissing in those times ... I never remember sitting on either my father's or my mother's knee – there were too many above me or below me ...' [2]

There were other memories that hint at a less-than-happy childhood. '... tea came at about 5 o'clock – we children went to supper in the Laundry, a room underground; cold and dark, where by the light of one candle ... we found a large wooden tray on which were basins of milk and pieces of bread ...' Or this '...we [Ann and her sisters] were shut in a room upstairs and told to amuse ourselves and not to make a noise as we must not disturb Mama. [Her mother had just given birth] We began to play, I suppose we made a noise, for Papa came to the top of the stairs and in what seemed to me a voice of thunder commanded us and threatened us to be still ...'

Ann was the fourth child of the seven born to James and Elizabeth Caldwell – though she outlived all her siblings by sixteen years. For the children it was not always a life of luxury, as the above quotations show. They were certainly not spoilt. When chickenpox broke out, a serious disease at that time, Ann was sent away to an aunt's house in Nantwich for safety. The food was no better there. 'Dry bread, – milk – very tasteless rice pudding and plain roast meat only allowed in certain quantities – butter in all its forms forbidden.'

But there were happy memories too – their father reading to them in the evenings, Christmas with all the aunts staying at Linley Wood and 'painting curtains' with her father and mother. Perhaps it is these events she was remembering when she talked later about having had a happy childhood.

Ann's father, James Caldwell, had married well. His wife,

Elizabeth Stamford, brought several thousand pounds as a dowry – added to by the death of rich relatives as time went by. Eventually James Caldwell was in control of upwards of £20,000 of her money (well over two million pounds today). He was a prudent Scot who was used to hard work and had seen poverty at first-hand as a boy. He managed the money well. With his wife's dowry, and the money he made as an attorney, they had enough to buy an extensive estate, Linley Wood, just outside Newcastle-under-Lyme at Talk o' the Hill. He paid £4,750 for the house in 1789 – half a million today – but immediately started to build a fine mansion on the site. It was finished by the time Ann was old enough to remember anything and she spent her childhood there.

Linley Wood, home of the Caldwell family

Ann had an older sister, Hannah Elizabeth, and two older brothers, James Stamford and Francis. Francis is not mentioned at all in the diaries and we do not know the reason for this. She also had two younger sisters, Catherine Louise and Margaret Emma – though it would appear that she did not share any tuition with them. The diaries that remain date from 1801 when Ann was ten years old – it is not known whether she wrote any before that date. In her diaries she often used initials to save writing out names in full. Her older brothers and sisters, who she always refers to by their second names, never their first, were Hannah Elizabeth (1785-1854, 'Eliza' or 'HEC'), James Stamford (1786-1858, 'Stamford' or 'JSC'), Margaret Emma (1792-1830, 'Emma' or 'EC'), and Catherine Louisa (1794-1814 'Louisa' or 'CLC'). Her parents are usually referred to as Mama and Papa but occasionally as 'JC' and 'EC'. There are also some initials that do not belong to her immediate family which remain unidentified.

She wrote copiously every day in her notebooks which are a mixture of diary entries, work set by her tutors, and huge chunks of books laboriously copied out. Often they are very difficult to read as she rarely bothered to use punctuation, but from them can be learned a great deal about her life and education, and indeed about the lives of other young women of a similar class at that time. She recalls her aunts, the sound religious upbringing she had from her parents and her mother's fickleness – sometimes kind, sometimes sarcastic and strict.

Elizabeth Caldwell, née Stamford, Ann's mother

James Caldwell, Ann's father

Her grandfather Caldwell, a devoutly religious non-conformist, had fled from the poverty of mid-eighteenth-century Scotland to start a small drapery business in Nantwich in Cheshire. The business did well; certain that education was the key to eradicating poverty, he set up a school in Nantwich with the well-known scientist, Joseph Priestly, for the poor children of the town – and made sure that his own son, James, was very well educated indeed. James Caldwell prospered. His father must have been proud when he became an attorney-at-law and Recorder for Newcastle-under-Lyme. Ann, aged fifteen, described the event in her diary. She had not been overawed by royalty.

> September 11th 1806: HRH the Prince of Wales came and the Duke of Clarence to Newcastle and had the Freedom of the Borough presented to them in the town hall Papa as Recorder made a speech and read an address which HRH answered in most pleasing manner. We were all present The Prince is

a very gentlemanly [crossed out] princely looking
man but he has lost all traces of beauty the Duke is
certainly everything rather than handsome.

James Caldwell was on visiting terms with many of the
great and the good in Staffordshire and Ann's diaries record
over a hundred people visiting, dining, or staying – sometimes
for weeks at a time – at Linley Wood between 1801, when the
diaries start, and 1808 when they finish. One of the families
the Caldwells socialised with most frequently was that of Josiah
Wedgwood and his wife and four children. Josiah was James
Caldwell's most important client. People with 'new money' –
money that they had earned, not inherited – came, including
doctors, lawyers and manufacturers, and also people with 'old
money' – money inherited over generations – including the
Marquis and Marchioness of Stafford, who, Ann noted in her
journal, 'behaved very agreeably towards us ...', Lady Fletcher
and her two daughters, Lady Thorne, the aristocratic Sneyds
of Keele Hall, and the Sparrows of Bishton Hall – John, his
wife Elizabeth and daughters Hannah Maria and Elizabeth,
and Hannah's young husband Sir George Chetwynd. Sparrow
was another lawyer and businessman, but he had not only
inherited money and married into more – he made a lot as well
both as a lawyer and speculative businessman. The Caldwell's
house seemed always full.

Ann also remembered, with some awe, her wealthy Aunt
Stamford who lived with them at Linley Wood. Her rooms
were elegantly appointed and she was very stylishly dressed
and completely self-assured. She had a fortune of her own
and had little use for men. When her attention was drawn one
day to a handsome man her stinging comment was, 'he has a
handsome horse!' Ann loved being with her aunt – perhaps
even as a very small child she saw what it would be like to be
in control of one's own destiny and not at the beck and call
of a husband. This aunt could go riding and on faraway trips
whenever she wished; she studied chemistry in her rooms –
there were shelves in her wardrobe filled with jars and bottles
– and she frequently burnt her fingers when experiments went
awry. And she was amusing too. With no children of her own
she could afford to spoil her little nieces and nephew and left

out raisins at night in rows of six, which the children could only take if they were as silent as mice.

Ann's brother Stamford went away to be educated, to Rugby then to Cambridge. Ann and her sisters were educated at home. This was the norm for girls of their class; that way their parents could be sure that they were only meeting people of whom they approved, people who would instil behaviour and ideas that befitted a young lady whose sole purpose in life was to attract a wealthy husband and live a life of probity. At the time of her notebooks and diaries, Ann does not seem to be sharing classes with either her older or younger sisters. Her principal tutors, Mr Alcock and Mr Fouchecourt, came on a Monday and Tuesday – weather permitting – and it did not seem to take much to put Mr Alcock, in particular, off from travelling out to Linley Wood. Occasionally Mr Fritch, her dancing master, came. Strangely, there is almost no mention of literature though she must have read extensively. Perhaps she was expected to do this by herself from books in her father's library; he read to his children and obviously encouraged reading. She was also expected to find out about things of interest for herself. Visits with her family provided the spur for that sort of study. Details of pottery manufacturing processes filled pages of her diary after a visit to a pottery in Burslem with her aunt and sisters, for example.

Mr Alcock and Mr (sometimes Monsieur) Fouchecourt, poured out before her a great rag-bag of information: history – anything from classical Greek through James I to Napoleon. Not in any particular order. Then there was arithmetic, natural history, astronomy, physics – of a sort – and 'speculative mathematics and optics hydrostatic hydrography' – whatever that may have been. Philosophy, French and Italian also exercised her mind. 'Mr De Fouchecourt came we have begun to study Italian and find it much easier than French'. The Bible, mining in South Africa, farming in Kentucky, life in Siberia, Adam Smith and the *Wealth of Nations*, the unimaginably convoluted workings of the French lottery system, in fact anything that caught her tutors' fancy on any particular day, made up Ann's education. And great events were recorded with no emphasis, just slipped in amongst comments about the weather and who had just visited.

Page from Ann's diary

Thursday November 9th: A glorious victory Admiral Collingwood and Lord Viscount Nelson 26 English ships of the line and 33 of the French and Spanish … the battle was fought near Cape Trafalgar … But the English loss was great for Lord Nelson was shot in the shoulder he was taken to the surgery and after confessing great anxiety to know how the day would be decided he expired.

And so it went on. There seemed to be no plan, no continuity. However, Ann was a diligent pupil and filled her notebooks with page after page of notes copied from the books her tutors brought with them or that were in her father's library. She wrote in French, copied out poems and newspaper articles and great chunks of Hume's *History of England.* At least her education could be called liberal and was not just restricted to reading safe English classics, or to drawing, painting and dancing – though she must have had some drawing lessons.

One sketch that she did while on holiday in Scotland with brother Stamford survives and shows her to have been quite accomplished.

Sketch made by Ann when she was on holiday

Later in life she was well able to see the limitations of her education, and writing to an acquaintance – in the third person – said:

> She certainly is clever in many ways, more by her own exertions, than by original education, which in a country place in Staffordshire, was limited, … but having by nature an enquiring mind, and an intuitive quickness of observation, and great energy, and having many clever and learned connections, she has improved herself …

When she was not working diligently at her studies, young Ann was sitting at her parents' table with their guests and absorbing – and writing down – the words of wisdom she heard from her father and his friends, though she was always critical. Like his father before him, James Caldwell was a devoutly religious man and there was church and Bible study every Sunday – Ann assiduously recorded both text and sermon.

> May 19th: Text. Keep thy heart with all diligence for out of it are the issues of life. Sermon on keeping the heart and its passions in order a very good one by Dr Blair.

Dr Blair was one of Scotland's most famous divines, a visiting preacher, and a frequent visitor to Linley Wood. He was even more tight-laced than her father. Ann wrote: 'When the theatre at Glasgow was erected Mr Blair preached vehemently against it declaring that not one of those that went to a play could possibly be saved.' Mrs Caldwell must have decided to part company with Mr Blair over that particular piece of teaching – she often took her children to the theatre.

It is not possible to transcribe all Ann's diaries and notebooks here page by page, but from an educational point of view what she studied is interesting. By the age of ten she was obviously already a very competent reader and writer.

This chapter concentrates on just a few months from her 1805 and 1806 notebooks as an example of her education, as they show the sort of information that was put before her. Whether this was general we do not know – but presumably Mr Alcock and Mr Fouchecourt had other pupils in the area and their subject matter was likely to have been the same. Ann was fourteen in 1805, and we have often only given a précis (the actual notes run to thousands and thousands of words) of the subject-matter in her notebooks to indicate the scope and complexity of that which was put before her. Some of it was difficult to read and a question mark in the text indicates an undeciphered word.

From her notebooks, it becomes obvious that if one of her tutors did not turn up Ann was expected to work by herself from one of the books they had left with her. Saturdays were no exception. It was challenging work for a fourteen-year-old – and she obviously did not always understand what she read. One of the main books that she mentions by name was *The History of England* by David Hume. He wrote it in installments while he was serving as librarian to the Faculty of Advocates in Edinburgh. It was published in six volumes in 1754, 1756, 1759 and 1761. The first publication of his *History* was greeted with outrage by all political factions as Hume was anti-clerical, anti-Catholic, anti-Presbyterian, anti-Puritan, anti-Whig, and pro-monarchy – but it became a best-seller. Hume's *History* spanned the period 'from the invasion of Julius Caesar to the Revolution of 1688' and it went through over a hundred editions.

Other books Ann read were *The Curiosities of Literature* by Benjamin Disraeli, *Dictionnaire Historique* and *The Life of Zicten*. Disraeli's book was issued in instalments between 1791 and 1823 and was all about books. The *Dictionnaire* was a multi-volume work detailing the evolution of the French language through ten centuries. It ran to over 50,000 words. Zicten was the Prussian General Lelen von Zicten, a distinguished commander under Frederick the Great, Colonel of the Royal Prussian Hussar Life Guards. In Ann's day, the *Life* was a recent work, published in 1803.

Another book she read was *The Cape of Good Hope* by Robert Percival. Percival was a traveller and writer; he became a captain in the 18th Irish infantry regiment, and in 1795 joined the fleet that was despatched to conquer the Cape of Good Hope, then held by the Dutch. The attack was victorious and he was the first man to enter Cape Town on September 16th 1796. On his return he published a narrative of his journey and a description of the country, under the title: *An Account of the Cape of Good Hope, containing an Historical View of its original Settlement by the Dutch, and a Sketch of its Geography, Productions, the Manners and Customs of its Inhabitants*. It was published in London in 1804, so when Ann was reading it, it was a recent publication. Percival's criticisms of the Dutch settlers – their laziness, inhospitality, low level of civilisation and especially their cruelty to the natives – are severe, but he commends the Cape climate as the finest in the world and advises the English government to reoccupy it. His work was warmly praised at the time.

Yet another tome on Ann's reading list was *Life of Washington* by John Marshall. He was the fourth Chief Justice of the United States (1801-1835) whose opinions as stated in court helped lay the basis for American constitutional law and made the Supreme Court of the United States a co-equal branch of government along with the legislative and executive branches. He was Secretary of State under President John Adams from 1800 to 1801.

There were many other books from which Ann made made notes. One by H Holland is mentioned several times; there was another by Adams on Siberia, one by Adolphus – in French – and one by Michour who apparently wrote about the soil in Kentucky. Work dominated Ann's life; there was no space in her daily routine for her to enjoy her childhood because she was being groomed to take her place as an educated young women who would know her place in a male-dominated world.

Below is a basic outline of what she was expected to learn day by day in 1805-6, interspersed with quotations from her notebooks. She did her best to record what she had read but it is obvious she did not always understand it. It seems strange that her tutors never attempted to correct her notes.

> May 11th: South African wine – Constantia –
> Percival's *Cape of Good Hope.*

> May 12th: A pound of cotton has been spun to the length of 160 miles.

> May 13th: When the Duke of Ormond was attacked in Parliament in 1681 … Hume's   *England.*

> May 14th: [Information on cowslips].

> May 16th: The condition of the poor in Devonshire is the most miserable that can be conceived in on hard winter [sic] if the frost continue long many may starve as the farmers cannot employ them and are too poor themselves to assist them their minds too are in a very low state of cultivation. A gentleman of the western circuit said that the further he travelled to the <u>west</u> the more he was convinced that the wise came from the <u>east</u>.

May 17th: [Spencer and the author of *The Turkish Spy*. *Curiosities of Literature*.]

May 18th: [Notes on James II from Hume's *England*. Entry on Nelson pursuing Spanish and French Fleets to Cadiz.]

May 22nd: [The conduct of the Prince of Orange towards James 2nd ... Hume's *England*.]

May 23rd: [Study entry – 'James II married a German princess...' Hume's *England*.]

May 24th: [More on James II from Hume's *England*.]

Saturday May 25th: [Entry about Ben Lomond and Loch Lomond and other British mountains from Mr H Holland.]

May 28th: [Calvinism in Scotland from 'M H' – this name seems to have been deliberately scribbled.]

May 29th: M H [again he appears as a deliberate scribble] Duke of Orange 'Hume's E.'

Saturday June 1st: Battle with the French on June 1st 1794.

June 3rd: Mr Alcock did not come.

June 4th: Mr Fouchecourt came. [Practice of the law in France.]

June 5th: [Notes on Malingra and a book about the Inquisition. *Dictionaire Historique*.]

June 6th: [Notes on General De Zicten from *The Life of Zicten*.]

June 13th: I went with the ladies to Burslem and saw the process of making earthenware. [This entry is followed by two pages of notes on the process of pottery making from the preparation of the clay to the finished product.]

June 14th: [Many more notes on pottery making.]

June 15th: I went to Trentham with the Ladies. [Two pages of notes on Trentham Gardens – the layout, trees, plants in the greenhouses, etc. follow this entry.]

Sun June 16th I will have mercy and not sacrifice. [Notes on dining traditions in St John's College, Cambridge, which her brother Stamford attended.]

June 20th: [More notes on St John's – reasons for expulsion etc.]

June 23rd: Mr Alcock came. [Some almost incomprehensible notes on mathematics eg 'speculative Mathematics comprehend geography optics hydrostatic hydrography…']

June 26th: Quotation – it has been said that true wit never made a person laugh it can always be translated into another language.

June 27th: [Notes about the Stoic philosophers.]
June 28th: [Notes on Plato.]

June 30th: Mr Alcock did not come a very warm day.
[More on Plato.]

June 31st: [Mr Fouchecourt. More about the French
and Spanish fleets.]

Sunday July 19th: [Text] and the 70 returned home
with joy saying Lord even the Devils are subject
unto us: and he said behold I see Satan as lightening
fall from heaven. Behold I give you power to tread
on serpents and scorpions and all the power of the
enemy: yet in this rejoice not, rather rejoice that your
names are written in Heaven.

July 20th: Mr Alcock did not come. The Lotterys
in France are very different from those in England
they are bets laid between the government and the
purchasers 90 numbers are put in the wheel of which
6 are drawn out the purchasers lays out 15 numbers
the names [?] drawn out suppose he lays on 12345
3 is drawn out and he receives 15 times the value of
his money /suppose 6d for which he pays 1 for each
number of his 5/- gain he lays that 1 and 4 will be in
the 5 drawn if only one comes up receiving nothing if
both receiving 64 times the value of his 6d Again he
lays that that 123 will come up if all three come up
he receives 400 6d's again he lays on 123 and if all 4
come up he receives 60,000 6d's again he lays that
123 may come up and receives a million 6d's on this
last bet he may risk no more than [?] on the other as
many pounds as he chooses. Mr Fouchecourt.

Ann dutifully wrote down what she thought she remembered
– but it makes no sense.

July 22nd: M De Fouchecourt came a violent
thunderstorm. [A very muddled account of how
lightning conductors work.]

July 23rd: Mr Alcock came. [Odd notes on sand in Siberia and laurel as a conductor of lightning.]

July 24th: The Pary's Mine cannot be worked the copper is so full of arsenic JSC.

July 25th: [More odd notes – about ascending mountains and more about Siberia.]

Saturday July 26th: [More notes about Siberia and its history from Adam's *Siberia*.]

Sunday July 27th: [Lots more notes on Moravia from Adam's *Siberia*.]

July 28th: Mr Alcock came. I learnt of Michour's *America* – In Kentucky peaches grow without cutting or grafting ... [This was followed by a complete page of notes on crops and farming in Kentucky.]

July 29th: Mr Fouchecourt came. [Short note on Nelson still being in pursuit of the French fleet.]

This was the period of the Napoleonic wars and M Fouchecourt was a Frenchman. Ann was obviously aware of what was going on – probably from conversations around the dinner table and snippets her father read out from the newspapers. As the months pass she includes more and more comments on the war, but the news was often unreliable and would often be contradicted a few days later.

July 30th: [More notes on farming in Kentucky.]

July 31st: [A short note on attar of roses in Kashmir.]

August 1st: [A short note on Ginseng being found in America and sold to China for its weight in gold.]

Saturday August 2nd: [Note on the soil in Kentucky from Michour.]

Sunday August 4th: [Notes on how etching is done and the materials that are used.]

August 6th: Mr Fouchecourt came [More about Nelson and his battles with the French and Spanish.]

August 7th: [A page of notes on etching.]

August 8th: [A note on a Danish astronomer from Jones' *Dictionary.*]

August 9th: [Notes on Lavoisier, the French chemist.]

August 13th: Mr Fouchecourt came. [Notes on Earth, Air, Fire and Water and the 'current view of Chemistry']. I believe that water is 2 kinds of air and that there are several kinds of earth those are called elements which cannot be analysed there are 46.

Saturday August 17th: [Some completely unintelligible notes about heat and particles.]

August 19th: Mr Alcock did not come.

August 20th: Mr Fouchecourt came.

August 21st: [Notes about a Phoenician called 'Sandioncatto' and references to Joshua and Moses.

It ends:] Cadmus did not introduce letters into Greece until 1519 therefore he could not be the inventor of letters. Tyler.

August 29th: [Notes on the thorny plant in Glastonbury associated with Christ that usually blooms at Christmas.]

August 30th: [A note on Constantine moving the empire from Rome to Constantinople.]

Saturday August 31st: Theododisius a Roman emperor first abolished paganism …

The following important entry has been transcribed exactly as it is written – lack of punctuation and capitals included – to show how Ann juxtaposed important news and trivial family affairs.

Thursday November 9th: a glorious victory Admiral Collingwood and Lord Viscount Nelson 26 English ships of the line and 33 of the French and Spanish being combined fleet the battle was fought near Cape Trafalgar the French and Spaniards commanded by Admiral Villeneuve and at Cape Gravina [?] Lord Nelson consented a new mode of signals which he laid before the officers the day before his ship was victory and A Collingwood's the Royal Sovereign The action began at twelve o'clock October 21st Admiral Gravina tacked and stood of for Cadiz with ten ships four more followed the rest were left for the victors But the English loss was great for Lord Nelson was shot in the shoulder he was taken to the surgery and after confessing great anxiety to know how the day would be decided he expired A Collingwood is made a Baron and the command of the fleet is left to him Sir John and Lady H Chetwood dined at Linley with Mr & Mrs J Wedgwood.

November 18th: Bonaparte had defeated General Mack and treachery is expected.

Saturday November 9th: A party from Newcastle viz Mr & Mrs & Miss Sparrow Mrs Mr W Bent Captain Mrs & Miss Furnival and Mr Swinnerton dined here. The King of Prussia has taken possession of Hanover for the English which the French evacuated a month ago The A Duke Charles has obtained a victory in Italy Oct 27.

Monday November 11th: Mr Alcock came and staid all night.

Tuesday November 12th: M de Fouchecourt did not come Sir Richard Strachan defeated the remainder of the combined French and Spanish fleets ten only are left now of the 33.

Saturday November 16th: I rode in the gig to Burslem a fine but cold day. The Paris papers say that the English and French have come to an agreement the only account of which is that ten ships Returned to Cadiz 'Not being wanted in the Engagement' Vive les francois pour les Gasesnaches.

Monday November 17th: [Notes about Adam Smith from his book *The Wealth of Nations* 'JC.' Maybe, since her father was a banker, he was instructing her about wealth and taxation.]

Friday November 29th: Bonaparte after making rapid strides through Swabia Bavaria and [?] the tyrant on the 10th of November entered Vienna. My Aunt Stamford in London died on Wednesday morn in consequence of which Papa Mama and my aunt set off for London.

Saturday November 30th: The Archduke Charles is dead of Fatigue and vexation in Italy my Aunts from Nantwich came.

Monday December 2nd: <u>Peace</u> signed between the Emperor of Germany and Bonaparte – It is astonishing what little stand the Germans have made apparently without any trouble Bonaparte has conquered the southern provinces of Germany and forced the Emperor to make peace The Russians have not time enough to [?] them.

Wednesday December 4th: It is untrue that the Emperor has made peace Bonaparte has entered Vienna the Archduke Charles is alive but Massena is driving him out of Italy.

Thursday December 5th: [Notes about stamp duty in America from Marshall's *Life of Washington*.]

Friday December 6th: [Two pages of notes about American politics.]

Saturday December 7th: [More American notes.]

Wednesday December 11th: A report that the French and Russians have had an engagement in which the last were defeated a French account the Arch Duke Ferdinand defeated a party of French in Bohemia My Uncle J S came.

Thursday December 12th: [Notes on a Latin poet born in Paris in 16 hundred and odd a [?] of the abbey of St Victor.]

Ann was not afraid of stating her own opinion of politics and current affairs. At fourteen she was, as all teenagers are, supremely sure that she knew everything.

Friday December 13th: It is my opinion that the further the French penetrate into Germany they are now in Vienna the further they penetrate into danger that the English or Russians through Hanover will cut off their rear and consequently their communication with Paris the Austrians will cut off the communication with Mapena in Italy. Bonaparte will have occasion to call off his forces from France and perhaps the event may be an insurrection of the people and the reestablishment of the Bourbons this has existed only in imagination … The Russians are entering Germany in Great numbers the first armies Have formed a coalition with the Austrians and the third is rapidly advancing My Aunt Anne set off for London.

Saturday December 14th: Silas Deane and Doctor Franklin concluded a treaty of alliance with Louis 16th …

Monday December 15th: A comet has been seen by Dr Hun[?] and another gentleman in the constellation Pisces.

Tuesday December 16th: M De Fouchecourt came for the last time Government requiring his services This gentleman had the rank of Count in his native country which he quitted in 1792 refusing to receive the oath directed to be administered He was in the Prince of Code's army and served as Lieutenant Colonel during the war succeeding the Revolution he was engaged in the unsuccessful attempt at Limberon out of 5,000 only 500 escaped he then returned to England and was allowed half pay The British government which he resigned to a brother in direst circumstances and taught French to support himself his manners were gentle but lively his face very plain and his figure small but well made he was well acquainted with the unfortunate Duke D' Enghien whose life he saved once when bathing and Bonaparte served a campaign under him in Constantin.

But then, the very next day –

Wednesday December 17th: Mr Fouchecourt came. [Notes about coral divers off the coast of Brittany – from Mr Fouchecourt.]

Thursday December 18th: A dreadful battle between the French and Russian Allies in which after 5 days combat the former were worsted the battle was fought near Wiskow in Moravia Though Bonaparte promised on his entry to the city that the property of the Citizens should be respected not one house was left unransacked and every outrage committed that was possible even had the city been taken by storm.

Saturday December 20th: More particulars of the Battle of Wiskow are arrived the French the first day charged the Russian took their artillery and several prisoners the second day the Russians charged with the Bayonet retook their artillery and prisoners and worsted the French at the end of the engagement the French fled in all directions The Emperor of Russia fought with the greatest valour he was lost for some time but fought his way to his army the guards under the Grand Duke Constantine performed prodigies of valour the slaughter was immense.

Sunday December 21st: A very fine day for the past week there has been a very deep snow which thawed on Thursday. Read a sermon of Dr Blair on the character of Hagael. Bonaparte it is said has offered an armistice and threatens if it is refused to burn Vilma to the ground.

Thursday December 25th: The good news is contradicted Bonaparte it is said was victorious at the battle of Wiskow but it is believed that it is not true that Alexander was victorious after.

Tuesday December 29th: [Notes on Renaissance painting in Italy from Tyler's *Elements.*]

At this point 'Thursday' is crossed out and there is a note – 'I have my dates wrong'. In fact she quite often got her dates out of sequence. She also had a cavalier disregard for punctuation – and in fact, even when she became a best-selling novelist, Ann Marsh Caldwell's grasp of punctuation remained shaky.

1806
Wednesday January 1st: The French Revolution … with the national Assembly then … the Legislative Assembly and then the national convention … Adolphus Fish of France.

Thursday January 2nd: An Armistice concluded between Bonaparte and Francis the Emperor Alexander has not agreed to it The Arch Duke Charles has made a most masterly retreat from Italy and had defeated Marshall Ney and after this victory he had this shameful Armistice to hear of it is supposed that the King of Prussia has had a great hand in it J C.

Friday January 3rd: Mama my Aunt Bessy and Eliza went to Newcastle Assembly.
Monday January 13th: Mr Alcock came.

Tuesday January 14th: Miss Bent came.

Wednesday January 15th: Miss Bent returned home taking Eliza with her. A <u>Peace</u> is concluded between the Emperor Francis and Bonaparte Alexander has returned to Russia Stamford was to have returned to Cambridge but the flood warning prevented the mail from coming.

Saturday January 18th: Stamford went. The position of the ships at the battle of the Nile was this. [She adds a rather scribbled diagram with squares, diamond and lozenge shapes labelled with letters to differentiate between the ships of different nations. It covers two pages.]

Sunday January 19th: Windy Text Not slothful in Business fervent in the service of the Lord.

January 22nd: Died William Pitt the greatest man that ever held the reigns of Government in England His last words were ' Oh My Country' – I have ever believed him to be the most wise and virtuous of Minister now he is dead I believe him still so to be and glory in the idea that I have always supported him – his enemies have broke his heart they may now all praise him but it is of no use Expressed views by J C on this occasion It is the general opinion here that since the meeting in the navy this reign has not seen a more lax government Mr Pitts death was occasioned by extreme anxiety about public affairs which quite exhausted his nerves so that he could get little or no sleep and having of a delicate constitution he had been accustomed from infancy to drink so much wine that it had injured his stomach so much as to destroy entirely his appetite.

Tuesday January 28th: Mr Fouchecourt came again he tells us that for 8 days the good news of the battle of Wiskaw was positively believed the Duke of York was so confident he gave him a Col's commission to raise a Regiment in La Vindee the report arose from this ... Mlle Jacobi the daughter of the charge d'affairs wrote to her father to tell him of the victory and gave the details which I inserted before the vessel which brought over the dispatches was lost or which Government believed would have confirmed the account.

Monday February 3rd: Mr and Mrs Bagley Miss Furnival M De Fouchecourt Mrs J Alcock dined here and we had some music handle was born at Halle in Germany Miss F went.

Friday February 7th: Mama my Aunt and Mary called at Etruria.

Saturday February 8th: ... the Ministry is fixed the offices of Chancellor of the Exchequer and First Lord of the treasury are separated The first is filled by Lord Henry Petty the 2nd by Lord Grenville who is consequently First Minister Mr Erskine with the title Lord Chancellor Mr Grey First Lord of the Admiralty Mr Fox Secretary of State for the foreign department Mr Wyndham do. For the Colonial Duke of Bedford Lord Lieutenant of Ireland Lord Moira Grand master of the Ordinance ...

Sunday February 9th: Mr Hindly drank tea here. The emotion in the city when the Ministry was doubtful was so great that the people were all in the streets in great agitation.

Monday February 10th: Mr Alcock did not come Mr Pitt died so poor that there was obliged to be a motion made in parliament to pay his debts one of the ministers mentioned that that ever to be lamented man had twice refused to his parents the pleasure of subscribing for him in 48 hours they raised 10,000 pounds for him but he declared that he had rather and would if necessary work in his profession than subscribe to such a proposal.

Tuesday February 11th: Mr Fouchecourt came.

Apart from her academic education Ann was also learning social skills and her notebooks afford a glimpse into 'society life' in Newcastle-under-Lyme. And 'society' was not always fun. A letter from one of her friends describes an assembly (dance) in Newcastle which they had both attended as, 'Boring, boring, boring!' – though the assemblies were one of the main forms of entertainment at which one had to be 'seen', to mix with the eligible young men of the neighbourhood – and find a husband.

Went to my first Assembly at Newcastle a dreadful snow so that we could not return home at night & all the beds were engaged so we stayed up in the Assembly Room ...

They sat in the room all night, and got home tired and dishevelled at midday the following day, being thrown about in a carriage pulled by four horses that bumped over roads heavy with snow. On another occasion she recorded – 'Went to a dance at Dr Brandreths crowded rooms full of company and not one face that I knew still I had a pleasant evening but shall I never learn to control my tongue ...'

Ann was still a gauche young woman finding her feet in society. She had not yet learned when to remain silent – or that it was not 'acceptable' for women to air their views. She comments elsewhere in her notebooks on women whom she met at her father's dining table who in company said little – or nothing of any consequence – yet alone with other women were full of interesting observations that showed a high degree of learning, wit and appreciation. She admired women who dared to be unconventional, and deplored that state to which she, as a woman, had to conform – even if the men who were airing their views so freely at her father's table, 'are little more than fools.' 'Miss Wedgwood and Miss Morgan dined with us there is so much refinement, sentiment and feeling in Miss M. that I never saw in a woman more inspiring confidence. Lettres de M Sevigne much admired by her – so to read them at the first opportunity.'

Ann Marsh Caldwell at the height of her career.
This is the image that appears in several of her books

Apart from the assemblies, attending the Newcastle Races and walking in the grounds around the course were supposedly enjoyable pastimes.

Wednesday July 1st: Went to Newcastle Races rained incessantly all day… took a long and most amusing walk to Mr Gilberts … rather fatal to gowns …

Then there were occasional travelling theatre groups that came to the town. Ann was frequently critical.

Went to see Little Betty in Frederick in Lovers Vows and the Citizen by Forte the play is wretched both in moral and interest the beautiful boy rather disappointed he speaks very ill … [The 'beautiful boy' was presumably a popular young actor]. Mama took JSC [brother Stamford] and we three girls to the play The Rival Queens ... I was so highly amused by the stile of acting that I could not attend to the stile of the dialogue but I think there are fine passages …

There were also concerts.

We girls and JSC to Etruria to hear Edwards upon the harp the sounding chords & all my poetic ideas of a Welsh harp were not exactly answered but when are they?

And of course there was the endless calling on people, and trips: to Trentham House to see the gardens and green houses, to Buxton Spa with her aunt to take the waters. With her aunt she travelled through Derbyshire – and described what she saw, perhaps becoming aware for the first time of the plight of poor people:

… as we advanced further on the country became more desolate consisting of large stone pastures of barren land separated by rough stone walls and now and then a wretched cottage and a few starved children …when we entered Derbyshire the moor lands were still more wild … starved cows now make way for sheep who roam or otherwise contrive to pick up the wherewithal to keep life in the body, which most other two legged or four legged animals would have a good deal of difficulty in doing …

On arrival at Buxton, Ann was definitely not amused when forced by her aunt to take 'the waters'. There was a lengthy trip to Liverpool to visit friends of Stamford's – and so on and so on. She had a very full social life indeed. To cope with it, both her mother and father fed her advice on how she should behave in society, the moral code she should follow and how she should guard her heart against inappropriate attachments. Ever the dutiful daughter, Ann wrote it all into her notebooks – page after page of good advice.

> I should most sincerely counsel every young person who is entering upon the Theatre of life to merit the good opinion of mankind by an unaffected easy and amiable disposition to all which will do more to render his walk through life respectable and happy than those more striking and splendid qualities which are forever the extremes of honour and disgrace – J.C
>
> … miserable will be your fate if you allow an attachment to steal on you before you are sure of a return. E.C

Ann was also flexing her writing skills – and by the time she was sixteen, in 1807, she had penned her first story, or novel, and shown it to her favourite aunt. She kept the letter her aunt wrote in response in one of her notebooks.

> My Dear Anne,
>
> Having perused this agreeable little book with great satisfaction I beg to propose that you will favour the world with giving it them in print. Should you wish for a dedication I shall be happy to use my interest with the most amusing fool I know to favour you with a suitable cover.
>
> Yours truly
>
> Emma Caldwell

Suddenly in 1808 the notebooks end. If Ann did continue to keep diaries then many are missing. Parts exist for 1825, 1826, the 30s and 40s – but they are very incomplete. They are mostly written on the blank pages of the diary belonging to her sister, Catherine Louisa, who had died in 1814 aged twenty. Reading them is made more difficult by the fact that the hand-writing of both girls is very similar and Ann's entries do not seem to be in chronological order. But during that period something of huge importance in her life did happen. In July 1817 Ann married – and she seems to have kept no record of it at all.

Ann's husband was Arthur Cuthbert Marsh, a junior partner in the bank of Marsh, Graham and Stacey. In the first

Cover of Mount Sorel *by Ann Marsh Caldwell, published in 1845*

six years of their marriage Ann bore him four daughters, and in 1824 she gave birth to their first son, Arthur, who only lived a few months. That year -1824 – was to be a truly terrible year for the Marsh family for as well as losing their child, it was the year the bank of Marsh, Graham and Stacey went under, largely due to the activities of Henry Fauntleroy, a junior partner who was involved in fraudulent activities on a gargantuan scale and had the dubious honour of being the last person in England to be hanged for fraud. Ann wrote:

> ... what a reverse of destiny! No home, no plan. A London life of pride and elegance, then hideous ruin which scattered all our hopes and left me and Arthur to make a miserable patchwork of life – without system and without prospects ... and striving to live on as little as we could.

But life went on. A second son, Martin, was born in 1825, quickly followed by two more daughters. Arthur never recovered from the scandal and it was Ann who kept the family afloat, taught her children at home when they could no longer afford school fees, took over the housekeeping when they could no longer afford servants, took the family to France to escape their creditors and kept up appearances as best she could.

In the 1830s she began to write. She became a novelist, producing over thirty novels and two histories. Though to the modern reader they seem turgid and moralistic, at the time her books were best sellers, running to numerous editions, translated into French, Dutch and German and serialised in *Harper's Magazine* in New York. She inherited money from her father and gradually the family finances recovered enough for Martin to be sent to Eton and on to Oxford. But in 1846 tragedy struck again; twenty-one-year-old Martin, the apple of his mother's eye and the family's hope for the future, died on a trip to Greece. Three years later Arthur died too. Writing seems to have been Ann's salvation, emotionally as well as practically – in the three years between the deaths of her husband and son she produced five novels.

In 1858 her brother Stamford died, and as the eldest surviving daughter, Ann inherited Linley Wood, on the condition that she added 'Caldwell' to her married name. But even her later years were unhappy – spent in lawsuits with her daughters about her inheritance. The sharp tongue, so evident in her early diaries, and her dismissive attitude to other people caused her to fall out not only with publishers and friends but also with her own family. She ended her life alone, a widow estranged from her daughters.

Endnotes

1   Sometimes spelt 'Anne'. However, her father always referred to her as 'Ann' which is the form we have chosen to use.

2   This memoir, and the notebooks from which we quote are all in private hands. For more information about Ann Marsh Caldwell and her family see www.jjhc.info/marshanne1874.htm

The obedient daughter

> 1840 June 20th: Returned home from school this day
> with Charles. My Father came to Liverpool for us ...
> I felt sorry at leaving Miss Davies as I perhaps may
> not return there again my Father having arranged for
> me to go to school at Miss Oates after the present
> holidays. I have been with Miss Davies since August
> 1836 and she had always been very kind to me and I
> had several companions in the school to whom I was
> attached.

'Felt sorry' was probably an understatement, but Emma had chosen her words carefully. Her father would read her diary and she did not want him to think she was being critical of the decision he had taken on her behalf. Emma Jane Longsdon was thirteen and she had already had a great deal of loss and upheaval in her short life. She was also old enough to be aware that there were things in her background that were better forgotten and memories and sorrows she should not share – she had learned the virtues of tact and discretion earlier than most girls her age. It must therefore have been a relief to record on June 23rd: 'Have been to see Mr James Longsdon's family and the Churchdale family and several others, all of whom have been very kind and friendly both to Charles and me.'[1]

The problem was that Charles and Emma Jane were illegitimate. They had been born in Charleston, South Carolina; their father was William Longsdon and their mother was Mrs Maria Lord. Maria's husband had abandoned her, and she and their two little boys were living with her mother, Mrs Smith, at 13 West Street, Charleston[2] when William Longsdon came into their lives. He was an Englishman who had arrived in town in 1816-17 and established a thriving cotton export business in partnership with his brother John.

John died in 1819. Perhaps William was lonely; perhaps, as some accounts suggest, he believed Maria to be a widow; perhaps she seduced him; perhaps he was genuinely in love with her – we have no way of knowing. Whatever the truth of their relationship, in January 1827 Maria gave birth to William's daughter, Emma Jane. William was a respectable, cautious, dutiful, hard-working, God-fearing man; fathering an illegitimate child seems totally out of character. In fact, his relationship with Maria Lord was probably the only injudicious episode in his entire life. [3]

William had enjoyed his stay in New York, though he did not think the buildings were as impressive as those of London or Liverpool and he found the Americans' constant talk of politics distasteful. He was also very much of his time. 'I cannot occasionally help thinking how you would like to be waited on by such uncouth looking creatures ...' was his comment on the black servants in his lodging house. [4]

But South Carolina was different: 'Much of the town [Charleston] is pretty well built and the streets are wide and regular, but the country is so extremely flat as to leave no sort of variation.' Areas in the forests were being cleared to make plantations, first by burning, then digging – 'the land is worth the labour of this process,' he said. There was a lot of marshland and 'all the roads in such places are obliged to have a foundation of wood, that is to say a multitude of sticks or the branches of trees, which forming a light and bulky body, will not sink.' No stone was to be found within a three-day journey, hence the dependence on wood. 'The Birds which we saw occasionally were really curious – One called the Red Bird is a brilliant scarlet, all except the tail which is brown, and has a small tuft upon the head. Another is the Mocking Bird which, exclusive of its imitative qualities, can sing very melodically, and there are many others of most beautiful plumage ...' William's letters to his mother are a joy to read; he was an observant traveller and recorded everything he saw in detail. Soon after he arrived in Charleston, he wrote to her to say:

> The people in this part of America have acquired a reputation for hospitality and, I suppose, justly so,

but if I am correctly informed, it certainly does not extend to too much familiarity, at least when ladies are in the case. At a party, should any stranger be present, the females range themselves on one side of the fire and the gentlemen composedly take the other, and after a length of time someone becomes bold enough to break the silence … The lady, if spoken to by a stranger, seldom returns any answer longer than a monosyllable, and, according to my informant, a person is expected after this to go home and say he has passed a pleasant evening.

Life in Maria Lord's household was evidently rather different. However, if Maria thought she had found a man to take care of her, she was sadly mistaken. A few weeks after Emma's birth, William Longsdon returned to England.

The Longsdons came from Little Longstone, near Bakewell in Derbyshire. They were an old established family – there were Longsdons in Longstone in the thirteenth century and family legend had it that they acquired their land from Serlo, an ancestor who had fought with William the Conqueror at Hastings. They were prosperous farmers, but in the late eighteenth century James Longsdon, William's father, had got involved in the cotton trade. To begin with he made money, trading with St Petersburg and with agencies in Manchester, London and Liverpool, but he was no businessman and by the time he died in 1821 there was not even enough money left to pay the bequests he had made to his children. His eldest son, another James, took over the family estate; it was heavily entailed and he could not sell the land to pay his father's debts. The younger James died in 1827, leaving a widow and a baby son.

William now had to come home to sort out the mess his father and eldest brother had left; this he did by somehow evading the entail and buying a large part of his brother's estate himself with the money he had made in Charleston, and by selling other lands to anyone who would bid for them. He provided for James' widow, Anne, and for her son, Henry John, his nephew and godson. Anne Longsdon was a difficult lady, given to histrionics; she had a grudge against her in-laws and was a hypochondriac who was convinced that she was about to die leaving her son an orphan – in a series of dramatic letters she begged William to take responsibility for him. William was now needed in Derbyshire and in 1828 he returned to Charleston to wind up his business affairs there – and stayed long enough to get Maria Lord pregnant again. Their son Charles was born in January 1829.

We do not know what promises William made to Maria, nor do we know how much his family back in England knew of the children in Charleston – however, he was not a man to shirk his responsibilities and he almost certainly made financial provision for Maria and the children. He had business contacts in the town and though there are no letters surviving that explicitly mention the family, one from a Mr Gardom (a distant relative) refers to visiting 'her Ladyship' and the children who were all recovering from whooping cough. But it seems Maria still wanted a man in her life and at some point in the early 1830s she ran off with a new lover, leaving her four small children in the care of their Grandmother Smith.

The Longsdons were hoarders and thousands of family letters and documents survive, but the coverage is patchy and it is not known exactly what happened next. At some point, probably early in 1836, William went back to America and collected his children from Charleston and brought them to England. They had lost their mother; now they were to leave their grandmother, their two elder half-brothers and the city they called home. They endured the rigours of the overland journey to New York, then the long sea voyage to a cold grey place called Liverpool. In Charleston the temperature seldom drops below 14°C and in summer it rises to a humid 32°C. The children had to get used to a chilly climate, cold rain, frost, snow, pollution and people who spoke with an accent they could not understand and who could not understand them. Even the food was different. Instead of shrimp'n'grits there was boiled mutton and potatoes; brown Windsor soup replaced she-crab soup; stewed apple took the place of watermelon; carrots and overcooked cabbage replaced field peas, okra and fried green tomatoes. And on top of that they had to adjust to boarding schools and make new friends. To nine-year-old Emma and seven-year-old Charles, the 'better life' they had been promised must often have seemed strangely uncomfortable. Their grandmother wrote occasionally and Emma answered her letters, but Mrs Smith was not an educated woman and Emma was a child – the letters said very little and gradually the correspondence ceased. The last surviving letter came in 1844 – seventeen-year-old Emma had saved ten dollars and sent it to her grandmother, which suggests she knew that her American family were in straitened circumstances.

But back in 1840 Emma and Charles were still struggling to fit in. Their father was often absent and it seems that when the children were not at school he left them with his friends, the Harrisons, in Liverpool. The Harrisons' daughter, Lizzie, became a lifelong friend of Emma's. In 1837-8 William went back to America. He was an able man, highly thought of in the business community, and his opinion was much sought after. He had a particular interest in railways and in America he explored the system, offered advice, investigated business opportunities and – who knows – perhaps spent time searching for Maria. He wrote copious diaries but unfortunately the American one is in faded pencil and all but illegible.

It is not at all clear how much time Emma and Charles had spent at Little Longstone before 1840, or how well they knew the people who were so 'friendly and kind' in June. The children had certainly been there in January that year for a rather curious ceremony, but it rather sounds as if that had been their only previous visit. Sometime late in 1839 William decided that it would be in everyone's best interests if the children took his surname – up to that point they had been known as Emma and Charles Lord – and on January 24th the local curate baptised them as Emma Jane and Charles James *Longsdon*. This seems to have been the point at which William decided to acknowledge them as his children rather than simply as a financial responsibility. Little Longstone and Great Longstone are small villages, a couple of miles apart – everyone in the district would have known of the baptism, discussed the pros and cons and been curious about the two little Americans – hardly an easy introduction for children desperately trying to be accepted.

*The Manor House, Little Longstone, where William,
Charles and Emma Jane Longsdon lived*

Throughout the remainder of June and most of July 1840 Charles and Emma visited neighbours and relatives and got to know their cousins – the five young Smithers at Churchdale who were the children of William's sister Kate and her husband, Sydney Smithers; Henry John Longsdon, son of their late Uncle James and their difficult Aunt Anne; and Mary and Selina Longsdon, daughters of 'Mr James Longsdon' at The Outrake who was William's contemporary but was actually his father's cousin. There was a trip to Chatsworth in the donkey cart (Uncle Sydney Smithers was agent to the Duke of Devonshire), a visit to Haddon, walks in Monsal Dale and endless tea parties. On July 27th Charles went back to school in Liverpool and Emma went to study with Miss Oates at The Cottage in Great Longstone. 'July 27th: This morning I went to school, Selina Longsdon and Elizabeth Mills [the minister's daughter] the only other scholars Miss Oates has at present,' wrote Emma. It was probably something of an anti-climax.

August 4th: Have been at school one week and like the change from Liverpool – but still feel sorry at having left all my old companions there. Am now learning Latin and French in addition to the several branches in English. My Father is anxious that I should pay attention to Arithmetic, as being the means of acquiring a great deal of useful information, and he tells me it is usually too much neglected in ladies' schools – I shall try to do as he advises me.

August 11th: I am going on comfortably at school. Generally say all my lessons over to my Father the morning before setting out which assists me a good deal especially in my Latin and French.

William Longsdon was critical and demanding; he had his children's best interests at heart but he was not a warm or affectionate man – there was more stick than carrot in his management of Emma. He was a meticulous record-keeper and had himself done exceptionally well at school. With his brothers he had attended Nottingham Academy. 'What can I say about your young man?' his headmaster wrote to his father. 'Where there is uniformity of excellence it is in vain to select what is most excellent.' William's children had a lot to live up to.

September 5th: Have begun landscape drawing instead of flowers. I like drawing.

September 14th: Morris dancers have gone around the neighbourhood. They are about sixteen young men dressed in white Trousers with blue Ribbons for ornaments. They had music and performed very nicely.

Like all children, Emma recorded the new and the exceptional – life in Little Longstone was probably quite dull after Liverpool.

View in Great Longstone where Emma went to school

September 15th: A cricket match was played today between the Ashford and Longstone players ... won by Ashford.

September 16th: Mr Mills, the Minister, told my Father today he would like me to be confirmed by the Bishop though I am four months younger than the age required which is 14 years.

The confirmation took place on September 23rd and it does not sound as if Mr Mills felt the need to provide any confirmation classes or prepare Emma in any way. He presented forty-two young people 'to undergo the solemn ceremony ... I hope always to remember this with proper feelings, for I am taught to consider that by this act I become a willing member of the Church of our Saviour,' Emma wrote piously. Miss Oates gave her a book of sermons addressed to young people to mark the occasion. It was obviously rather heavy-going and she did not finish reading it until mid-December.

On September 26th William Longsdon had a visit from a Mr Matthieson and they played chess. Emma does not tell us who won but we can guess that it was not her father as Mr

Matthieson 'is considered a first rate player having once beaten the famous Automaton managed by Mr Maelstrel.' This may have been the 'Turk', a machine constructed by Baron Wolfgang von Kempelen in 1769. It was not an automaton at all, but a box in which a man was concealed, pressing levers to move the chess pieces mechanically.

For months Emma struggled to net a purse as a present for her old schoolmistress, Miss Davies. Netting is an extremely ancient technique and at its simplest consists of a series of loops secured by knots. Nets made in this way were used for fishing and hunting. In the eighteenth century netting developed as a craft for making ladies' bags and purses, with fine mesh, fancy knots and embroidery over the net. It continued to be popular throughout the nineteenth century. The knots are made with a special needle over a 'mesh' or bar – the difficulty lies in creating a neat, even net. There was no-one to help Emma and perhaps she had not fully mastered the technique – a competent needlewoman could have made it in a week. She also sewed but it sounds as if her father did not approve: 'September 28th: ... Took some playing [plain?] sewing to do at school but did not inform my Father ... Wet today – had my dinner sent to me at school.' It seems the girls usually went home to dinner (lunch), but when the weather was bad dinner was sent to them from home. Presumably one of the servants brought it – their employers did not care if they got cold and wet.

On September 29th, she wrote: 'I knew my Father was anxious I should get the habit of making a few notes of this kind daily.' William Longsdon was a stickler for order and method – it was not enough that Emma keep a diary, it had to be written on a daily basis.

Mr James Longsdon seems to have taken a shine to little Emma and often invited her to tea with his own daughters, Mary and Selina, who were a few years older than she was. In October he gave her a book called *Children and Bread*. 'It is a very nice little book,' Emma recorded dutifully. 'October 12th: Mr James Longsdon would have taken me to Eyam [where another branch of the family lived] with his wife and daughters but my Father did not wish me to neglect my studies.' On October 15th she was again invited to The Outrake but her father wanted her to do her lessons and finish writing a letter instead. She accepted the invitation against his wishes and afterwards meekly recorded in her diary 'It was very kind of Mr James to ask me to tea but I did wrong in going.' No doubt William Longsdon had reprimanded her severely. He was a difficult man to please – even when Emma earned his praise he would usually follow it up with an admonition of some sort:

> October 13th: … showed Father my drawings and he thought I was improved. Told me again of the danger of following a habit of delaying to do things we know must be done.

> October 23rd: … finished a copy book today and brought it home. Miss Oates told me that I improved my writing and my Father thought so too.

> October 24th: My Father found fault with me for not having my clothes from the Wash put by in proper time, and the necessary repairs done to them.'

> October 29th: I got scolded for not writing my Journal with more care and neatness.

That week her father arranged for her to begin to acquire another accomplishment appropriate to her status: 'On Saturday I am to go to Churchdale to commence a Quarter's dancing under Mr Fritch, with Katherine, Rosa and Elizabeth Smithers, Selina Longsdon and Elizabeth Mills.'[5] However, it was still her academic attainment that concerned him most: 'October 30th: In accounts I have got as far as the Rule of 3 Inverse. In Latin I have learnt one verb of the first conjugation – "Amo"'. The Rule of Three in its various forms relates to proportion – the student would have to answer questions like 'If it takes two men a week to dig a ditch, how long will it take three men?' Arithmetic and account-keeping were useful skills for a young woman who might one day run a home of her own, but it is difficult to see what use Emma would ever make of Latin. Nonetheless:

November 2nd: Miss Oates told me today that I have no occasion to learn any more English Grammar but gave me a portion of the Latin Grammar to learn every morning instead. She also gave me additional French lessons.

November 9th: I began again with landscape today having finished a flower that I was painting to keep in practice.

November 12th: I began the Double Rule of 3.

December 12th: Arithmetic – I am doing fractions which now begin to be easy. In Drawing I go on with Cottages and Trees – finished one this week.

She was nearly fourteen and by modern standards was still doing very simple arithmetic. She was also expected to acquire social skills appropriate to her position.

November 27th: Played a little on the piano for the first time … My Father did not give me my usual allowance of 2d because I had neglected writing up this Journal since the 18th inst. His wish and instruction to me are that I should make notes of each day's occurrences as they take place.

William Longsdon was keeping her on a short rein. On December 9th they were invited out to tea but she was not allowed to join him until she had done her piano practice and 'after returning home my Father reproved me for a habit of contradicting people and for using vulgar expressions.' On December 17th, she wrote that she practised at the piano for one hour every day and expected 'to take lessons from Mr Fritch soon.'

The dancing lessons at Churchdale had petered out. The Smithers girls were all delicate – none of them survived into middle age – and were often too unwell to take lessons.

Perhaps William wanted Emma to concentrate on another ladylike accomplishment. She hadn't been very good at dancing, admitting on November 14th that she found 'Mr Fritch's steps rather difficult to learn.'

School broke up on December 18th and she took all her books home for her father to see:

> I brought home all my Books. During the half year I
> have done 14 small pencil drawings and two flowers.
> In Latin I have gone through the Grammar as far as
> 'Defective Verbs', in French translated Belisaire but
> only with the assistance of Miss Oates. In Accounts
> I am in 'Practice'. Of Sewing I have done scarcely
> anything. School recommences 25th January.

Charles was to travel home from Liverpool by himself for the Christmas holiday – he was not quite twelve and it was a long journey with various changes of coach, tips to give to coachmen and so on – and Emma worried about him and awaited his arrival with impatience. Christmas was a lesser celebration than it is today but there were still some festivities. On December 21st it was Selina Longsdon's sixteenth birthday and Emma and Charles were invited to a party with Harriet Harris, Elizabeth Mills and Susanna Barrow. 'We danced, played at Bagatelle and made ourselves merry till nearly 10 o'clock.' On Christmas Eve the house was 'dressed in greens', they had their usual Christmas Eve supper of 'posset, hot apple pie and Yule cheese' with their relatives and then the young people dressed in masks and red coats and danced. Christmas Day was marked by going to church and a visit from carol singers in the evening.

On December 28th Barbara Hill, the dressmaker, arrived to make Emma a new dress for New Year's Day and it was completed by the following day – the poor woman must have sat up all night to finish it. In the country, dressmakers travelled from house to house and shared the servants' quarters while they worked on whatever garments the household needed making or altering.

New Year's Day was the day for present-giving and William Longsdon announced to both children that he would double any money they had saved from their weekly allowance of 2d in the last half year – Emma had saved 3s, Charles just 1s. 'I have in my purse 10s-2d,' Emma wrote, 'Charles has £1-0s-6d.' Given that she had saved more than he had it is difficult to account for the discrepancy. William also gave them presents:

> My Father gave me a nice drawing box for a New Year gift but under a promise that I will try to take better care of my clothes and see that they are always mended in proper time – that I will always attend to the putting of them in proper place – that I will learn to sit upright and avoid lazy habits, and above all things not to deviate from strict truth at any time in what I might say.

Even presents came with conditions – William Longsdon was a real kill-joy. Charles got a shilling and if any promises were required of him Emma does not record them.

1841

> January 4th: Charles' 12th birthday. Charles and Henry dressed in masks and red coats to go from house to house and to Great Longsdon collecting money. Henry's mother thought they were very silly.

Henry was their cousin, the son of William's brother James who had died in 1827, and his mother was the difficult and complaining Anne Longsdon, née Oates. She was the sister of Eliza Oates who was Emma's teacher and lived in the same house. Emma must have seen her on a daily basis and no doubt part of William Longsdon's plan in sending Emma to Miss Oates' school was to support his sister-in-law's family. Henry and Charles were much of an age and as boys they were good friends.

On January 6th, Emma recorded that she had spent the day making herself some new chemises. On the 12th she set off for Liverpool; she was to stay with the Harrisons and she was to visit Miss Davies, her former schoolmistress and present her with the painstakingly netted purse. It is not clear whether Emma was expected to pay for this visit out of her own savings

– certainly she recorded all her expenditure, including tips and 'a halfpenny to a poor man', in the back of her diary for her father's scrutiny.

She made several visits to Miss Davies and her sister, Mrs Carter, and played with Mrs Carter's little children. There were parties, she and her friends danced, played 'Ladies Toilet' and 'Hunt the Slipper', and on January 20th Emma celebrated her fourteenth birthday. She must have enjoyed the change of company and seeing her old friends again. Five days later she set off for Manchester and met Charles and her father on their way to Liverpool – Charles was going back to school and William was off on some business of his own.

Her father was away and would be away for several weeks, leaving Emma alone with the servants – a situation she would experience often. She quite enjoyed having Selina come to tea and going visiting wherever she was invited. She went back to school on January 27th and began taking music lessons from Mr Fritch again. In February the weather was bad and there was thick snow; initially too deep for Emma to get to school. Eventually there had been enough people toing and froing to make a track and she walked to school, but she recorded 'Selina and I went to school but had a very ruff walk. We had our dinner sent to us.' William Longsdon finally arrived back home on February 14th.

The new year sees a subtle change in the diary entries. At fourteen Emma was a young woman and though she was still going to school, her focus is no longer on her school work. She writes of games of 'La Grazie'[6] with Selina, of playing Battledore and Shuttlecock by herself 'for a long time', but she also notes when the rooks are building their nests, when she sees the first water wagtail of the year, when the hawthorn and lilac are in bloom, when her father plants potatoes in the garden and when 'the Green Gage and the Ocean Plum are beginning to blossom.'

She had begun to take an interest in village matters back in 1840. 'October 4th: Went to the Sunday School with Miss [?]Asted and taught some of the little girls. I found it very pleasant work.' In 1841 she starts to take Selina's Sunday school class regularly, and on 10 April says: 'I made a frock for one of the little children in the village.' Three days later, she made another for little Hannah Stone – 'it fitted her very nicely.' William Longsdon was heavily involved in parish affairs, on the board of the Midland Railway, a good friend of Joseph Paxton and on close terms with the local MP. Emma was beginning to find her own place in the community, albeit a much more limited one as befitted her gender.

Her father also began to treat her as a young woman. On March 27th he bought her 'a very nice pair of kid gloves in Bakewell', and towards the end of May the dressmaker came to 'alter my silk frock it having got very much too short for me.' She recorded that on May 6th it was 'Fashion Day in Bakewell' though we do not know if she was allowed to go. Even in small places, drapers and milliners would have days at the beginning of each new season when customers could come to view the new fashions, fabrics and fashion plates.

Emma also starts to take an interest in the farm: 'May 15th: One of the Lancaster cows died suddenly by overfeeding' and 'May 29th: The sheep have been all washed today ready for shearing.' Her father still occasionally finds fault with her, and from May he seems to be trying to ensure she rises early – day after day he makes her record what time she comes down to breakfast – but he seems less interested in her schoolwork and spends an increasing amount of time away from home.

School broke up on June 3rd 1841 and the diary comes to an end. It seems likely that at that point Emma left school. She would live at home for the rest of her life, acting as her father's housekeeper. William rather hoped she would marry his nephew and ward, Henry, but Henry had other ideas. He fell in love with Fanny Lace, daughter of one of William's business contacts, and married young. We do not know whether Emma had any other suitors or whether she was happy with her lot.

In 1852-3 William visited America for the last time. Many people in England had taken out shares in the various American rail companies, and the English shareholders deputed William to go and review the systems in which they had invested – he seems to have actively enjoyed travel, so was happy to oblige.

Emma wrote to him regularly. The drawing room was being done up and she sent regular reports on how the work was progressing: 'The Drawing Room now seems in a fair way to get on – all the ornamental moulding is put

Monsal Dale, just down the road from Emma's home

on the arch, the walls are covered with their white paper preparatory to the other and the maple paint is replaced with a coat of white.' The colour scheme of white and gold seems to have been Emma's choice. 'The handles for the Drawing Room doors and windows are just come and are very simple and pretty, being white with a little gold ornament. I hope everything else will look as chaste,' she wrote in her next letter. She sent news of the farm – how many ewes had lambed – 'William [the shepherd] says he never knew them take such a deal of nursing as this year'- what potatoes had been planted, how much manure had been spread, which fields had been harrowed, which fences were being repaired. Her friend Lizzie Harrison came to stay and one day they found 'the Horse' was not being used for farm work and went for a ride – but mindful of her father's work ethic, she promised that they would never go riding if the horse was needed on the farm.

She told him about a book they were reading about America, *Hesperos, or Travel in the West* – 'it seems, which is rather unusual, to be written with an unprejudiced mind, for though not sparing the peculiarities of the people, the writer does not withhold anything which she knows to their advantage.' Emma had been in England for twenty years but she still felt a loyalty to the land of her birth.

In a letter to Henry and Fanny, Emma wrote: 'as moving about is not irksome to [my Father] I am pretty well satisfied although it does leave me a good deal by myself' but in actual fact she was quite worried about him – he was sixty-two and travelling was strenuous. All her letters end 'I long to see you, dear Father.' However, her biggest disappointment was that, despite the fact that Charles was living in America, William had not been able to see him.

Although William had bought the family estate, he was quite clear that Henry, his eldest brother's son, was the rightful heir. That meant there was no land for Charles to inherit. William had considered apprenticing him to a draper or chemist, claiming that both trades could provide a good income for someone who was prepared to work hard, but in the end it was settled that Charles should return to America and farm. Whether this was Charles' choice or William's is unclear. Charles was not yet eighteen when he left England and settled in Whiteside County, Illinois, bought land with money his father advanced to him, and set about creating a farm out of virgin territory. There was some problem with one of his associates, a man called Hankey, who in some way did Charles out of money, but little by little Charles began to make a living. The problem was that his father would not leave him alone. He demanded detailed accounts, criticised Charles' methods of record-keeping and accused him of wasting money. William knew about farming in England – but he had no experience of creating a farm from virgin land in Illinois. While in America in the 1850s, William tried to see for himself how his son was faring – but Charles made endless excuses to avoid meeting him.

Charles did, however, return to Little Longstone for a four-month holiday that winter, much to Emma's delight. The willingness with which the Longsdon men embarked on transatlantic travel is quite amazing. William's first voyage in 1816 took 65 days. By the 1820s the journey time could be as short as four weeks if the weather was good but the average was still around seven weeks. Nonetheless, William made the round trip at least seven times.

No doubt William enjoyed Charles' visit but overall his son was a problem to him. No school reports survive and nor do any letters Charles wrote home from school – one gets the impression that at some point someone did some heavy editing of the Longsdon papers. In a letter to William in 1848, Mr Cornish,[7] the former Vicar of Bakewell who had for a time tutored Charles, wrote of him in glowing terms, saying what a likeable boy he had been and how delighted he would be if his own son showed the same qualities of 'honesty and truthfulness.' But by the 1850s William was more concerned with his son's apparent inability to make money. Charles, for his part, was hurt and angered by his father's lack of respect and understanding.

It is difficult to know who was in the right. Copies of some of William's later letters to Charles survive, including details of how to value a farm that are almost insulting in their simplicity. William attributed Charles' 'ill success to always acting contrary to my advice and wishes' and his lack of 'systematic economy'. Sometimes Charles tried to make light of the criticism and attribute it to 'your affection [which] still preserves undiminished' but it is clear that he was deeply hurt by his father's lack of trust and craved his approval: '[your] love and confidence it has been the daydream of my ambition to win,' he says. The letters between them become more and more acrimonious and resentful. In 1866 William wrote, 'It has always been a matter of pain and surprise to me that when asked about your accounts and business operations you generally show irritation ... Let me remark for the last time I shall ever do so [William thought he was dying but in fact he lived for another ten years], that unless you adopt some system of kind you will never know from what causes your property dwindles away.' By this point Charles was a man of thirty-seven and had been making a living from farming for twenty years. There is a final letter in 1870, including what, to anyone other than William Longsdon, look like very adequate accounts. Charles values his land in Illinois at $8,000 and considered that in total, with stock, buildings and farm implements, after all debts and taxes were paid, his farm was worth $11,765. Given that he had bought it for $2,765, and that he also owned some property over the state line in

Wisconsin, it is difficult to see Charles as the failure his father believed him to be.

Emma died in 1874 at the age of forty-seven. She left £10 apiece to her cousin Selina Shaw (née Longsdon) and her friend, Lizzie Postlethwaite (née Harrison) to buy themselves a ring apiece in her memory, and she left two pictures, one by her father's friend, J Horsley, to her cousin Henry John Longsdon. Everything else was to go to Charles – but she described him as 'formerly of Mount Pleasant, Whiteside County, Illinois, now living in Canada', which suggests she did not have his address. Her estate was valued at just £183-5s-7d.

William died two years later, aged eighty-six, a disappointed man. In one of his last letters to Charles he wrote:

> … if my duties in life have ever been performed to the full, it is in the acknowledgement of you and your sister as my children and the care that has been taken of you. Every impulse of my heart tells me that I have a claim to gratitude from both of you, and perhaps if you will reflect on what might have happened if you had both been left in Charleston, to work for a precarious living, you will not refuse to confirm it.

By the standards of his time, William had indeed done right by his children when he had no legal obligation to do so. His tragedy was that he could not accept that they had done their best to love and please him; he was a man for whom nothing they could have done would ever have been good enough.

The estate at Little Longstone went to Henry and a little over £1,000 went to Charles. By this point Charles was back in Whiteside County, farming at a place called Genesee. The legacy enabled him to marry. His wife, Gertrude (née Stiles) was some fourteen years Charles' junior, and she bore him three daughters. They named the eldest one Emma. [8]

Endnotes

1   Derby RO D3580/FP/5 Emma Jane Longsdon's Diary.

2   Hagy, James, 2002. *Directories for the City of Charleston, South Carolina: For the Years 1830-1831, 1835-1836, 1836, 1837-1838 and 1840-1841,* Clearfield, Baltimore.

3   The *Memoir of William Longsdon* D3580/ZP/560. This is particularly useful, albeit rather too upbeat an account to be entirely reliable.

4   This letter, and all the other documents quoted in this chapter (unless otherwise stated), are part of the Longsdon Collection in Derbyshire Record Office, ref D3580/. They are readily traceable in the excellent and detailed schedules.

5   John Fritch lived in Bakewell. Over in Staffordshire in the early nineteenth century both Ann Caldwell at Linley Wood and John Sneyd at Ashcombe Park had lessons from 'Mr Fritch the dancing master.' It cannot have been John Fritch because he was only in his 30s in 1841, but it seems likely that it was a relative.

6   This was a game that was thought to be particularly suitable for young girls because it looked pretty and graceful. It consisted of one person spinning a beribboned hoop through the air while others tried to catch it on a stick.

7   No relation – as far as we know – to Mr Cornish in Debenham who taught Ralph De Tunstall Sneyd.

8   American Federal Census 1880; Barbee-Otjen Family Tree (1), Public Member Trees, Ancestry.com.

'Must work harder'

> ... Premature debauchery that only prevents men from being corrupted by the world by corrupting them before they enter the world ... A system of abuse, neglect and vice in which a boy who began as a slave was likely to end himself as the tyrant.

So wrote Sydney Smith in the *Edinburgh Review* in 1810 in his tirade against the public schools, and he was in a position to know – he had been a pupil at Winchester. It was the beginning of a sustained attack on the public schools from various sources, but mainly led by Smith. The schools, revered by almost all as the citadels of decency, were now being shown to be hotbeds of iniquity. They were increasingly being watched and their hidden inner workings revealed to a horrified public. It was a biased view of course, but it did expose things that had been going on for a very long time under the cover of decency and gentlemanly behaviour.

Public schools had started, like grammar schools, as schools for bright boys from impecunious families. Winchester claims to have been the first, set up in 1382. In 1440 a charter was issued by Henry VI to found Eton College – though the main purpose seems to have been not education but so that the Provost and Fellows might constantly say Masses for the founder's soul. Westminster School dates from 1560, Rugby from 1567, Harrow from 1571. They were not set up as places for the privileged, but as places where those who had academic ability could enter by getting a scholarship. In 1661 John Evelyn – the renowned diarist, writer and gardener – was attending the selection of boys up for scholarships for Westminster School and marvelled at the wit of little boys of twelve and thirteen years of age who could be heard sparring with each other in Chaldee (an ancient language in which passages of the Old Testament had been written), Arabic, Hebrew, Greek and Latin. Like the grammar schools, the early public schools taught classical Latin and Greek, but what set them apart was the fact they not only accepted scholarship boys attending on a daily basis, but also took in paying boarders from wealthy families. Over the years the difference between the public and grammar schools widened. Grammar schools broadened their syllabuses to take in the growing interests and needs of a blossoming industrial age, while the public schools became the sole domain of the elite and wealthy and taught almost nothing but Greek and Latin. Where the basic aim of grammar schools was education, the most important objective in public schools was robust Christianity and turning out 'gentlemen'. In the nineteenth century there were nine schools which we would now call public schools: Eton, Winchester, Harrow, Charterhouse, Rugby, Westminster, Merchant Taylors', St Paul's and Shrewsbury.

One father, on deciding to send his young son to Rugby School in the late 1840s, wrote:[1] 'I don't care a straw for Greek Particles or the Digamma[2]... if he'll only turn out a brave, helpful, truth-telling gentleman and a Christian. That's all I want.' This was a view which had been espoused by the famous headmaster of Rugby School, Thomas Arnold. 'What we look for here,' the headmaster wrote of his school, 'is first religious and moral principles, secondly gentlemanly conduct; thirdly intellectual ability.'[3]

In public schools the boys were not only encouraged but forced to be the custodians and shapers of their own morality and order. The eldest boys and the elite few were almost more powerful than the masters in the school. Fagging was well established by the early 1800s – the youngest boys were at the beck and call of the Vth and VIth form boys. They accepted it, knowing that when they reached that age they too would have fags to wait on them. Telling tales to parents or teachers, even if you were beaten or abused by an older boy, was totally unacceptable. You grew by learning to bear pain and shrug it off; that way you became strong and able to cope with whatever the world might subsequently throw at you. *The Times* remarked in 1858[4] that it remained an unsolved mystery how, 'Those fierce passions are tamed, how the licence of unbridled speech is softened into courtesy, how lawlessness becomes discipline and all this within two to three years without external assistance.' The article went on to suggest that parents would do well not to seek too hard for answers but to content themselves with the good result. So basically, a self-governing regime of boys by boys was at the core of the public school. The less a boy complained and the more he bore, the higher his status became among his peers. To be admired by one's peers and thought a 'good chap' was the goal. But it was a regime that shy, timid or frail boys found very hard to cope with. They suffered and – as some later revealed – the agony stayed with them all their lives. 'I cannot say that I look back upon my life at a Public School with any sensation of pleasure, or that any earthly consideration would induce me to go through my three years again,' wrote Charles Lutwidge Dodgson (Lewis Carroll) in his diary. Some, like Anthony Trollope (who attended Winchester and Harrow), felt that the ordeals that they had suffered were responsible for permanent injury to their personalities.[5] But for those who had not only coped with the system but grown within it, there was a sense of loss. The fourth Lord Lyttleton, describing the poignancy of his loss at leaving Eton, wrote: 'It was over: I had left Eton. It was one of the heaviest and deadliest feelings I ever knew, to find that I was no longer a boy.'[6]

For most people the most complete picture we have of life in a public school is *Tom Brown's School Days* by Thomas Hughes. Published in 1857, just before the rigorous investigation of the public school system by the Clarendon Commission,[7] it gives a somewhat idealistic view of school life. Though it was based very closely on Hughes' own time at Rugby School it was written for boys, and he disguises and softens some of the shadier and harsher sides of school life. At precisely the same time as Hughes was writing his novel, Gerald Upcher – a boy at Harrow – was writing his diary, which is now held in the Norfolk County Record Office.[8] Upcher, too, is careful in the way he records things and this suggests that perhaps the diary was kept at his father's insistence and was likely to be read by him.

Sheringham Hall, the Upcher family home. It was designed by Repton and building was begun under Gerald's grandfather, Abbot Upcher. Gerald's father, Henry Ramey Upcher, moved in in 1839 and oversaw the completion of the building

Gerald Upcher was born in 1841, just three years after his family moved into Sheringham Hall in Norfolk. His father was a wealthy landowner and a magistrate. Gerald had seven brothers and sisters and there were eight servants in the house. He attended Harrow School from 1854 to 1860, as did his father before him, and his brothers after him. From there he went on to Trinity College, Cambridge.

His school diary dates from 1858 and it is full of self-castigation, but it does throw light on to the subjects he was taught, the method of teaching and the games he played. It is resonant in all respects with the account of public school life in *Tom Brown's Schooldays*.

The entry for every single day starts with a long and very detailed description of the weather – omitted here – but the weather was an important factor in people's lives in the days before central heating or hot running water, and when many journeys had to be made on foot.

On the front page of the diary Gerald wrote: 'Diary of General Observations of Ocurrences during School and Holiday Time beginning January 1858':

> January 14th: Came back to Harrow ... determined to work hard in spite of finding this very difficult.

For the rest of January there is little reference to work – but lots of descriptions of very long walks, ice-skating and falling though the ice when it broke. He was not injured and simply says 'just got very wet'. Almost every entry contains 'must do better' or 'must work harder'.

On February 2nd there is a long description of a snowball fight which ended in a 'scuffle' and during which he says he used 'strong' language – he later reprimands himself for doing so.

Although there are no references in the diary to any sexual practices in the school, there are sexual overtones. For example Gerald describes a game he has played with a

Harrow School

younger boy that he had also played at Cromer with young ladies who did not understand what it was about – '… a good case of ignorance is bliss. Missed my Greek Grammar this morning. I must not miss any more lessons this quarter. I must work harder.' This entry is interspersed with descriptions of football, catching birds, cricket – though it was still only February – and numerous very long walks: 'I only do half my work … I only do half my work … may God help me.'

The football he mentions was what we now call Rugby football – rugger not soccer. Rugby football started in Rugby School in 1830 and very quickly became popular throughout the UK – especially in the public schools. A description of a match in *Tom Brown's School Days* shows just how rough and violent it was, but it was thought a good thing by the masters as it let the boys take part in what were essentially fights-with-a-few-basic-rules. Also described is the drinking that went on after football matches, the beer being provided by the school and the older boys having innocent-looking bottled beer which was in fact laced with gin.

Harrow Football XI 1860

As at Rugby, the boys at Harrow had their own studies where they were expected to work – mainly preparing Latin and Greek texts for the next day's lessons. They obviously used them for socialising too, but they slept in dormitories. Gerald was a conscientious young man, anxious to do well and almost neurotically self-critical:

> ... I have wasted a good deal of precious time today ... I have let myself down. This evening I went to a lecture given by Mr J Baker about the Philosophy of Water. It was very interesting ... he showed us some pretty experiments.

The Philosophy of Water was propounded by Thales of Miletus in the fifth century BC who argued that water was the basis of all matter. There is no way of knowing whether Mr Baker was presenting the theory as fact or as a historical curiosity.

After this Gerald records nothing else of real interest for several weeks – just more football, cricket, smoking in the barn and visits from relatives. He describes going to breakfast with various boys, going out to buy biscuits and beer and going back to his room in the afternoon with friends and discussing parliament and politics. 'Much laughter with young Brazely and Deversle. Lecture in the evening in Latin – the cause of Earthquakes' – which he then had to write about. 'I got 6/10.' The 'mark' system used at Harrow was similar to that at Rugby where each boy was given a mark for the work he had done and that decided where he would sit in class. At the end of January Gerald was placed 25th – but by the end of February he had moved up to 11th.

One of the other things he records fairly often is chasing and catching cats. This was obviously a very cruel game as the boys then put the cat into a box and left it there. '... in the afternoon we turned out the cat we had caught on Friday but it had hurt its leg so that it could not run – poor brute.'

Jumping over hurdles seems to be another sport engaged in frequently and in which the boys seem to have been obliged to take part. Gerald writes several times about how bad he is at hurdles and how frightened he is of jumping over them.

Classroom at Harrow

Finally he breaks his leg and on March 25th his parents come to Harrow to collect him and take him home. He then gives lengthy descriptions of much home-nursing and visits from relatives. Finally he returns to school, where it is more of the same – walking, cricket and now games of racquets.

He records sermons in great detail and how good the various vicars are who give them – and he still writes almost every day 'Must do better.' He continues to miss lessons but he must have been doing some work as, by November, he is first in his class, and even goes to evening lectures and discussions. One topic was the difference between British and foreign education. Gerald recorded confidently that 'British is superior.' He does badly in Divinity and Mathematics examinations, so there is more self-deprecation and claims that he 'must work harder.' The fact that he records Mathematics and Divinity exams at all is interesting as those subjects had certainly not always been on the syllabus. The headmaster kept a copy of the 1845 sixth-form programme in his notebooks, which shows that the subjects studied at that time were exclusively Latin and Greek.

Sixth Form Programme

From The Head Master's Book, 1845

Sunday: 8-9 a.m. in the two winter terms and at a variable hour between 6 and locking-up in the summer term.
  Greek Testament
  Jahn's Archæologia Biblica
  Show up Latin or Greek exercise from Arnold's Latin Prose, or Greek Prose Composition

Monday: 7.30 - 8.30 a.m.   Greek Testament
                           Theophilus Anglicanus
       11 - 12   Odyssey
                           Hermann's Manual of Political Antiquities of Greece
       3 - 4   Repetition of Saturday's Greek Play
                           Latin Prose. Cicero, Tacitus, or Livy
                           Historia Romana
                           Theme set

Tuesday: Whole holiday.

Wednesday: 7.30 - 8.30 a.m. Philosophia Graeca
                             Verses shown up
          11 - 12   Horace's Odes
          3 - 4   Repetition of the Horace
          5 - 6   Pindar &
                             Lyrics set

Thursday: 7.30 - 8.30 a.m.   Cicero: de Officiis
                             Theme shown up.
         11 - 12   Juvenal
                             Greek Iambics set
              Half-holiday

Friday: 7.30 - 8.30 a.m.   Septuagint
                             Lyrics shown up.
        11 - 12   Lucretius, etc., in Pitman's Excerpta
        3 - 4   Repetition of Lucretius, etc.
        5 - 6   Aristophanes
                             Verses set.

Saturday: 7.30 - 8.30 a.m.   Translation from Greek into Latin
                             Greek Iambics shown up
                             Arnold looked over.
         11 - 12   Greek play

VIth Form timetable for 1845

By Gerald's time, German and French seem to have been introduced as well. The Clarendon Report on the public schools would be published in 1864 and included the recommendation that the public school curriculum should consist of classics, mathematics, a modern language, two natural sciences, history, geography, drawing, and music. Harrow seems to have embraced this suggestion well before the report came out. Change was in the air.

117

The rest of 1858 is blank except for detailed accounts of shooting on the family estate, family visits and Christmas at home. Early in 1859 he writes:

> January 14th: I returned to Harrow.

> January 16th: Got my exams into Upper Fifth which I am very glad of. Football this afternoon. I did my lesson alright.

> January 18th: ... Concert given by Turner our Organist. Some of it was very pretty indeed. It wasn't to my taste.

> January 26th: ... Did not do my German ... must do better next time.

> January 27th: ... I joined the Musical Society and had my first practice, got on pretty well considering.

He does not record which instrument he played but continues practising until he can play it 'pretty well'. There is more smoking with his friends in the barn but he writes that he prefers a pipe.

> February 17th: Thackeray gave us a lecture in the Speech room at 12 pm ... very amusing indeed, enjoyed it very much.

It is just possible that 'Thackeray' was in fact the novelist, William Makepeace Thackeray, who was writing satirically at that time, both in articles and in his novel, *Vanity Fair*.

Like all young men of his class and time, Gerald Upcher was also honing his social skills:

> ... walked after school with Cruikshank and Druselle and enjoyed it very much. In the evening had tea with Mrs Campham, met Mr & Mrs Tindell and Mrs Parsonby. Spent a very pleasant evening indeed.

February 26th: ... Tried catching with the cricket ball. Found my hands were rather tense, had a good practice for a couple of hours. Was rather lazy in the evening.

Sunday February 27th: ... went for a six mile walk.

This was with friends. It was church as usual in the evening and he makes comments about the sermon. He always recorded the reference to the Biblical text on which the sermon was based.

March 1st: ... evening lecture – scientific.

March 3rd: [He describes a long walk then going to the music room for practice.]

March 4th: ... then chess again.

March 5th: [He played more chess, then watched a racquets match which he describes as 'excellent and worth seeing.' Afterwards he played cricket, then met up with friends in the barn. There is no mention of any school work at all that day.]

March 9th: [He started taking part in hurdles races again.]

March 21st: [He signed a declaration with his friends promising to refrain from 'Bad Language', to 'put it away' and promote decent language. He records lectures in the evenings on a variety of topics.]

Saturday March 26th: ... The two Miss Elliots came to spend the evening. Very nice girls indeed – they played some duets together without notes, uncommonly prettily. Spent the evening very

Playing a game of racquets, mid-nineteenth century

pleasantly indeed. Got to bed about 12 after doing my map.

March 30th: ... Did my final Latin Prose 4th school. Hope I did it well.

'4th School' means the fourth lesson of the day, '2nd School' the second lesson of the day and so on.

April 1st: ... Did Euclid Paper Second School, History Third. Hope I did well.

April 2nd: ... Did French and German 2nd School ... practised a bit in the music room

Sunday April 3rd: ... There was sacrament in the morning. I should think there must have been nearly

100 boys there. May God grant that we all received it to our benefit. Swatted Divinity in the evening.

April 4th: Did Divinity 1st School, mathematics 2nd School ... I'm afraid I did not do them very well.'

April 5th: ... Babylon after [?] Levalteodus, Virgil con, in the evening Cicero.

April 6th: ... Latin Paper 2nd school. Latin tenses. I'm afraid I did not do very well.

April 7th: ... 1st School Greek Prose. 2nd School Latin ...

He spent the afternoon in races and jumping, and from this time onwards there is virtually no reference to any lessons, teaching or exams. Cricket fills up most of his time with a little music and some socialising. He mentions his eighteenth birthday on Monday June 19th, and in late June and early July he begins to pepper his entries with French phrases, such as 'I shall do goodness mais J'ai peur.'

During July he records almost nothing in his diary except cricket and the cricket practices that he goes to. A record of one of the matches he played in still exists. Harrow played a wandering amateur club called I Zingari ('The Gypsies') founded in 1845 by three old Harrovians. They grew in strength and expertise, even playing once against 'The Gentlemen of the South', a team that included the famous cricketer W G Grace and two of his brothers. Gerald was in the team that played against I Zingari on July 2nd 1859. His part in it was not memorable – he made only two runs.

July 17th: ... I am busy getting up Divinity Mal which we do First School tomorrow, puis le faire bien ... Had 2 splendid sermons from Smith in the morning and Laughton in the afternoon.

He found with the result of his exams that he was not in the first ten but hoped not to be much lower. He then went home and spent the summer holidays in Cromer and Sheringham.

> September 14th: ... I came back to Harrow. Got here safely at about 7 ... may God make me more diligent during this Quarter and enable me to get on better and also manage to keep all of us from every evil way and take us home again in his safely.

> September 15th: ... holiday tasks in the morning, played cricket in the afternoon. I intend to try and write an abstract of everything I read and try to improve.

> November 16th: [He records a lot more Greek Grammar then there is a very interesting entry about friction between staff and the new headmaster which he calls 'shocking'.]

On September 16th Dr Charles Vaughan, the much respected forty-three-year-old headmaster of Harrow School, suddenly resigned. During his fifteen-year tenure he had been responsible for raising the standards and prestige of the school. When he took over there had been only seventy boys; when he resigned there were over four hundred. His resignation was totally unexpected and none of the boys at the school had any idea why he had left. In fact nobody would know until after his death.

What had happened was that Vaughan had been having an illicit sexual love affair with one of the boys – Alfred Pretor. Pretor made the mistake of showing the love letters that he had received from Dr Vaughan to his friend, John Addington Symonds (later to become a poet). Symonds was unhappy at school – a homosexual himself, he later revealed – and was fascinated by the rampant carnality that was taking place. His own sexuality was repressed and he was jealous of the love and attention that his friend Pretor had received, and in a fit of anger after leaving school, he had shown copies of the letters to his father, a Bristol physician. His father was outraged that this should have been going on in a school for which he had paid high fees and from which he expected high standards, and he wrote to Vaughan demanding his immediate resignation, threatening to send the letters to *The Times* if he did not comply. Vaughan met with Dr Symonds and pleaded with him – his wife also pleaded, on her knees, knowing of her husband's 'weakness' – but to no avail. Furthermore, the doctor insisted that Vaughan should not accept any high position in the church if it was offered to him – which it was. He refused the post of Bishop of Worcester, again leaving everyone completely bemused, and it was not until after Dr Symonds' death that Vaughan finally accepted the post of Dean of Llandaff Cathedral in Wales.

Gerald Upcher remarks in his diary, on November 16th, that there is friction between staff and the new [acting] headmaster, which he calls 'shocking'.

In December, among accounts of exams, he mentions dining with Mrs Vaughan and a farewell sermon from Dr Vaughan:

> November 21st: ... Did a Latin trial in the morning and Greek translation in the afternoon.

> November 22nd: ... Had a good swat at History.

> November 23rd: ... Had a good game of House footer. Socrates. History ... Greek in 3rd School.

> November 24th: ... Did Roman History 2nd School ... Footer in the afternoon. Had a good game.

> November 26th: ... played footer in the afternoon then tea afterwards, we had a good spread. Then did Sophocles paper 2nd School.

> November 27th: ... Swatted all my spare time for Greek test trials ...

November 28th: ... Did Divinity 2nd School, Euclid and Algebra 3rd School. In the evening I got through half the school Cicero and half Thucideros. A good night's work.

November 29th: ... Finished Cicero, ... Aristophanes, Aulder the Juvenile ...

November 30th: ... I took my exams.

December 1st: [He lists more exams – nearly all Greek or Latin and]... played House Football in the afternoon.

Saturday December 3rd: [he played sport nearly all day then dined in the evening with Mrs Vaughan – followed by a party which he didn't leave until 12 o'clock].

December 4th: ... A farewell sermon from Dr Vaughan. The chapel was crowded with old Harrovians ...

These last two are interesting entries as it seems that although Dr Vaughan had resigned and a new headmaster was in place, he and Mrs Vaughan still lived in the vicinity, and – as the reason for his resignation was unknown – he was still socialising with the boys. The following day Upcher made several social calls during the day and spent the evening with Mrs Vaughan. He then took a trip to Cambridge:

December 7th: ... I went down to Cambridge by the 11 train, had lunch with Barclay then explored Cambridge. Dined with the "Quare hoc" club at 7 pm. Had a most excellent dinner then went to a supper party at a fellow called Bagge then walked about the streets

There follows a lengthy description of the shambles that the journey became after Fakenham. There was a 'carriage fault' and there were to be no more trains for eight hours. He had a meal of bread and cheese and then set out to walk the eighteen miles home.

The rest of the diary consists of his holiday at home: socialising and going to church – and this last section is very pious – full of praise for God, seeking God and so on.

Gerald did not live long to benefit from his time at Harrow. He went on to Trinity College, Cambridge and took his degree in 1864. The following year he married Annie Louisa Hamond, daughter of Robert Nicholas Hamond of Fakenham Hall, but the marriage was tragically short-lived. She died in 1867. Gerald continued to keep a diary and his last records his work as a missionary in Buenos Aires and later as a sheep farmer on the family estate, and is full of spiritual reflection – 'I want to make this my book of remembrance, a picture of my inner life,' he says. In September 1872 he writes 'Dr Churchill told me today I was in consumption'. The diary ends on September 20th 1872 with a final pious hope: 'I want to walk as indeed a stranger and pilgrim here, journey to a home of glory, an entrance to, and a meetness for, which I received simply through the Great Love of another who died for me.' Gerald died four days later, just a month before his thirty-first birthday.

The Clarendon Commission produced its report in 1864, and this led to the Public Schools' Act, which became law in 1868. Thereafter, life in the public schools began to change dramatically. Rules were laid down by the staff, not the boys, to govern behaviour in the school. Riotous behaviour – like travelling on coaches and shooting peas at unsuspecting labourers and other people on the road – ceased, as did late-night rowdy parties and visiting the houses of well-known whores. Violent beatings of younger boys by their older schoolfellows were outlawed.

The schools were ripe for reform and had been under attack from various quarters ever since Sydney Smith's clarion call in 1810. An old Etonian, Matthew Higgins, wrote an article in the *Cornhill Magazine* in 1861 applauding the changes that were taking place in the education of the poor – but wishing that a comparable improvement could be seen in the education of the rich which seemed to remain static and inadequate. He complained of the small ratio of masters to boys at Eton, calling it 'dishonestly' small, as upwards of 800 boys were being taught by just nineteen masters – and those masters also took on private tuition to earn extra money. The changes must have been difficult for the 'old guard' of public school masters to accept, but gradually the new regimes came into force – and the public schools continued to flourish.

Endnotes

1   *Tom Brown's School Days.* Based on the experiences of Thomas Hughes when he was a pupil there.

2   'Digamma' – an archaic letter of the Greek alphabet.

3   See Dudek, Mark, *Architecture of Schools; The New Learning Environments,* Architecturla Press, 2000, p.11

4   On Friday 15 January.

5   Wikipedia – Anthony Trollope.

6   Frost, Thomas, *The Life of Thomas Lord Lyttelton,* Tinsley Brothers, 1876.

7   In 1861. For further details of the Clarendon Report recommendations, see Gillard, Derek, *Education in England, a brief history,* 2011 www.educationengland.org.uk/history/chapter03.html. The Public School Act was passed in 1868.

8   Norwich CRO ref UPC 179, 642X1. This diary records entries for 1858 and 1859. The second diary, which is also listed as a school diary, is in fact just a very few pages about his social life in Sheringham in 1860.

'They are so absurdly prejudiced ...'

My tongue is perfectly aching to speak English ...

Edith was sixteen and she was writing a diary about her time at a boarding school in Nîmes, in the south of France.[1] No doubt she had been sent there to learn French, and as most of her teachers were French it seems probable that that was the language in which she was being taught, but this particular comment was written because 'Mary, Annie, Sophie and I have made a resolution to speak French all the day except the half hour we get up in, and whoever speaks English has to pay a centime each time she breaks the rule.'

Mary Edith Hughes – always called 'Edith' – was born in the autumn of 1867, the fifth of the seven children of William and Mary Hughes. William Hughes was a Welshman, a clergyman's son from Swansea, and Mary Hughes, née Jones, came from Hereford where her father ran a bookshop. The couple married in 1856 and for a time lived in Preston where William had a job in a shop, but this was only a stepping-stone in his highly successful career, for by 1861 he was running a hotel in Scott's Yard in the City of London – behind Cannon Street Station – and employing ten staff. Sometime between 1861 and 1871 he changed direction and went into the tea business. The family seems to have moved around a lot but by 1873 they were living in Redhill in Surrey, and by census time in 1881 the eldest son – also called William – was working with his father in the family firm.

In the same census Morgan, the second son, was a medical student – he would later become a dentist. Eighteen-year-old Ernest was at Bootham School in York; Emily, Edith's only sister, was sixteen and at the Friends' School in York; twelve-year-old Geoffrey was at school in Hitchin; and little Arthur, the baby of the family, was still being taught at home by a governess. Edith may already have been in France by this time. This was a family that took their children's education very seriously, and by sending the boys to a variety of schools they were widening the family's range of contacts.

The whole family wrote to Edith while she was in France, both jointly and individually, though she was not always grateful – one letter from the then thirteen-year-old Geoffrey that arrived on March 11th 1884, for example, was dismissed with elder-sisterly scorn as 'Very uninteresting and short'!

Arthur, Mary Edith and Geoffrey Hughes in 1879.
Edith was almost 12

At the end of January 1884 the family were preparing to move to a new house in Primrose Hill – 'It is near Regent's

Park and from what they say of it I think I shall like it', wrote Edith, having received a favourable report of it from her sister Emily. However, it would be some months before Edith saw the house for herself. The Hughes' house in Redhill no longer exists, but the new house – 30 Elsworthy Road in Primrose Hill – still stands. It is one of a row of uncompromising, square, semi-detached houses built of yellowish London brick, with four storeys including a basement, and overlooks the park. There is a wide flight of steps spanning the basement area and leading to a front door which has an elaborate stained-glass panel and is topped by a simple triangular arch; there is a little garden at the front with a much more spacious one to the rear.

Elsworthy Road, the house to which Edith's family moved in 1884 is probably the one on the far left

Edith's diary begins on January 1st 1884 and on the flyleaf she wrote 'Ye Diarie of Edith Hughes who abodeth yn ye merrye towne of London.'

The Hughes family were Quakers and the school Edith attended was a Quaker foundation. When she began the diary, she was at Congénies (Edith usually spelt it Congéniès), a village about 15km from Nîmes, which boasted the only purpose-built Quaker Meeting House in France. English girls at the school in Nîmes seem to have been sent there at

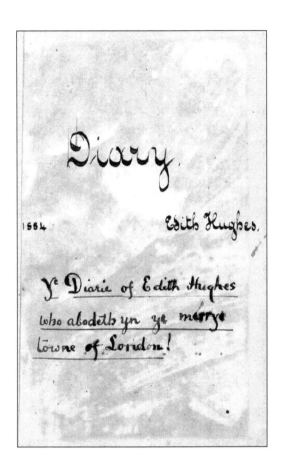

The front page of Edith's diary

Christmas and Easter as it was too far for them to go home. They seem to have had quite a good time, visiting members of the Society of Friends who lived in the area, going for long walks in the countryside and being taken to visit places of interest. On January 2nd, for example, Edith and her friends went to the picturesque little town of Aubais and borrowed a donkey, taking it in turns to walk or ride as they explored the narrow streets.

Their school in Nîmes was founded in 1882 by a group of English Quakers at 21 Rue Cité de la Foulc and the first headmistress was a Mme Tayssaire. However, by the time Edith joined the school, the headmistress was Mme Matthieu, number 21 had become the girls' living quarters – the Pensionat Tayssaire – and the school itself was across the road at number 16.[2] There were quite a number of English girls there – including Annie and Sophie Stephens who were Edith's first cousins, the daughters of her mother's sister, Elizabeth. Elizabeth had married a Cornishman, John Stephens, who had a rope-making business; they lived in Budock in Cornwall and produced twelve children. Annie was the same age as Edith; Sophie was two years younger.

Annie (standing) and Sophie (right) Stephens, Edith's cousins, with their younger sister, Nellie (seated). Annie and Sophie were at school with Edith in Nîmes

The diary also mentions girls called Edie, Rachel, Jessie, Mary, Isabel, Marion and the two Newman sisters. There were also some French girls – Adolphine, Rose-Marie, Emilie, Pauline and Lydie and some 'externes' (day girls). They all seem to have been much of an age as there is no suggestion of different activities for the older or younger girls. Edith had been at school for at least a term before the diary begins and it is probable that most of the girls were only there for a year or two. The two Stephens girls were there between 1883 and 1885,[3] for example.

Edith did not much like her headmistress. She frequently refers to Madame's temper and occasionally makes comments like 'Mme was in a good mood – for her' 'Mme Matthieu came and was very horrid' – and she never missed an opportunity to criticise. 'January 10th: Mme Matthieu came also and was very cross and had a cold. I was very cross too as while she had a nice hot chauffe-pied [foot warmer] my feet were nearly frozen and my hands also ...' Even when Madame's mother died, Edith was not particularly sympathetic. On February 22nd she wrote: 'Mme Matthieu came arrayed in black with an enormous crape veil down to her knees, and much to my astonishment, kissed me. (I afterwards discovered it was the custom to do so after the death of one's mother or grandmother) She sniffed a good deal during the lesson and said she was very 'triste'. Had oranges for goûter [snack].' On March 14th Edith was forced to admit: 'Mme Matthieu in an <u>extremely</u> good temper and gave me a book of duets which she said were very pretty and good music too, not "little bêtises" [little nonsenses]' but it does not seem to have altered her opinion of the poor woman.

A Miss Thompson seems to have lived on site but it is not clear whether she was a teacher or the matron. In fact, for most of the diary Miss Thompson does very little as she is suffering from a 'dislocated foot' and spends a good deal of time resting. Edith describes her as 'paresseuse' – lazy – a term she also often applied to the French girls when they did not want to go for walks.

Other teachers came in from the town – Monsieur Chaudard, Monsieur Perrot and Monsieur Fabre among them. Edith was not overly impressed by any of them: 'January 26th:

M Chaudard came, awfully fussy and excited because he had given us some maps to paint instead of doing them in pencil as usual.' M Chaudard seems to have taught geography – on another occasion he brought a 'map of Amerique'. Monsieur Saradon taught Art and Music and Monsieur Paradon taught Bible Studies. On January 6th his lesson was 'more interesting than usual as he told us all about when he was in the east.'

Mademoiselle Gain taught gymnastics which Edith hated, writing: 'January 7th: Mlle Gain came and tortured us' and 'January 10th: Mlle Gain came and made us hang head downward with our legs through one of the bars of the ladder and other disagreeable things.' This must have been quite a shock for the English girls. In most girls' schools in England exercise took the form of drill – bending, stretching and arm movements with the feet planted safely on the ground. Hanging upside down would have been seen as positively indecent. Part-way through the diary Mademoiselle Gain becomes 'Mollie Gain' – perhaps a joke based on the fact that 'Mlle' written carelessly or mispronounced might look or sound a bit like 'Mollie'. However, one day the girls were invited to visit Mademoiselle at home and Edith recorded that 'it was very jolly as she had all the proper things to do gymnastiques'. Such visits to teachers' homes were not uncommon – the Paradons and the Fabres seem to have been particularly generous in this respect. The girls met other Quaker families at Meeting – French Quakers, British ex-pats and visitors – and received various invitations. Like all children, Edith records the exceptional rather than the everyday, but it does sound as if the girls had quite an active social life.

In her diary Edith grumbles a lot about the school and her teachers and sometimes even about the other girls – 'March 6th: Pauline will not return till Sunday (tant mieux!) [so much the better]'. The endless complaining may have been something of a pose, however, reflecting teenage melodrama and contrariness rather than any real unhappiness or dislike. Indeed the girls seem to have had quite an enviable time. In February, for example, when Edith and Annie were both unwell, they were apparently given a good deal of leeway to decide whether they wanted to spend the day in bed or get

The Roman arena in Nîmes. Edith often writes of walking 'under the arches'. Rue Cité de la Foulc where the school was is a short road leading directly to the arena

up late and attend some of their lessons. Day after day Edith records 'breakfast in bed.'

The school seems to have been run by a committee and some, if not all, of the members were English. On February 2nd it was the 'Quarterly Meeting. Heaps of Friends came …' One of them was Thomas Hambury and he put up the money for the girls to go on an excursion to Aigues-Mortes and proposed that he provide the school with a 'mazet', a little rustic building, near 'La Fontaine.' 'He really is a member of the committee worth having' wrote Edith. Her diary is peppered with French words that the girls obviously used even when they were speaking English to each other. 'La Fontaine' was the fountain in a large park in Nîmes – les Jardins de la Fontaine – and Edith and her friends often went there to listen to the band and watch the townspeople promenading.

Les Jardins de la Fontaine. The 'mazet' was somewhere near here

The proposed outing to Aigues-Mortes took place at the beginning of February – it was all very educational. They visited the old town, once a port on the Mediterranean, and walked round the ramparts. Edith recorded the snippets of history she could remember – they had seen some cannonballs that Charlemagne had used in battle; they had been told St Louis had led two crusades that started in the town; they had visited 'an old house to see a beautifully carved chimney piece'. She seems to have particularly enjoyed a visit to the Tour de Constance and recorded at length gory stories about the persecution of Protestants imprisoned there. There were trap doors through which boiling oil could be poured on intruders and 'oubliettes' into which people disappeared for good. This was the fate that befell three Huguenots who managed to escape the tower by sawing through the bars of a window but who were caught and brought back. At one point ninety-eight ladies were imprisoned in the tower:

The name of one was Marie Durand. She was shut up for 48 years, she went [in] when only 8 years and every day a priest came in to ask them to recant but one day she wrote "Resiste" with her knitting needle on the stone floor and always when the priest came she used to go and sit there and look at the word.

The Tour de Constance, Aigues-Mortes, which Edith visited

The visit took place on a Monday and the following Thursday Edith wrote angrily, 'Disgustingly cheated out of our half-holiday by Mme Matthieu who said we would work all afternoon as we had a holiday on Monday.' The girls usually had a half-holiday on the first Thursday of the month, but Mme Matthieu's ruling seems to have been quite fair. Edith, however, insisted that as they had done an hour's work before they set out on Monday morning and more 'études' (study) when they got back that should have been knocked off the time they spent in lessons on the Thursday afternoon.

On February 18th there was another trip out for many of the girls with the Crosfields, a family of English Friends visiting the area. This time they went to the Pont du Gard, the great Roman aqueduct that spans the Gardon river valley. This trip included a walk and a picnic, and by the sound of it the girls actually walked on top of the aquaduct.

The Pont du Gard which Edith visited with the Crosfield family

The 'mazet' Thomas Hambury had promised was made available to the school at the beginning of March: 'March 7th: Chose our gardens, worked hard trying to get them into a little order. Had goûter there'. 'Goûter' is a French word Edith uses a lot and it means the snack they had at tea-time, usually bread-and-butter, sometimes with jam, and sometimes with cake if it was somebody's birthday. 'Jan 24th: ... had a cake at goûter in honour of Annie's birthday.' Occasionally there was fruit.

Food features largely in the diary – Edith was a growing girl and she was often hungry. 'Souper' – supper – seems to have been particularly important to her. Often this was soup or eggs, but on January 20th she was outraged to be given bread and milk with macaroni: 'went to bed hungry and cross.' On January 28th she wrote that they had had 'a new mess for supper' but she does not say what it was. On February 7th she wrote: 'Marion and Edie made some apple pies which we are going to eat tomorrow. What a <u>delicious</u> change from the French messes,' and the following day she recorded, with unconscious irony, 'All the French liked it [the pies] for a wonder as they are so absurdly prejudiced against anything English.' Among the highlights of the many outings they went on were – for Edith – picnics, trips to cafés for coffee or 'sirop' and the opportunity to buy treats. On May 13th, for example, a visiting Friend, William Smith, took the girls to Arles and in between sightseeing they sought out a pastry-cook and bought 'lots of cakes which Mr Smith paid for'. He also bought them strawberries and cherries to eat on the way home. William Smith and his bevy of English teenage girls apparently attracted a lot of stares and comments. They saw us as 'rowdy English trippers' Edith reported happily.

Strawberries had a particular significance for the English schoolgirls. They meant summer had come. On May 10th the school gave them strawberries for dinner 'and afterwards all the English rushed upstairs and put on cotton dresses, determined, as <u>strawberries</u> were ready we would <u>not</u> wear thick dresses any longer.' It gets hot in the south of France and in May and June Edith recorded temperatures of 84, 85 and 86 degrees. She also described seeing lots of lizards on the walls of the old town and disturbing a nest of scorpions when they were cleaning out the mazet – but for the most part there is little to tell the reader that she is in a foreign country. Only once does she report a local event: 'May 5th: ... when we were in bed we heard a great deal of noise of fireworks and music in the distance, as there had been an election for the mayor late Sunday night and a Republican had got in ...'

Edith does not tell us much about what she actually studied either – and when she does, she grumbles. On February 26th she complained that she 'had eighteen pages of the most atrocious French history to learn for tomorrow.'

Exams began on March 31st with 'Botany and Physique'

[sic], and after they had 'Made April Fools of everyone we could' on April 1st, the girls went on to sit exams in 'Dictation and Composition'. The following day the exam was on 'Histoire de France' and after the weekend there was one on 'Histoire Ancienne Romaine et Grecque'. It seems Edith passed them all.

With exams out of the way it was time for the Easter holiday and another trip to Congénies. Mrs Sturge – a relative – was 'very sympathising' and brought her son, Robert, for Annie and Edith 'to amuse' while she went off on some business of her own. He was much the same age as they were but Edith writes about him as if he was a little boy. The girls took Robert to the home of their friend Lydie Margolier and tried to teach him to make oreilletes. Oreillettes are a local speciality and they are a little like deep fried pancakes, flavoured with lemon peel and dredged with sugar – the secret is to roll them out very thinly. 'RS was a very bad cook and made fearful holes' in the dough he was rolling out, much to the girls' amusement. They visited Lydie several times, and another school friend called Emilie. On April 19th, Edith wrote that they had been on 'a foraging expedition to Lydie's for books and came back with 'Harry Beaujoy' for Sophie, 'Sandford and Merton' for me and 'Popular Tales' by Miss Edgeworth' for Annie. *Harry Beaujoy* has proved untraceable, but the other two were children's books which seem rather juvenile for sixteen- and eighteen-year-olds, but perhaps they were the only English books Lydie had.

The girls were obviously getting rather bored. Various expeditions had been laid on for their entertainment – to Trois Moulins, a local beauty spot; to the quaint little village of Aujargues; and to the pretty medieval towns of Sommières and Aubais. There were also walks and picnics by the Vidourle river – but Edith and her friends were teenage girls, so rural views and picturesque places were of limited interest.

In the summer term there was less pressure to study and more excursions. On May 13th William Smith took them to Arles.

Edith records conscientiously the sights the girls were taken to see, including the amphitheatre; the church of St Trophime where they all dutifully dipped their hands in the

*Tympanum of the Church of St Trophime, Arles, which
Edith visited. It is stunningly beautiful –
and she makes no mention of it at all*

Les Alyscamps, the Roman necropolis in Arles

stoops of holy water; the rows of stone coffins in what Edith calls 'the Alis Champs' (more properly 'Alyscamps' – a famous Roman necropolis); and the museum, which she dismissed as 'uninteresting'.

She did however comment on how attractive most of the women in the town were and how pretty their costumes were – in 1884 many people in France would have worn national costume – but she was simply amused by the Algerian soldiers 'who looked very funny in their red baggy trousers (a sort of divided skirt I should think) and white gaiters and red caps.'

Over Whit weekend Edith and Annie went to St Gilles on the edge of the Petit Camargue. They seem to have stayed overnight in a pension but they visited people they knew there – Mrs Sparkes, Marie Breen and Jeanne. They walked by the Rhône canal and visited the Cathedral and museum. However, it is the journey that Edith records in most detail:

> May 31st: Started at 4.00 from the school for the diligence office. It should have been an agreeable journey had it not been for an old woman, a man and a woman with a child. The grease on the child's hair and the smell of tobacco combined did not make it a very agreeable odour.

Edith and Annie spent the journey pulling faces to terrify the little girl and making her 'shriek with fright.' There are times, and this is one of them, when Edith comes over as much younger than her sixteen years.

On June 8th a group of girls was invited to visit the country house owned by a family by the name of Dumas. This was about an hour's journey from Nîmes, halfway to St Gilles. Again the girls stayed in a pension, but they visited the house and gardens, went for long walks and picked and ate cherries.

On June 12th the school arranged another outing for the English girls, this time for a day at the seaside town of Palavas. They got up at 4am and caught a train at 6am, changed trains at Montpellier and arrived at Palavas by 8am. By this point Miss Thompson's foot seems to have got better, for she accompanied them. Mme Fabre had arranged for them to have a room for the day to use as a base but they do not seem to have spent much time in it. They went to the beach and 'waded' – the term Edith uses for 'paddled' – and at 11.30am Miss Thompson allowed them to bathe.

> [The woman] gave us all nice bathing gowns (quite new, had never been used) and we went into little "cabines" in a sort of long low house divided into little partitions. We were soon undressed and all rushed down to the water (the woman offered us hats but of course we all refused immediately). We had a delicious "time" in the water and stopped in ever so long.

They explored the town and then in the afternoon went out in a rowing boat with an old sailor and they all took turns at rowing – 'no-one was ill, tho' Lucy Newton did not look very happy', despite the sea being 'perfectly blue and calm,' and 'it was a lot hotter at Palavas than at Nîmes'. It sounds like an idyllic day out – but Edith was never satisfied. They got back to Nîmes at 6.30 and 'after supper Mme drove us off to Meeting in the most heartless manner' ignoring the fact that they were all very tired. Edith was not one for pious reflection and she always seems to have found going to Meeting a bit of a chore.

The school year was almost at an end but lessons continued for a further week until on June 19th they 'fixed the trains we were to go home by'. They made many visits to say goodbye to people; there was a party at the Paradons with an impromptu concert and charades; and on the 24th 'after supper we had a very affecting parting with the French'. Several of their French friends from the town were at the station to see them off the following morning.

Edith met up with her father and sister Emily in Paris. They spent nearly a month in the city, sightseeing and having fun, and Edith abandoned her diary. The last entry consists of several rows of neatly inked stars – perhaps in celebration of the end of her time with Mme Matthieu – and a final note of explanation:

> During our sojourn in Paris I had no time to continue my diary but left it, thinking to copy out of

Emily's what I had missed. However, on looking at her diary on our return home, I was dismayed to find what I had missed; and also the number of pages left in hers to copy.

At that point she seems to have been happy to give up. Edith was seventeen later that year and it seems likely that her schooldays were at an end. At the end of August they returned home and Edith saw for herself the new house in Primrose Hill. However, they did not stay there long. By 1888[4] William and Mary Hughes were living in Ross-on-Wye with Edith and Geoffrey, and William seems to have been semi-retired. There was a flourishing Quaker community in Ross which may have informed their choice. By this point young William and Ernest were running the family business in London, Morgan had a dental practice in Croydon and was married with a family, and Arthur was at school in Lewisham. Geoffrey went on to become a dentist like his brother and Arthur went into banking.

Emily married in 1894. Her husband, Herbert Sefton-Jones, was a patent agent and inventor, and a prominent Quaker, best known for his opposition to Quaker pacifism in the face of the Great War. Emily was a member of the Royal Historical Association, travelled extensively, and published several articles and two books under the name 'Margaret Sefton-Jones' (Margaret was her second name) – *Old Devonshire House by Bishopgate* in 1923 and *Friends of the East* in 1930.

Rather more interesting is a book she seems to have compiled with Edith shortly before her marriage to Sefton-Jones – *Selections from the Philosophical and Poetical Works of Constance C. W. Naden,* which was published in 1893. Constance Caroline Woodhill Naden was an atheist, a poet, philosopher and science writer from Birmingham. Many of her poems dealt with nature, myth and religion and her questioning of Christian teaching. From a modern perspective, her most interesting works deal with science and the relationship between men and women. The quotations below give a flavour:[5]

The Nebular Theory

This is the genesis of Heaven and Earth.
In the beginning was a formless mist
Of atoms isolate, void of life; none wist
Aught of its neighbour atom, nor any mirth,
Nor woe, save its own vibrant pang of dearth;
Until a cosmic motion breathed and hissed
And blazed through the black silence ...

Natural Selection

... But there comes an idealess lad,
With a strut and a stare and a smirk,
And I watch, scientific though sad,
The Law of Selection at work.

Of Science he had not a trace,
He seeks not the How and the Why,
But he sings with an amateur's grace
And he dances much better than I.

And we know the more dandified males
By dance and by song win their wives –
Tis a law that with *avis* prevails,
And ever in *Homo* survives ...

Scientific Wooing

I was a youth of studious mind,
Fair Science was my mistress kind,
And held me with attraction chemic;
No germs of Love attacked my heart,
Secured as by Pasteurian art
Against that fatal epidemic.

For when my daily task was o'er
I dreamed of H_2SO_4,
While stealing through my slumbers placid
Came Iodine, with violet fumes,
And Sulphur, with its yellow blooms,
And whiffs of Hydrochloric Acid ...

The Lady Doctor

Saw ye that spinster gaunt and grey,
Whose aspect stern might well dismay
A bombardier stout-hearted?
The golden hair, the blooming face,
And all a maiden's tender grace
Long, long from her have parted.

A Doctor she, her sole delight
To order draughts as black as night,
Powders, and pills, and lotions;
Her very glance might cast a spell
Transmuting Sherry and Moselle
To chill and acrid potions.

What was it in these sentiments that attracted Emily and Edith? Or was it the fact that Constance was not much older than they were and had died tragically young? She seems an unlikely heroine for two girls from a very conventional and religious background, and it gives us an intriguing glimpse into the way they thought – and makes Edith seem a good deal more interesting than do her teenage diaries.

But it seems she made no further essays into print. Of the seven Hughes siblings, only Edith seems to have made little use of her expensive education. She lived at home until her parents died – William in 1902 and Mary in 1911. What became of her after that? Did she stay in Ross-on-Wye? Did the Great War give her the opportunity to do something useful? She was not quite forty-seven when it began, young enough to have forged a career if she had so wished. Did she ever revisit France and use the French she had acquired so painfully at Mme Matthieu's school? There seems to be no way of knowing – 'Edith Hughes' is too common a name to be able to trace her with any degree of certainty.

Endnotes

1   Birmingham University Special Collection MS6.

2   Bibliotheque Chretienne Online, Chapitre XXIV. The school closed in 1889.

3   Cornwall Record Office, ST/224 Stephens family correspondence.
     Information from Friends' House. The family joined the Ross-on-Wye Meeting in 1888.

4   Ancestry.co.uk, Public Member Tree TREE8112010. We are extremely grateful to the Stephens family for making this information available and for allowing us to use some of their family photographs.

5   For more examples, see *The Complete Works of Constance Naden* at www.searchengine.org.uk/ebooks/67/70.pdf

Quaker values

November 10th 1897: When Sarah Ostle went to her desk to put her books away after school, she found it in great confusion and a large rat jumped out. Of course, all in the schoolroom screamed as loud as they could, and those who were outside rushed in to see what was the matter ...[1]

Needless to say, the rat escaped.

This is one of the last entries in a rather curious diary kept by pupils at another Friends' School, this time one at Wigton in Cumberland. The school was usually known as 'Brookfield', from its location, and it has to be said that the disordered scene described above was far from typical.

The diary was a group effort – some of the diarists signed or initialled their entries and at least eighteen pupils and teachers took part. Some were regular contributors and wrote the diary for several weeks at a time, others contributed just one or two entries. Some obviously enjoyed writing as a literary exercise, other entries are very pedestrian. Keeping the diary does not seem to have been set as an exercise – there seem to be far too many in-jokes for it to have been written in class. It begins:

1892

December 1st: Model Drawing Exam

December 2nd: Literature Exam

December 3rd: French Exam

December 5th: Grammar, History and Model Drawing Exams

December 6th: Science Exams

December 9th: Geography and Geometry Exams

December 10th: Mental calculation and Algebra Exams. Herr Barstel came and told us our French places.

December 12th: Etymology Exam from 9 to 10. We got our papers given out. At half past 12 we got our final places.

Brookfield was a co-educational boarding school – quite unusual for the period – and it had been founded in 1815.

Brookfield school

At the time of the 1891 census it had forty-seven pupils of whom eighteen were girls, and they were all between the ages of eleven and fourteen, although the school could take children as young as seven. Pupils do not seem to have stayed long – most were there between one and three years.[2] The majority came from Cumberland and the surrounding counties, but the three McCracken children, Elizabeth, Mary and David, came all the way from Johannesburg and several others came from Scotland. Some were paid for by their local Quaker Meeting if a parent had died or if their families were experiencing financial difficulties.

The headmaster in post when the first diary entries were made was Martin Lidbetter, a man in his seventies who was nearing the end of his thirty-three years at the school.

Martin Lidbetter, Headmaster of Brookfield
until the summer of 1892

He was replaced in the summer of 1893 by one of the junior masters, Joseph Jopling. Other masters during the 1890s were Messrs Gower, Geeson, De Vit, Grone, Heald and Harrod; the girls' teachers were Miss Burtt, Miss Williamson – the gym teacher – Miss King, Miss Cumine and the redoubtable Miss Shields. In his memoir Joseph Jopling claimed that he did not know girls could 'get into disorder' until after Miss Shields left the school. All of the teachers feature in the diary.[3]

Girls and boys had separate living quarters and classrooms, they sat at different tables in the dining room and were allocated different playgrounds, but nonetheless there seems to have been a good deal of interaction between the two groups – both boys and girls contributed to the diary for example – and there was a good deal of friendly rivalry between the sexes.

Girls' classroom at Brookfield

In 1919 the school celebrated its centenary – four years late on account of the war – and William Walpole Lidbetter, son of the former headmaster and who had himself been a pupil at Brookfield, penned a lengthy poem to mark the occasion. William had left the school in 1891 and by 1919 he was living in South Africa and unable to attend the centenary celebrations in person. His poem casts an interesting light on various aspects of school life, not least on the relationship between the boys and the girls. He starts by remembering the girls he knew:

> Ye bright Brookfield lasses! the years roll away,
> As I knew you in boyhood I see you today;
> Though you never dear ladies, suspected the truth,
> In my heart you're endowed with perpetual youth.
> There was sweet Williamina, the dearest of girls,

And the glint of the sunshine in Josephine's curls,
Wild Winnie the wayward and Bessie the tease,
And my Mary, who went to the Antipodes.
Oh! the pain of that parting, it still makes me
squirm.

When you passed from my life at the end of the term;
But mischievous Maggie restored me to bliss,
And I've never forgotten that one stolen kiss;
And you, last of the legion till now unconfessed,
Do you still in the gloaming sing "Gates of the
West."?
Dear lasses I loved in the days that are gone.
Are you mothers and grandmothers thirty years on? [4]

Young Master Lidbetter obviously had an eye for the ladies. Later in the poem he describes how that 'one stolen kiss' may have happened:

In the long winter evenings we'd many a spree
When the teachers were safe in the parlour at tea;
'Twas the hour most propitious in which to engage
In a cousinly "crack" on the dark playground edge;

'Cousinly crack' indeed!

The school year was divided into 'halfs' and there was a holiday at Christmas and another over the summer – about three weeks each time. Children occasionally went home for the Easter weekend and family and friends visited, but the children spent an awful lot of time away from their families.

Alas the change – we come once more
On to the old familiar floor
And in the classroom now we stand
Beside the well-known door.

No longer Esther's cheerful voice
Is heard in the playground race
And the first class girls feel almost lost
Without Lilian's teazing face.
But a bright little spark of a sister
Has come in her stead – quite gay
And the many tales of her doings
We will find out the truth of today.

Yes, do ring the bell, please,
For I've heard it said
We are to go
Very shortly, to bed
And bed, delightful bed
Is heaven on earth to the homesick head.

The bell doth toll, its echoes roll
We know that sound full well
Its old, old ringing – how it calls to 'Reading'
With its ding-ding-ding dong bell.

Sleeping (weeping), sleeping, sleeping (dreaming) in
the old, old bed as of yore
Snoring, snoring, snoring, thro' the open chamber door.

One of the diarists – probably Margaret Wright – penned those
lines on her return to school on July 31st 1895. It is the single
indication in the diary of any sort of unhappiness – and in fact
it reads more like adolescent melodrama than real sadness,
though no doubt Margaret and her friends really did miss
their homes and regret the absence of former schoolfellows.

Even when they were ill, children remained at school. The
diary refers to pupils going into, or coming out of 'the nursery'
– the name for the school sick bay – but they were usually only
there for a day or two. Even hospital appointments were

Outside Brookfield School

arranged by the staff: 'October 22nd 1895: Mr Jopling took Willie Hinde to London to see about his eyes.' Poor Willie was left there in hospital. There are a couple of instances recorded of boys breaking limbs, but they seem to have recovered well and been able to carry on with their lessons while the bones healed. The only recorded incidences of long-term sickness were the measles and mumps epidemics in the spring of 1896 and the diarists seem to have regarded these as amusing rather than serious – especially when the sufferers were convalescent:

> April 6th The Mumpers and Measlers are enjoying their liberty and roaming the fields and lanes with pea-shooters and are getting into mischief whenever they can.

Brookfield pupils were a hardy lot – indeed, in his memoir Joseph Jopling wrote that he could only recall one case of serious illness in all his time at the school, and that was a girl who went down with typhoid fever the day after the holidays ended – so clearly she had contracted it elsewhere.

Mr Jopling and a group of teachers, including Mr Harrod, the bearded gentleman at the back

Several things come across quite clearly. First of all, this was an excellent school with a modern curriculum that stretched the children and kept them interested. Secondly, the children were busy and happy, encouraged to participate in a wide range of extra-curricula activities and with a good deal of freedom to entertain themselves and roam the countryside. And thirdly, it shows just how unremittingly dismal Cumbrian weather can be.

Weather had a much greater significance in the nineteenth century than it has today. Most journeys were made on foot, few people had truly waterproof clothing or footwear and most roads were un-metalled and could easily become impassable in bad weather. Houses were not centrally heated, there was no hot water on tap and in winter frost formed on the inside of the windows of unheated bedrooms. Rain and snow made life profoundly uncomfortable – and Cumberland had plenty of both:

> March 1st 1894: Another fearful storm in the night and when we came down in the morning the classroom floor had pools of water and the rain had come into Miss Shields' room so much that it was dropping from the parlour ceiling below ...

> February 9th 1895: 26 degrees of frost

> February 10th: Washing is still done under difficulties as bowls are so frozen in the mornings that often the plugs will not go in. If it were not for the exertions of our top girl every morning, many of us might deserve the fingers of scorn that the old woman of Pears' soap fame showed when she exclaims "You dirty boy!"

That particular cold snap lasted for several weeks and the railway companies ran special excursion trains to Windermere for people to skate, as the lake had frozen over for the first time in sixteen years. The children had snowball fights, went skating, and enjoyed writing their names in the fresh snow and taking photos of each other alongside them – photography was a hobby the headmaster enjoyed and encouraged. The school had foreseen at least one of the difficulties the snow would cause: 'February 1st 1895: The girls got galoshes to keep the snow off their feet and prevent us getting colds.'

The school timetable was adapted to make the most of the snowy weather: 'January 30th 1895: We had lessons in the afternoon instead of the morning and went to Moorhouse Tarn to skate in the morning.' The boys made slides by pouring buckets of water down the slope in front of the school, getting up at four in the morning to do so, supervised by their seventy-year-old headmaster.

William Walpole Lidbetter fondly remembered his days on the icy slide. All his former schoolfellows are referred to by their nicknames and the giving and using of these seems to have been a Brookfield tradition.

Come along all you chaps there's a slide on the front!
On a cold winter's morning what more can you want?
What matter though falls and hard knocks may be rife
You'll have harder knocks yet on the long slide of life.
Come, keep the pot boiling! Look sharp! Off we go,
With Peiler and Frazer, Tom Ed. and Joe Crow;
See old Snipe does "spread eagle" and trips on the side,
There's Wigs cutting "cannels" he'll ruin the slide
There goes Peck and old Putty and Abey the fat
And clever young Kitten and smart Andypat,
Then Paddy sails past with his dignified frown,
And Bunky does "little man" all the way down.

Children sliding at the front of the school

The school favoured healthy outdoor exercise and – unusually for the period – had its own swimming bath. This was used for swimming but it also seems to have been seen as an alternative to washing.

> June 19th 1893: The girls bathed for the first time this year in the outside bath.

> August 8th 1894: Bathing still continues – tho' today it took place during the rain. Fresh bathers made their first plunge today and all the new girls but one have now had a 'dip' and as nearly all the old girls bathe there are only a few to reckon among the 'great unwashed.'

On September 3rd 1894 the diary recorded that Miss Burtt, one of the teachers, was the only one of the 'noble fourteen' still taking regular dips in the pool.

Miss Burtt was something of a favourite; in summer she would allow the younger girls to swing in her hammock and both she and Miss King were invited to contribute to the diary. The children seem to have got on well with their teachers – certainly there are no unkind descriptions of any of them in the diary – and the teachers seem to have had fun with the children: 'April 1st 1893: We were all made April Fools by W and M Lidbetter [the headmaster and his son] putting empty eggshells the wrong way up in the eggcups with paper inside with 'April Fool' on.' It is also notable that the entries make no reference to any punishments being meted out – there must have been some, but corporal punishment was probably against the Quaker ethos and the staff seem to have shown their charges a good deal of kindness and respect.

It would be difficult to reconstruct the school timetable from the diary entries – the writers knew the times of their classes and saw no need to record them – but certain aspects of the school routine become apparent. The children got up early – 6.15am or 6.30am, depending on the time of year, though at the end of March 1896 they had a week of late rising: 'March 30th 1896: We got up at 7 o'clock and are going to continue getting up late all the week seeing as we are not going to get home for the weekend this Easter.' Birthdays were celebrated and recorded in the diary. Every fortnight there was 'head washing' – presumably that means 'hair' – and it was considered sufficiently important to mention almost every time.

Wigton was a Quaker school and the diary was filled with entries about going to Sunday Meeting, about which teachers went to Monthly Meeting, who spoke in Meeting and so on. Monthly Meetings were on Wednesdays, so one day a month classes were disrupted and the fact was solemnly written in the diary each time. Their Quaker faith was reinforced: 'Sunday February 11th 1894: Mr Jopling has begun to read to us in Reading the little book called "Why we children are Friends" by G. Crookfield.' The children were also encouraged to do good works: 'February 17th 1896: Susannah Hall has been collecting to send to the Armenians and Becca Bigland collected 3s-6d amongst the girls and took it to Waverton in the afternoon.' Speakers came to introduce Quaker values. There were lectures on the harmful effects of alcohol and on October 22nd 1896 a Miss Robinson gave a lecture on Peace and brought along a book for the children to sign to say they were pacifists.

But there were plenty of other talks and magic-lantern shows that had no particular religious context. Speakers talked of their travels in places as far afield as Palestine and China, and Mr Jopling, proud possessor of a Kodak camera, gave a talk with slides he had made himself entitled 'Around the World with a Camera'. The lectures were an eclectic mix. On November 1st 1894 'A gentleman named Mr Enoch gave us a very interesting lecture on the Trap-trap Spider. They get their curious name from the little trap door the foreign ones make at the top of their nests.' One talk that went down particularly well was about 'relics of the inhabitants of England thousands of years ago, then of those of the Druids, Romans, Normans, etc. It was a very interesting lecture, especially as some of the slides were photos of places around Cockermouth Brigham which were familiar to us.'

But far and away the children's favourite visitor was Joseph Spence Hodgson, always known as 'Spence'. He visited the school for a few days every summer and taught English, but the children loved him because he gave funny recitations and told stories. *The Locusts, The Bear and the Baker* and *Noo Bairnies, Cuddle Doon* were particular favourites, but each year there were additions to his repertoire. He was also an accomplished swimmer and gave demonstrations at the school pool – diving, doing backward somersaults and so on – and he would act as swimming coach for some of the new pupils. In 1894 he even sent the girls 'many-jointed dolls, all wrapped up in cotton wool' after his visit – perhaps to use in drawing class. He styled himself a 'Professor of Elocution', and though Yorkshire born, he lived in Lancaster. He was a prominent Quaker and seems to have been involved with many of the Quaker schools.

Loyalty to Brookfield ran deep and there was – and is – a flourishing Old Scholars' Association. The annual cricket match against the old boys was always eagerly anticipated:

> July 12th 1893: Six visitors arrived before dinner to play in the Old Scholars' cricket match. The rest arrived soon after and batting began about 2 o'clock. The home side went in first and made 54 runs: The Visitors had a better team the last time but in the first innings their wickets fell in rapid succession before the severe bowling of Mr Jopling and Mr Gower. Rain came on a little but this did not prevent a second innings when the Old Scholars made a better score but did not succeed in equalling our side – so that the match ended in a decided victory for the school.

The Old Scholars were often generous to the school, both individually and as an organisation. They offered prizes for swimming and natural history studies, put up money for outings and sent gifts: 'August 22nd 1895: Prizes are given again to be offered for Natural History and we expect to have 10£ [sic] worth of pictures as a gift from the Old Scholars before long.'

There were other traditions like the twice-yearly 'Toffee Joins' when the girls made pans of toffee – with varying degrees of success – in which were hidden two small tokens, a ring and a button, a bit like sixpences in a Christmas pudding: 'October 10th 1896: It was toffee-join day: the results were pretty good with the exception of one panful.' For the most part boys and girls were treated equally, but cooking the toffee was a girl's job, as was darning stockings: 'May 9th 1896: The second great mending of the boys' stockings has been accomplished today and appropriate pence distributed to the darners, a valuable source of income to some.' At least the girls got paid.

There were girls-versus-boys cricket matches which the girls always lost, even though the masters chivalrously joined their team, but there were other occasions when the girls managed to defy expectations. In August 1896 Sir Raylton Dixon, one of the old boys of the school, sent £5 to enable the pupils to go on an outing. The original plan was to visit Ullswater and there was some disappointment when the staff decided it was too far for a day's journey and opted to go to Bassenthwaite instead. The children set out to climb Skiddaw:

> The steepest part of the mountain being just at the beginning and the wind very strong against us, a good many gave up before they had got halfway and returned to recruit their strength at the sweet shop. Four of the girls, however, pressed on and reached the summit, thereby falsifying the prediction of the boys "the lasses would never do it."

Cumbrians are great walkers, and going for long walks was one of the children's main pastimes. They did 'the three mile round' and 'the six mile round', trekked across to 'Old Carlisle' or up to High Pour or went looking for wild flowers in John Peel's Wood. Collecting wild flowers was a school passion. Each year they kept a book of how many different flowers they had collected, when and where, and the tally usually came to around 200.

> March 4th 1896: We went a walk to John Peel's Wood in the hopes of finding anemone, field wood rush and spotted dead nettle, only succeeding in finding the last one.

April 3rd 1896: ... many new flowers were found –
among them dog violet, stitchwort, broom and marsh
Andromeda.

May 30th 1896: ... the boys found 13 fresh flowers
and broomrape was found at High Pour. It appears
that this is only the second time broomrape has been
found in Cumberland.

Common broomrape (orobanche minor)

The children were often accompanied by the school's
pet dogs – Guess, so-called because the children had been
invited to guess his name when he arrived as a puppy, and
Pat, an Inishmore terrior, properly named 'Patrick Dragon',
who arrived on May 25th 1895 'in a hamper from Ireland'.
He was not always well behaved and on one occasion, out with
a group of boys, he caught and almost killed a hen, and was

soundly beaten with an umbrella 'but it had no effect.' He was luckier than the white kitten, however, which was found dead on March 6th 1893 – '… some boys declare the girls fed it and squeezed it too much'.

The children all had gardens and it was their responsibility to keep them in good order, a task which seems to have been done only intermittently 'Gardened instead of going for a walk' is a very occasional entry in the diary. But when an entry recorded that the gardens were in a 'very wild state', the girls decided to do something about it and turned out in force:

> Many and varied were the costumes for the occasion – some wearing their skirts as short as possible, others putting on large pinafores and making them as long as possible – some in dirty old dresses – others in clean blouses … Some of our number seemed to think it ought to be a regular Spring Cleaning affair and dug up all their plants so as to have a regular turn-out. These were afterwards replaced, looking slightly the worse for being disturbed.

The children also established an essay club where pupils – and sometimes teachers – read their own work out loud and invited discussion of the topic. These meetings at their best were funny and noisy, or, when one of the teachers was involved, simply instructive: 'November 9th 1893: Mr Geeson's essay on the electric telegraph was very edifying and interesting.' They also staged impromptu plays and concerts, as on November 7th 1895: 'Then we had a concert, singing, dancing, musical performance, the instruments being: poker, tongs, Jews' harp.' Music did not play a major part in school life, however – the school did not even acquire a piano until 1894 and apparently even then some of the staff disapproved. This may seem strange, but the early Quakers had tried to distance themselves from the Church of England and its hymns and psalms. Quaker worship was largely silent and many regarded music as frivolous and not in keeping with their emphasis on 'simplicity'. By the mid-nineteenth century attitudes were changing but it seems that even in the 1890s some Brookfield teachers clung to the old values.

Boys and girls played cricket, tennis and croquet in the summer, and in the winter the boys played football and the girls played hockey, but alongside these official sports the children played a range of games of their own choosing:

> March 2nd 1894: Rounders has become the fashionable game and the squealing and yelling that seems to be its necessary accompaniment is something startling.

> August 19th 1894: Skipping has quite gone out and the girls are playing a new game which Thomas Little taught us about two years ago when he was here from Brumana [sic].

Brummana was a Quaker school in the Lebanon which had been founded by a Swiss, Theophilus Waldemeier, in 1873, and it maintained a close link with Brookfield.[5] The game seems to have been 'Prisoner's Base', a team game played with two lines of children and a chalk square – the 'prison' – in the middle. Each side chose a 'prisoner' from the other side and the objective was for each team to rescue their prisoner without being caught by the other side. Another favourite was a game called 'Fox and Dowdy', the rules of which seem to have completely disappeared.

> March 17th 1896: A skipping fever has set in, as we had to play in the playroom we all turned out ropes and had various races.

> November 6th 1897: We were skipping and Arthur particularly distinguished himself by jumping two times for every turn of the rope.

Like all children, Brookfield pupils enjoyed novelty and breaks in routine, however banal. The diary records such excitements as the arrival of a man with a weighing machine to weigh and measure the children (January 21st 1895), Miss Williamson teaching Swedish Drill (August 20th 1896),

Miss Burtt showing the girls objects under a microscope (November 1st 1894) and the barber being unwell: 'March 22nd 1895: [He] had not been at work an hour when a little boy came into Mr Jopling's arithmetic class and announced "Please, the barber's bad" so the bus had to be sent for and he was taken down to Wigton.' Even the arrival of new jam dishes merited a full entry: 'February 22nd 1894: Jam pots at meals are a thing of the past and instead we are using thin, elegant, shapely vessels of white edged with gilt. Unfortunately these overturn much easier than the aforementioned jam pots and more than one upset took place the very first day.'

Occasionally something really exciting did happen: 'August 29th 1894: Great excitement was caused amongst the children by three rather obstreperous tramps who shouted threats and imprecations and ... when we would not give them anything threatened to blow up the school.' On March 26th 1895 there was an eclipse of the sun which the children 'espyed [sic] through coloured and smoked glass'. In early November 1896 the school celebrated Guy Fawkes Day – not something they did every year – with an enormous bonfire 'in Carr's Field'. The fire was eighteen yards in circumference and could be seen six miles away on the Allonby Road. There was a guy with 'a broadly smiling mask' and the children contributed towards the purchase of fireworks – that event merited almost a full page of description.

New pupils were always a source of interest, particularly so if they had something interesting to offer. Louis and Henri Anderson arrived at the school in 1895:

> August 2nd: Two of the new boys have been brought up in France and can speak very little English; it is interesting to have them among us, and tables shall sound quite exciting when beginning "deux fois un deux – deux fois deux – quatre" etc., etc..

School meals were probably fairly stodgy, as any deviation or treat was eagerly recorded:

> June 9th 1893: Percy Corden gave us each two oranges.

August 26th 1895: At supper the boys and girls were delighted to find pleasant surprises in the way of honey and cake presented by Mrs Grone – unusually large meals were made on either side of the room.

September 19th: We had bramble jam to tea.

September 28th: Brambling. The boys got 16 ½ lbs, the girls 17 ½.

October 6th: We each got three biscuits sent by Josiah Hall.

February 19th 1896: The Miss Halls gave us each a large bun which we all greatfully [sic] received.

March 10th: We had rhubarb pie to dinner today, the first we have had this year.

William Lidbetter's poem tells us more:

Or when grub-boxes failed, the occasion we took
To make warm cupboard-love to Eliza the cook ...

However, the main purpose of the school was to educate, and this it seems to have done exceptionally well. The curriculum was broad as the list of exams at the beginning of this chapter shows, and both boys and girls learnt 'modern' subjects like algebra and chemistry. Even more avant garde was Mr Jopling's decision to offer shorthand as an alternative to Latin. Those boys – and it would nearly always have been boys – going on to university could still study Latin, but those whose parents were in business often opted for shorthand. At the time of the diary, there were two sets of exams a year at the end of each 'half', and on the basis of these, children moved up or down a standard or stayed where they were.

The science labs at Brookfield, c.1900

Alas the change, we used to stand
High top of all the class,
But "places" come, the marks are scanned
And down the line we pass.
The mumpers, true, have some excuse
And measle-coughers sore,
But there are some, an idle few
Must work a little more ...

wrote Margaret Wright in the diary in the spring of 1896 as the children were preparing for the summer exams. She was, of course referring to the recent mumps and measles epidemics.

Three years later, Mr Jopling decided that two examinations a year was too many and abandoned the winter ones. However, like his predecessor, he still encouraged children to go in for the South Kensington (Department of

Science and Art) exams in Drawing, Chemistry and Maths so that their achievements could be measured on a national scale rather than simply against that of their schoolfellows, and by 1898 he also had them working for the College of Preceptors examinations. Brookfield children were getting the best academic education he could secure for them.

It is probably unwise to read too much into a single document, but Brookfield children also seem to have had a fine social education. They were encouraged to think for themselves, girls were allowed to have aspirations like their brothers, and relations between staff and pupils seem to have been cordial and respectful – at least if the diary entries are to be believed. Sadly, the school closed in 1984 and the buildings were burnt down in 1989; however, its memory is still kept alive by WOSA, the Wigton Old Scholars' Association.[6]

Not all the contributors to the diary could be identified, but the following were certainly amongst them:

>Becca Bigland
>Mary Ann Brown
>Annie S Hannah
>Margaret D Wright
>Mabel (and/or Matthew) Wigham
>Sarah Scott
>Florence S Pickering
>J Herbert Walker
>Robert C Bell
>Joseph Williamson
>Miss Katherine L Burtt
>Miss Florence M King

In many ways Quaker children were lucky. Even if their parents could not afford to send them away to school, their local Society of Friends often paid for their education at schools like Brookfield. But for the vast majority of children from modest backgrounds, access to education was a lottery, dependent largely on where they happened to be born. The next three chapters look at the education available to children from less fortunate families. Such children seldom kept diaries and they lived at home so had no reason to write letters; these chapters still use contemporary sources but more reliance has had to be placed on 'official' documents than on the children's own writings.

Endnotes

1   The diary is in the Cumbria Record Office, Carlisle DFCF/7/1992.

2   Pupil lists published in Reed (see below).

3   Other information about the school comes from Reed, D W, *The Friends' School, Wigton 1815-1953*, WOSA, 1954.

4   The authors are indebted to Marjorie Taylor of WOSA for this information, for her advice and support and for a copy of the poem.

5   As above.

6   www.wosa.org.uk

The young lace-maker

We were all so excited! Miss Bidney came to see us all – looked over our work – she needed to pick the best lace-makers, you see. To think – the Queen was going to wear lace made in Branscombe!

S arah Jane would have heard her mother's story many times over.

The Perry family – Mary, Solomon and their children – lived in Branscombe, a village on the Devon coast some five miles east of Sidmouth. It is a picturesque little place, thatched stone cottages straggling for two miles along a deep valley which finally meets the sea at Branscombe Mouth.

View towards Branscombe Mouth

But it was also a place of great poverty. There were no gentry in the place to distribute charity; just a few well-to-do farmers and lace merchants, all intent on making money. Some of the village men were fishermen and sailors but most worked on the land or in the limestone quarries, for wages well below the national average. Their young sons went cockling on the beach to earn a few extra pence and their wives and daughters made lace. Out of a population of around 1,100 in 1841, some 123 were lace makers – and by 1851 that number had risen to 310.

Branscombe beach where the village boys went cockling

Custom died hard in the little villages around Axminster and Honiton. Branscombe women made lace – it did not occur to them that there was any other way of earning a living. And so, when they were old enough, Mary Perry sent her elder daughters, Mary Ann and Sarah Jane, to lace school. Concepts of 'old enough' varied. Some lace schools took children as young as four – though the younger children were only at school for four hours a day. Many of the mistresses spoke of how trying it was to teach small children and the short hours were probably as much for the teacher's benefit as for the children's. But while they were at school the little ones were expected to learn the simple repetitive movements by which the two bobbins known as 'runners' produced a basic weave ('cloth stitch') or the equally simple but prettier 'half stitch'. Later they would graduate to making decorative holes in the weave by twisting bobbins together in a pre-ordained pattern and learn to make 'lead works' – a simple form of infill stitch. Creating lead works that were not too fat, too thin or mis-shapen was a skill that required a good deal of practice. Some people believed that learning the stitches early, while hands and fingers were small and pliable, was an invaluable way of developing the speed and dexterity needed to make fine lace – but children kept at such work from toddlerhood often grew up small and feeble, with bent backs and weakened limbs from hours of sitting hunched over their lace pillows in cramped rooms – if indeed they grew up at all.

Honiton sprigs made using basic stitches (these have been enlarged so the detail can be seen more clearly)

1. *Sprig made of whole stitch (eg. bottom three leaves), half stitch (eg. top two leaves) and with 'ladder trail' design in the leaf on the middle left. These are all very simple basic stitches.*

2. *Butterfly sprig. The outline is in whole stitch with a pearl border, the solid parts of the wings are in half stitch, the open parts are filled with leadworks. Again, these are all very basic stitches.*

3. *Diagram showing how to make leadworks, sometimes called 'cutworks'.*

171

By the time Mary Ann and Sarah Jane were old enough to go to school, most mistresses did not take children before the age of six. Indeed, in the 1860s, Mrs Treadwin in Exeter, one of the most respected lace-makers of her day, settled on ten as the ideal age at which to begin learning. Mrs Treadwin also considered that it took a full seven years to turn girls into proficient lace-makers[1] – so by the age of fourteen Sarah Jane would have learnt almost all she needed to know about the craft with which she would earn her living for the next quarter of a century.

She was seventeen when Mr White of the Children's Employment Commission came to Branscombe.[2] The commissioners were given guidelines about what to ask and they usually had an agenda – in Mr White's case it was to find out about hours of work, the age at which children went to lace school and how this affected their general education. He developed his own way of doing this by getting the children he interviewed to read for him and asking them general knowledge questions – it was an unusual approach, not followed by most of the commissioners, and the results were revealing.

Most of the lace school teachers claimed to teach the children to read as well as to make lace, but in reality many of them only allotted a few minutes a day to reading and Mr White discovered that very few of the girls could read fluently. Most could read 'simple words'; others seemed able to read parts of the Bible but probably only because they knew them by heart; many spelled words out loud as they went; few could write, and even fewer could recognise numbers when they were written down. Whether this also meant that they could not count or do basic addition is not clear. Certainly Sarah Jane was recorded as being unable to recognise a large print version of the number '2', she could only read simple words, and when she was asked to name foreign countries she listed France, Australia and California. They were not surprising choices. France was not far away, the old enemy, the country from which men in nearby Beer smuggled silks and brandy. No doubt there were tales in the village of local men being transported to Australia for what today seem petty crimes – the practice did not cease till 1868. And the Californian gold rush would still have been a recent memory – perhaps some

Branscombe men had gone there in a desperate bid to improve their fortunes. What we do not know is how long Mr White gave Sarah Jane to come up with those answers, or whether he asked for three countries or as many as she could name

She did tell him she had been to 'reading school'. This could mean she had been to Saturday or Sunday School or possibly, between the ages of four and six, to the dame school in Branscombe run by Rachel Goldsworthy, the dairyman's daughter. School was often seen as a convenient baby-sitter by hard-pressed parents with children who were too young to help or earn – and when Sarah Jane was four her mother had two-year-old Oliver and a sickly baby to care for as well as two older children. She may well have seen the penny a week charge as money well-spent to keep her little girl occupied until she could begin the important business of earning her keep.

Most of Mr White's interviewees were found in lace schools and were interviewed along with – and probably in the presence of – their mistresses. It is not surprising, therefore, that none of them reported any ill treatment. However, a description of the lace school in Exmouth, given by a Mrs Dixon in the 1940s when she was ninety one, suggests that not all mistresses were kind:

> The Principle [sic] was a middle aged spinster named Mary Ann Long. An out and out martinet, her word was backed up with a cane of extra length. Her backward charges had to sit at the door on a small stool with a dunce's cap on their heads. [3]

All the girls Mr White talked to told a similar story of the hours they worked – and most of them clearly said very little at all. Most were younger than Sarah Jane and were no doubt over-awed by the gentleman from London in his black frock coat and top hat with his strange accent and ridiculous questions.

Sarah Jane's interview was unusually long and she comes over as talkative and confident:[4]

I am a lace-maker. I went to the lace-making at six years old to a lace school with twelve girls. I only had to work four hours a day in my first year but it did not suit me because I could not sit so long. I very often had dreadful headaches from keeping my eyes steadfast upon the pillow. My eyes used to ache dreadfully and so they do now very often and my sight is weak. I have been at four different lace schools. Most girls change about because their parents think the mistress is not strict enough and doesn't bring the children on.

The interview does not state which schools Sarah Jane attended. In 1851 when she was five, just a year before she started to learn lace, only the Purse sisters, Mary and Ann, described themselves as 'lace mistresses' to the census enumerators. They were still in business in 1863. Mr White interviewed Ann and recorded the conversation:

Has twelve lace girls from nine or ten years old up to about sixteen. A task of eight or nine hours is set, and they never come by candlelight though they did formerly. Does not have learners or apprentices now because there is no sale for children's work.

This was not always the case. In 1841 little Mary Ann Driver, aged seven, could make sprigs that sold for 7d a dozen after just two weeks of instruction – though she thought it would take her another two weeks to make up her dozen. Mr White had other concerns about the Miss Purses' school.

The room in which they work (shut up now) is much larger than this (a room about 12 feet by 10) and the windows open but there is no fireplace. It is too close sitting to want that. Has had seventeen or so in it. Has known two or three children begin lace-making at five years old, but they must be big healthy children to do it.

Branscombe village. We know from the census that the Perry family lived in this part of the village

Ann Purse was also anxious to show that she took education seriously. 'My girls read verses of the Testament when they come in the morning,' she told Mr White. 'Five or six of them can do so without spelling, and the others can read the easy words.'

It is almost certain that this was one of the schools Sarah Jane attended. Miss Purse was probably wise not to let the commissioner see the room that was shut up, for Mr White was not impressed by the rooms he did see. 'These rooms are generally the living rooms of small cottages, with the fireplace stopped up to prevent draughts, and sometimes, even in winter, the animal heat of the inmates being thought sufficient ...' ran his report. He criticised the lack of ventilation, windows that wouldn't open, the overcrowding – and above all, the smell: 'The crowding in these rooms and the foulness of the air produced by it are sometimes extreme ...' But conditions were probably no worse than those the girls experienced at home – baths and regular changes of clothing were not something impoverished village homes could provide.

Mrs Eliza Woodrow also ran a lace school in Branscombe in 1863, and Samuel Coombs' wife ran a rather less formal establishment with three or four pupils. Sarah Jane probably knew them both and they may have been among the four establishments she says she attended.

> At some of these schools I worked from 8 or 9 in the morning till 11 or 12 at night, and in summer from 6 or 7 in the morning till 7 in the evening. I have sometimes gone in the morning before 6 and once at 3, having been at work till 10 the night before and up till 11. This day I worked all through the day till 8 or 9 at night, only stopping for ten or twelve minutes for breakfast and about twenty minutes for dinner and taking my tea at my pillow. That was half a year ago when I was sixteen. I was at the school but working on my own account, none of the other girls worked so long. I have many times sat all through the night and first did so when I was about thirteen or fourteen. I took my pillow home from school to do this. It is when an order comes in that we work so.

The lace mistresses were all careful to minimise the length of time children worked when talking to the authorities, but Sarah Jane's version is probably nearer the truth.

'I am a quick worker,' Sarah Jane told Mr White proudly, 'but I have never earned more than 3s or 3s-6d in a week. My parents have all that I earn. I could never get enough to put in the Post Office bank, indeed I don't get paid in money much. The best kind of work is that paid in ready money, but for all other work you cannot get more than 2s-6d in ready money out of 12s worth of earnings. The smaller shops never give money at all.'

This refers to the 'truck' system that was in force in the lace-making villages and was the cause of many complaints. Mrs Harriet Wheeker of Sidbury gave Mr White a very full account of the problems it caused. Her girls were expected to take two loaves and half a pound of butter each week as part of their wages. Sometimes they were desperate for cash. 'The other day,' she said, 'a girl who had been working long hours to earn more came to me and asked me if I would buy a pound of white sugar for 6 ½d if she could get it, 6 ½d being the proper market price, though the price of this sugar would be put down to the girl herself at 8d.' She gave other examples – five-shilling boots were sold to the girls at 10s-6d, calico which cost 7d a yard would be 9d or 10d, candles would be 8d not 6 ½d and an extra penny or two would be added to the price of a pound of bacon. Furthermore, if a girl took a private commission and was paid in cash the shop would boycott her work and worse still, all the members of the lace-maker's family were expected to shop with the dealer, even when they had cash. 'I wish the Government could do something to stop this: it is so cruel,' Mrs Wheeker went on. 'I could myself if I had capital to spare. Any shop that would pay ready money and sell on fair terms would make a fortune …' Clearly none of the local dealers agreed with her.

In Sarah Jane's time in Branscombe, the monopoly of the lace trade rested with John Tucker. He took over his mother-in-law's business in 1845 and was deeply unpopular. He had a reputation for meanness and the women particularly resented his practice of weighing lace thread as he gave it out and weighing the sprigs the lace-maker brought back. His excuse was that he was avoiding wastage – but in reality he was making it impossible for his workers to do private commissions. John Tucker was a wealthy man with premises in London as well as Branscombe – but he had no intention of sharing his good fortune with his employees.[5]

Mr White was keen to hear about under-age children working and Sarah Jane was happy to oblige. 'I know of one girl who was put as an apprentice to a lace school at four and a half years old,' she told the commissioner:

> She was clever and worked hard but was delicate and the work hurt her health. I heard that after two or three years she died of a brain fever. This child had a very kind mistress and only worked four hours a day. But I did hear her mother say she would never send another so young.

The case was obviously well known for a number of bystanders joined in the discussion, tut-tutting, with one pointing out that the mother of the unfortunate little girl did not send her next

Another view of Branscombe village

daughter to learn lace until she was nine. They probably shared the opinion of Mary Ann Gay, the village schoolmistress, which was that the children sent to lace school at five had 'cruel parents – though it is surprising,' Miss Gay admitted, 'to see what little girls can do, and what nice little sprigs they make.' She, of course, had a vested interest in keeping girls at school long enough to get them reading and writing.

Mr White also interviewed Branscombe's curate, Reverend Gidley, who spoke of a Saturday afternoon writing class and explained that Miss Gay only taught infants. 'These girls can just read, but barely know the meaning of any but simple words,' he sighed, but he did show himself to be quite knowledgeable about the financial arrangements in Branscombe's lace schools:

> The girls can earn out 1s-6d a week, but out of this they have to pay 4d for schooling (lace), and pay for thread, pins, pricking patterns, etc. besides and get hardly anything else.

Lace schools varied in their practice but most charged the parents a small fee and allowed the children to keep (and sell) the lace they made.

The vicar of the neighbouring parish, Reverend Mamerto Gueritz in Colyton, was more concerned with the unhealthy conditions in which children worked, which he was sure led to consumption being rife in the district, and also with the potential for immorality. 'The employment also lowers the morals by making children early independent of their parents, girls of sixteen and seventeen going off to live by themselves,' he said. 'It diminishes the wages of the men because employers know their wives and daughters are earning.' The Reverend Craddock Glascott in Seaton, another lace-making parish, felt girls would be better off going into service but said that lace-makers made poor housewives: 'They grow up untaught, and ignorant of plain household duties such as sewing, washing, etc. and this makes it difficult to get situations in service for them, though I endeavour to do so.'

Clergymen nationwide found many reasons to worry about the morals of their poorer parishioners, and women in working-class households were forever being accused of being incompetent housewives when in fact they could not afford such luxuries as soap, needles and thread, or proper food for their families. Several interviewees commented that the local wage for a labourer was seven or eight shillings a week plus three pints of cider (probably well-watered) a day. Even with a wife and two daughters working hard and earning another eight shillings a week between them this still left families well below the threshold for respectable living, which throughout the century was reckoned to be £1 a week.

The lace made in East Devon is known as Honiton lace, but it was made across an area south of the town, stretching from Exmouth in the west to Axminster in the east. Honiton was the staging point for coaches to London and later for the railway, hence when West Country lace arrived in London it was known as 'Honiton lace' regardless of whether it had been made in Beer or Branscombe, Ottery St Mary or Newton Poppleford, or any of the other villages and towns in the district. When it reached London it was sometimes sold as 'Bath-Brussels' lace, a name chosen for its associations, deftly (but dishonestly) linking the most fashionable city in the West Country to the part of the Continent where most people expected fine lace to come from.

Two sorts of lace were made in East Devon. Firstly there was 'trolly' lace, a simple edging lace made by the yard, in various widths, and secondly there was 'head' lace – more usually known as 'Honiton' – which was considered much more difficult to make. Both were made with bobbins on a lace pillow, but Honiton lace was composed of a series of small motifs known as 'sprigs', made separately but then assembled into a pattern, either by being mounted on net or joined with needle-made 'brides' or bars.

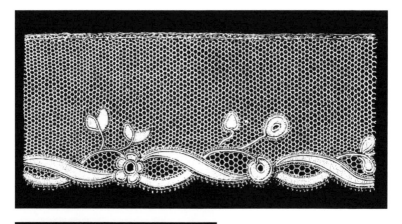

Above: Honiton lace 'sprigs' mounted on net known as 'Honiton application' or 'Honiton appliqué'

Left: Honiton lace 'sprigs' joined with needle-made 'brides' or bars, sometimes called 'guipure' lace

The motifs could be several inches across or 'as small as swan-shot' to use the delightful phrase employed by Mr White in his 1863 report. This meant that most large pieces of Honiton lace were the work of a number of people – skilled hands making the complex motifs, less experienced workers making spots or leaves for which they were paid a few pence a dozen, and 'sewers-on' assembling the whole into a collar or veil or whatever the customer had ordered.

'Sewing-on' was quite easy, according to Elizabeth Filder of Honiton in 1841 – a capable girl could learn the craft in a few weeks – but it was important that she had 'taste' and a sense of design. The way the motifs were laid out made all the difference to the finished article and because this part of the work was so important the sewers-on were paid more than the lace-makers – around five shillings a week.

Sarah Jane's mother, Mary Perry – then Mary Eveleigh – was just a girl when news came through that the young Queen Victoria had placed an order for a large amount of Honiton lace. Mary was a lace-maker. Women of *her* mother's generation remembered the glory days of the industry, when a single lace sleeve frill could cost hundreds of pounds, and hand-made net traditionally cost as many shillings as it took to cover the piece – Mrs Bury Palliser wrote of a wedding veil for which the net alone had cost £20.[6] But in 1808 John Heathcoat had set up a factory in Tiverton with machines making net that was virtually indistinguishable from the hand-made variety at a tiny fraction of the price. By Mary's day, lace-workers were using this as the ground for their sprigs – but demand was low. Fashions had changed. By the early nineteenth century men no longer wore elaborate lace cravats and sleeve frills while women preferred embroidered muslin to lace and liked their sleeves fitted tightly at the wrists with no room for a frill. In 1800 a lace-maker could easily earn ten shillings a week[7] but in the 1830s Mary Eveleigh was lucky if she earned three shillings – and that was seldom paid in cash. By then, the lace dealers had a stranglehold on the trade. They took orders from customers and divided out the work between the workers, making impossible demands that had the women toiling through the night when a rush order had to be completed and sitting idle at other times. These lace dealers also sold provisions and drapery and they insisted the lace-makers take their wages in goods, not money. In Mary's day, the Branscombe trade was in the hands of the redoubtable Abigail Chick, an able businesswoman – and a martinet much feared by her workers.[8]

But the royal order was to be paid for in cash. Miss Bidney had come down from London specially to commission the work – a deep flounce and frills for the Queen's wedding dress, sprigs for a veil and lace to cover a morning dress in the trousseau. The designs had been created by William Dyce through the Government School of Design at Somerset House, and it looked like the lace Mary's mother and grandmother had learned to make – motifs close together and elaborate filling stitches, making a rich flowing design like old brocade.

True, it was mounted on Heathcoat's net – no-one could be found who was able to make net in the old way, with bobbins on a pillow, painstakingly linking the motifs with carefully concealed 'sewings'. Jane Bidney came from nearby Beer Regis but she had done well for herself – she had a shop in St James' Street in London selling lace to grand ladies who knew nothing of the villages where it was made. Miss Bidney struggled to find women sufficiently skilled to follow William Dyce's design (there are no records to reveal who they were) – but even those who were not chosen would have watched the motifs being created by their older or more talented colleagues and would have hoped against hope that others would follow the Queen's example and order lace for their own weddings. That had been Lord Melbourne's plan when he urged the young Queen to patronise British manufacturers rather than the French designers she had favoured before her coronation.

The wedding dress was simple, of white Spitalfields silk with the full skirt, wide neckline and low waist coming to a point at the front that was typical of 1840s fashion. A wide 'bertha' of Honiton lace edged the neck, double flounces of the same lace extended the short silk sleeves to three-quarter length and a deep flounce covered the lower part of the skirt. The Queen's veil was of sprigs mounted on yards of net, doubled over and attached to the back of her bun, quite separate from her wreath of mock orange blossom. It was widely reported that the lace had cost a total of £1,000 and

Key to names of stitches

Braid stitches

1	Whole (cloth) stitch
2	Half (lace) stitch
3	'Mittens' (vein of leaf)
4	Plain hole
5	Four pin bud
6&7	Six pin bud
8	Twisted leaders
9	Zig-zag holes

Leaves and flowers

10	Half and whole stitch vein of sewings
11	Raised leaf worked in sections called 'taps'
11a	Raised flower
12	Serrated whole stitch leaf vein of ten stick and cutworks
13	Whole stitch with vein of 'mittens'
14	Whole and half stitch with vein of cutworks and winkie pins
15	Half stitch with raised veins

Groundings

16	Purl pin bars
17	Point d'Angleterre Net
18	Trolly net

Fillings

19	Cutwork/leadwork
20	Diamond
21	Brick
22	Pin
23	Cushion
24	No pin
25	Toad in the hole
26	Blossom
27	A swing and a pin
28	Point d'esprit
29	Pearl
30	Double ground
31	Double ground with Cutwork
32	Bars and cutworks
33	Bars and cutworks with hole
34	Cartwheel

(Taken from Maidment, M., 'Bobbin Lace Work', 1931)

Honiton lace sampler of filling stitches and diagram with key

183

the commission had been executed by two hundred women in and around Beer between March and November 1839, though in fact the only surviving bill for the lace is for £250. [9]

Young Mary Eveleigh and Queen Victoria were much of an age and Mary too was planning to marry. Her husband-to-be was Solomon Perry, a farm labourer in Branscombe, a neighbour's son she had known all her life. Victoria married Albert in February 1841; eighteen months later Mary Eveleigh wed Solomon and settled down to the hard life of a labourer's wife. [10] Their wedding would have been a homespun affair – no white silk dress but something plain and serviceable. Young girls like Mary would usually marry in a new frock that would do for 'best' for years to come – but Mary Eveleigh was seven months pregnant on her wedding day and she probably crammed her swelling figure into corsets and an old dress let out as far as it would go. Perhaps she made herself a lace handkerchief or a little bonnet veil for the occasion.

Her lace-making enabled her to contribute a shilling or two a week to the family budget – she could work at her lace pillow when she was not busy cooking and cleaning and having babies. Her first child, Mary Ann, arrived just two months after the wedding, followed three years later by Samuel, then came Sarah Jane, Oliver, Ephraim 1 and Ephraim 2 (both of whom died in infancy, barely a year apart), Eliza, Henrietta, John and Charles. Baby Charles only lived a few weeks, and five months later, in June 1864, Mary herself died. She was just forty-four, worn out by a lifetime of poverty, hard work and child-bearing. Her youngest surviving child, little John, was just three and her eldest, Mary Ann, was twenty-one. Mary Ann and Sarah Jane were both lace-makers, contributing their meagre earnings to supplement the eight shillings [11] a week their father would have earned on the farm.

Queen Victoria's order did give a boost to the lace trade. Mary Driver who kept a lace school in Beer boasted that in 1839 she 'had to the value of £100 worth of lace on her pillow ... for the Queen's dress.'

Victoria placed other orders – Maria Hutchins reported in 1841 that she had made part of a gold work-bag for the Queen and had also made some of the sprigs for the Princess Royal's christening robe. Some members of the court followed

Queen Victoria in her wedding dress, by Franz Xaver Winterhalter,
painted in 1847 as an anniversary present for Prince Albert

the Queen's lead, but there was probably a more important reason why the well-to-do began to buy hand-made lace. By 1850 technical developments made it possible to produce more and more types of lace by machine and lace had become fashionable again. However, there was a cachet attached to wearing 'real' lace rather than machine-made and for a time the Honiton lace workers benefitted.

A different type of customer arrived with the railway. The main line from London to Exeter opened in 1844 bringing middle-class tourists to Devon, some of whom bought pieces of locally made lace as presents or souvenirs of their holiday. The numbers of lace-workers quadrupled – but the quality of what they made hit rock bottom. 'The demand for lace had now so much increased that in 1850 the quality of the work was much deteriorated,' sniffed Mrs Treadwin, 'for the work people, finding that whatever they produced met with ready sale, were not desirous of improving their patterns,' and she spoke derisively of sprigs that looked like 'turkey tails and frying pans'.[12] Few workers bothered to use the more complicated decorative stitches – brick, blossom, no-pin, pearl, toad-in-the-hole and so on – even if they had learnt them. They were fiddly to do and the customers valued quantity over quality. This was the period when young Sarah Jane Perry began to learn lace-making and for a time it must have looked as if the future was rosy.

But the boom was short-lived. By 1860 the interest in hand-made lace was declining. Customers became more discriminating; they recognised the poor quality of much of the work being produced in Devon in contrast to the lace made on the Continent, and the increased number of workers in the market drove prices down and down. Girls began to look for jobs that paid them in ready money. This time there were no royal commissions to boost production and the industry stagnated.[13]

Prices to the customer remained quite high, however. In 1853 a collar cost £3-3s-9d, in 1865 a veil would be upwards of £2-5s-0d, a pair of sleeve frills was £1-7s-0d and a deep flounce was around £3-1s-6d a yard. By 1871 single motifs were sold at between three farthings and two shillings each and veils were anything between five guineas and £52-10s. In 1875 a lace edged handkerchief cost a guinea, by 1897 the price was anywhere between 7s-9d and 10 guineas according to size and the quantity of lace used.[14] Of course, the lacemakers only ever received a tiny fraction of those sums.

In or around 1850 the villagers began to make a new kind of lace – Branscombe Point, developed by John Tucker the Branscombe lace dealer. It originated in Branscombe – but it was soon made in all the lace-making villages around. It was a needlepoint lace, using machine-made braid which was tacked down on to a printed paper or cloth pattern to form the outline of the design. The spaces between the braids were then filled with decorative stitches – usually a type of buttonhole stitch worked over a single thread. When the work was complete the tacking threads and pattern were removed to leave an openwork design. Branscombe Point was much coarser than pillow lace and was sometimes used for collars and corners of handkerchiefs, but more often for furnishing lace in the form of tablecloths and mats to go under vases and knick-knacks or on a lady's dressing table.

Mary Jane Perry. Mary Jane was the wife of Sarah Jane's cousin. She was seven years younger than Sarah but would have known her as they both grew up in Branscombe

Sarah Jane left Branscombe for a time in the 1880s and moved to Exeter; her elderly father moved to Chard to live with his younger daughter, Eliza. Eliza had married Reginald Elliott, a painter and decorator, in 1883. Solomon

Perry died in Chard eleven years later at the ripe old age of seventy-six.

In 1888, aged forty-two, Sarah Jane married an old neighbour who had recently been widowed. He was William Selley Brown, a cattle dealer and farmer who appears to have been quite well-to-do – in 1891 the couple had a live-in servant. They had moved back to Branscombe and William died there in 1897. Sarah Jane then moved to Chard to live with Reginald and Eliza. In 1901 Sarah Jane Selley Brown proudly described herself to the census enumerator as being 'of independent means' – her William had obviously left her well-provided for. She died in 1907. For a village girl from a poor working family, apprenticed as a child to a failing trade, and with little formal education, she had done remarkably well for herself.

Endnotes

1   Treadwin, Mrs, *Antique Point and Honiton Lace,* undated.

2   Unless otherwise stated, the information in this chapter comes from the two reports of the Children's Employment Commission into the lace making industry of East Devon. The first (Volume 10 in the Irish University Series of reprints) was published in 1843 but based on interviews conducted in 1841. The second (Volume 13) was published in 1863 and the interviews seem to have taken place that same year. It is in this volume that the interview with Sarah Jane Perry appears.

3   Mrs Dixon was interviewed by the Devon novelist, Eric Delderfield, in the 1940s. She was then 91.

4   There was no standard format for recording interviews. Some interviewers reported the interviewees' words verbatim, others used reported speech. Mr White favoured the latter approach but we have taken the liberty of converting the words back into the first person. Phrases like 'steadfast on my pillow' are almost certainly the ones Sarah Jane used.

5   Tomlinson, Margaret, *Three generations in the Honiton lace trade; a family history,* 1983.

6   Bury Palliser, Mrs, *A History of Lace,* 1865.

7   Yallop, H J, *A History of the Honiton Lace Industry,* 1992.

8   Tomlinson, op cit

9   Staniland, K, *In Royal Fashion,* 1997.

10 The biographical information in this chapter comes from standard family history sources – the census, parish registers and trades' directories. In the case of Branscombe all this material is available on line at www.branscombeproject.org.uk/

11 Several of the interviewees in 1863 gave this as the standard wage for a farm labourer in the district.

12 Treadwin, op cit.

13 Yallop, op cit.

14 Ibid. Much of his evidence comes from an account book in All Hallows museum in Honiton.

'My vagabond boys'

On Monday evening upwards of one hundred and
thirty of the women of the parish were regaled with
tea and cake, by the benevolence and liberality of the
Reverend George E Bruxner, the worthy vicar, who
on Wednesday supplied a plentiful supply of good old
English roast beef and plum pudding for upwards
of one hundred and fifty of the male population,
who, presided over by the rector himself, enjoyed
themselves until a late hour ...

So reported *The Leicester Chronicle* on April 24th 1854 on
the opening of the beautiful new school in the village of
Thurlaston.

The Reverend George Edward Bruxner,
Rector of Thurlaston from 1845 to 1876

It had obviously been a memorable and very enjoyable
celebration. Thurlaston is in Leicestershire, about eight miles
south west of Leicester and three miles from access to the
railway network at Desford. Both the design and building of

the school had been overseen and paid for by the Reverend George Bruxner, Rector of Thurlaston, and it was built on the Rectory glebe land. The *Abstract of the Education Returns* presented to the House of Commons in 1833 tell us that there were already:

> Two daily schools, whereof one contains 53 males and 32 females and is partly supported by an endowment of 7L 10s per annum, and partly by payments from the children; in the other school 16 females are instructed at the expense of their parents – Two Sunday Schools, in one whereof 63 males and 49 females, and in the other, 30 males and 41 females, are instructed gratuitously; the former school is of the Established Church, and the latter appertains to Baptists. [1]

This suggests an enthusiasm for learning in Thurlaston that is not borne out by the research done for this book, and it may be that the returns reflect the numbers that had enrolled in the schools over a period rather than the numbers that ever actually attended.

Soon after this report was submitted, the Rector of Thurlaston, the Reverend Joseph Arkwright, was instrumental in getting a National School built in the village. The National Society for Promoting Religious Education had been established in 1811 with the intention of establishing a Church of England school in every parish in the land to teach basic literacy and numeracy to the poor along with Christian values and some practical skills. This was not pure altruism but was conceived as a way to draw people back into the church. The rapid development of towns during the industrial revolution had seen a significant decline in churchgoing, and the rise of nonconformity in the late eighteenth century had also had a devastating effect on attendance at Anglican churches. While the National Society had hoped to target large working-class parishes in the towns where there was no educational provision, a preponderance of the new schools were actually built in villages, often in places like Thurlaston where some schooling was already available.

Architect's drawing for Thurlaston School 1853

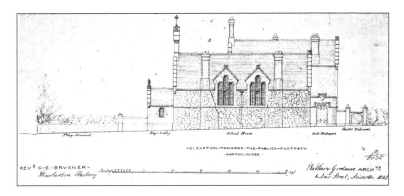

Another elevation

In the 1840s Thurlaston was growing. The vast majority of its population were agricultural labourers, but there were also many framework knitters and seamers, men and women engaged in the knitting and making up of stockings. There were dressmakers, butchers, grocers, a post office, men employed as grooms and gardeners on the estates, bricklayers, carpenters and shoemakers. The population was 694 in 1841, and when the Reverend George Bruxner arrived in the parish in 1845 the school was already too small and so he began negotiations for a new building to be provided at his own expense. In 1853 the school moved into new premises on Desford Road, which could accommodate seventy children of both sexes, hence the celebrations referred to at the beginning of this chapter.

The building cost £1,000. An infants' school was added to the elementary school in 1855, taking the capacity to 100 children. Mr Bruxner was a wealthy man. When he arrived in Thurlaston he built a grand house for himself to use as a rectory, and when he retired he remained there and built a new rectory for the next incumbent. The school he built was much more ornate than most National Schools but – magnificent as it looked – it had serious structural defects, as the log-books and journal make clear. However, the building, though much altered, is still in use as a school to this day.

Thurlaston School in 2015

Forster's Education Act came into force in 1870 and was the first step towards making education compulsory for all children between the ages of five and thirteen. Documents survive that give a very detailed picture of what it was like in Thurlaston school between 1872 and 1875. Both the headmaster and the mistress of the infants' school were required to keep a weekly log-book. The vicar also expected his curate to write a daily journal – which he checked and signed every week – the initials 'GB' can clearly be seen in the margins. For those three years the log-books and journal overlap, and by reading and comparing them it is possible to get a very clear idea not only of what life was like in the school, but also in the village, for the curate devoted as much, if not more, of his journal to other aspects of village life and its inhabitants as to the school. The three accounts present very different pictures. Whereas the headmaster and the head of the infants' school were largely concerned with recording the syllabus, the attainments and attendance of the pupils – mainly to satisfy the National School inspectors – the curate's journal shone a clear light on why there were so many failures, and on what he was trying to do to raise standards in the school and to try to make life more enjoyable for the children.[2] There was also some additional information in the Manager's Minute Book.[3]

The headmaster in 1872 was William Anscombe – he had been appointed head in 1858 when he was only twenty-five, and by 1872 he was a married man with four children. The other school log-book was kept by Mrs Rhoda Warren, head of the infants' department, who was appointed in 1872. Mrs Warren was then a thirty-six-year-old widow with two young daughters. She had been working in Leicester before coming to Thurlaston, but she was originally from Devon. The curate's journal was kept by the Reverend James Marshall who took over the curacy in March 1873. He came from Lancashire. He had studied at Durham University, was ordained in 1866 and had held two previous curacies, both in Northumbria – one at Brinkburn from 1866-70 and one at Alnwick from 1870-3.

Both the headmaster and the infants' headmistress were certificated teachers – which means that they had passed the exams set by the National Society for Promoting Religious Education; a system of training for teachers in National Schools had been in force since the early nineteenth century. They and their school would have been inspected annually. There was an assistant teacher named in the log-books, Mrs Anne Turner, a labourer's wife, who was paid £22 a year, and Ann Archer, aged fifteen, was a pupil teacher – the daughter of a carpenter, she seems to have been paid £14 a year. Neither she nor Mrs Turner were qualified teachers, though Ann could have gone on to become one had she so wished. At this date most teachers started as pupil teachers. This was an extension of the 'monitorial system' the schools had espoused earlier in the century by which the teacher taught the older or brighter children and they, in their turn, passed on what they had learnt to lower groups.

The headmaster received a salary of £64 a year, plus £5 for coal, and he was also required to collect rates due to the school from parishioners and to teach music – both of which duties he quickly off-loaded onto the Reverend Marshall when he arrived in 1873. As headmaster he was provided, free of charge, with a very nice house and garden which the architect's plans show had a parlour, kitchen, scullery and three bedrooms. The plans also show the general layout of the school, which was similar to that of other National schools. The children were divided into ability groups, called 'standards', separated by partitions but all facing the master.[4]

The various levels each child was supposed to reach had been defined by the Newcastle Commission in 1862[5] and at the annual inspection the inspectors would decide whether children should 'pass the exam' and move up a standard, or stay where they were. In theory, the children would pass Standard I at the age of seven or eight and then move up one standard a year until by the age of thirteen they would leave school having attained Standard VI or at least Standard V – but practice was very different from theory. Children whose attendance was erratic, who were tired, poorly nourished or unhealthy – or who were just plain bored – made slow progress. Each Standard group, therefore, would contain children of different ages – bright ones who did move up a standard each year and others who might be stuck in one of the lower standards for the whole of their school career, no doubt becoming more and more frustrated and disruptive as the years went by. Teaching so many children of such very different ages and abilities, all at the same time, must have been a real challenge.

Mrs Warren's log of 1872 shows that she found difficulties in her new school right from the beginning. She obviously taught in the main school as well as in the infants' department:

January 8th: Attendance smaller this morning.
Several children in the Upper Standard seem not to

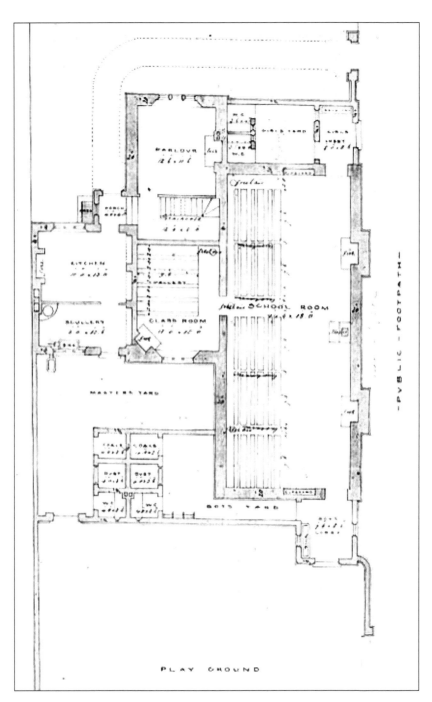

Architect's drawing of the ground plan of the school, 1853.
Note the five blocks of desks all facing the one teacher.

have understood their arithmetic or are inattentive. The Fourth Standard seem to know nothing of long division the First Standard have not started subtraction.

January 22nd: Attendance this morning very small, the Hounds meeting in the neighbourhood. The Fifth Standard have made little progress in arithmetic during the past week. Scripture 1st Book of Samuel chapter 15. Average attendance 36.

January 29th: Attendance better this morning. Several children in the 2nd Standard are not at all fit and the lessons are far beyond them. The children have begun learning a new song. The 1st class girls have begun cutting out and making garments. Average attendance for the past week 37.

The table below explains the level each set of children was expected to achieve:

The following are the six *Standards of Education* contained in the *Revised code of Regulations, 1872*

STANDARD I

Reading	One of the narratives next in order after monosyllables in an elementary reading book used in the school.
Writing	Copy in manuscript character a line of print, and write from dictation a few common words.
Arithmetic	Simple addition and subtraction of numbers of not more than four figures, and the multiplication table to multiplication by six.

STANDARD II

Reading	A short paragraph from an elementary reading book.

| Writing | A sentence from the same book, slowly read once, and then dictated in single words. |
| Arithmetic | The multiplication table, and any simple rule as far as short division (inclusive). |

STANDARD III

Reading	A short paragraph from a more advanced reading book.
Writing	A sentence slowly dictated once by a few words at a time, from the same book.
Arithmetic	Long division and compound rules (money).

STANDARD IV

Reading	A few lines of poetry or prose, at the choice of the inspector.
Writing	A sentence slowly dictated once, by a few words at a time, from a reading book, such as is used in the first class of the school.
Arithmetic	Compound rules (common weights and measures).

STANDARD V

Reading	A short ordinary paragraph in a newspaper, or other modern narrative.
Writing	Another short ordinary paragraph in a newspaper, or other modern narrative, slowly dictated once by a few words at a time.
Arithmetic	Practice and bills of parcels.

STANDARD VI

Reading	To read with fluency and expression.
Writing	A short theme or letter, or an easy paraphrase.
Arithmetic	Proportion and fractions (vulgar and decimal).

February 23rd: The stove has been very troublesome this week smoking badly every day notwithstanding the flues have been cleaned which has caused the children to cough and affected their eyes.

March 10th: The frequent changes in the weather has caused nearly all the children bad colds, consequently attendance much less.

March 28th: Attendance better this week. Several still away with bad feet. Reading and writing and counting by the older ones every day. Alphabet and pictures to the lesser ones with the usual singing exercises.

In January and February that year there was very bad weather and as we shall see, the school was poorly heated. Things did not improve. On March 3rd a year later, Mrs Warren recorded 'attendance has been smaller, children ill with bad colds and bad feet.' Most of the children would have been poorly dressed. Clothes were handed down in families or acquired secondhand; they were not necessarily warm or waterproof and were often ill-fitting. The last part of her sentence is particularly significant: 'poor feet'. Children had to walk to school, some covering quite considerable distances, and walking in bitter weather with broken, leaking boots – or no footwear at all – would have caused chilblains – a scourge in the nineteenth century and extremely painful – something people seldom have to endure today though some can remember them from our own childhoods. The floor of the school would also have been extremely cold in the winter. In poorer schools it was just compressed mud – better ones, like Thurlaston, probably had wood or stone, but it would still have been cold and damp.

Sadly Thurlaston was not unusual. In a report into another village school, Colwich in Staffordshire, in the late 1850s[6], the inspectors wondered whether the teacher's desk should stand on wooden flooring, rather than just tiles or mud, as 'they would be less likely to suffer colds in the winter'. The children received no such consideration. It was an ongoing problem, making both teaching and learning exceedingly difficult in very cold weather, but not one that was properly addressed in Thurlaston, it would seem, as Reverend Marshall recorded in 1874, two years after Mrs Warren's initial entry:

January 6th: Mrs Warren complains of her difficulties in the way of obtaining coal. School very cold. Windows so imperfectly closed.

February 27th: Mrs Warren complained bitterly of cold and irregular attendance.

October 12th: Studies in the Infant School unbearable due to smoke from the stove. This state of things will probably last all winter. The fire roars admirably and splendidly flamed by open doors and windows which act as chimneys.

November 17th: Smoke from the fire insufferable and very bad for the children as all the windows and doors have to open.

November 18th: On going to the school I found Mrs Warren not there, too ill to come, consequently I have taken the school entirely today. Mrs Warren cannot speak and her chest is very painful.

November 23rd: Went to school as soon as possible as I heard Mrs Warren was ill in bed with the prevailing influenza cold.

November 24th: Mrs Warren still ill. Took the school myself.

November 25th: In school again all day as Mrs Warren still not much better.

November 26th: Still at school in Mrs Warren's place ....

December 1st: Mrs Warren fairly recovered but attendance in both schools very bad as there is quite an epidemic amongst the children of the village of the serious bronchial influenza, especially severe in the infants.

December 4th: Succumbed to my cold and stayed in the house.

December 17th: Intense cold and frost.

Coal for warming the school was expensive and the school relied on donations from villagers to pay for it. The accounts from 1875 show that fuel and lighting, presumably candles, cost £9-3s that year. The task of collecting money from parishioners to pay for this seems, like so much else, to have fallen on James Marshall:

1874

January 9th: Mrs Warren having asked permission to be away this afternoon I took the school. The sewing which I overlooked I do not consider to be satisfactory though I do not venture a reason for this as I believe that the prevalence of seaming[7] in the village renders it uphill work. To Mr Scott's to ask for his subscription for the school. On being asked Mr Scott also promised to draw up a load of coal for the school which example I hope will be followed by the rest of the farmers.

February 22nd: School. Only Mrs Turner and myself present as teachers.

The next few weeks are dominated by his accounts of colds, raging influenza and bronchitis which were rife in the village, but these were not the only illnesses in the school, and cold and smoke were not the only problems that interrupted teaching and learning. On September 17th 1873, just two months after he had arrived at the school, Reverend Marshall noted, 'Some satisfactory way of lighting the school must be found to light the school for the winter. Candles are insufficient, dirty and expensive ...' With doors and windows open to combat the smoke from the fire, candles must have been all but useless, especially at night when there was a school for adults and for those children who could not attend during the day because they had to work. The idea of providing a night school was admirable, the outcome less so, as in the summer all available hands were needed for all the hours of daylight in the fields or on the allotments, and in the winter the dark, cold school was not an inviting place – not to mention the fact that adults and children had to walk to school in the dark after having worked all day. In 1872 Reverend Marshall recorded:

> November 7th: Mrs Warren thinks she will be obliged to give up the night school as the parents will not send their children and she has not enough scholars present for examination. The apathy of the villagers is very remarkable.

> November 14th: Mrs Warren reluctantly gives up the idea of continuing night school. So few present.

Maybe Mrs Warren was 'reluctant'. But maybe she was also relieved that having spent all day in the cold, smoky school she did not have to go back again at night.

A letter from Mrs Warren is also in the School Minute Book and indicates that she accepted the post as Mistress of the Infants School for a salary of £52 a year, which included £7 for teaching needlework. It was raised by £2-8s in 1873 – but she obviously felt this was not enough given the difficult task she had undertaken and the dreadful condition of her classroom, and she must have asked for a rise. Reverend Marshall presented her case for her but recorded on July 6th 1875 that 'Mr Wesley thinks it is sufficient.'

While colds, influenza and bronchitis were still affecting many of the children and adults in the village, in April and

May 1872 there was also a potentially much more serious problem. The school log-books for those months record a significant spread of 'blisters' and many children were sent home ill. This seems to have been smallpox, and many parents kept their children away from school for fear of infection.[8]

The government had been trying to enforce smallpox vaccination since 1853; it was regulated by a series of acts of parliament and powers were delegated to Vaccination Officers who were paid between 1s and 3s per child vaccinated. Finally, in 1873, vaccination was made compulsory, and parents could be fined for failing to present their children for vaccination, though records show there was still considerable resistance to it – and that was certainly true in Thurlaston.

By July 1874 children were still being sent home with 'the itch' and messages were sent to their parents to withdraw them. A vaccination date was set to ensure that all the children were vaccinated, but Reverend Marshall recorded on October 30th that Mr Bessford (the Vaccination Officer) had complained that no children had been presented to him for vaccination. On enquiring further it appears that Mr Bessford had not turned up at the specified time and so the parents had taken their children home – only to find out too late that he had arrived in the village but left again before they could get to him. Marshall wrote to Bessford to arrange another day – but again the children of the village missed the opportunity due to 'a postal delay in the message reaching Thurlaston'. It was not until November 12th that all the Thurlaston children were vaccinated and James Marshall was able to record, 'None remain undone.' This was yet another responsibility that had landed on the shoulders of the unfortunate curate.

The headmaster and Mrs Warren mentioned quite a lot of children by name in the log-books – always to say how bad their attendance or work was, never to praise. Since many of the parents in the village would have been illiterate, they would probably not have seen sending their children to school as a priority. Helping in the fields or in the home were felt to be more important and the teachers struggled to teach children who were not very interested, had little encouragement at home and were frequently absent. But they also did not seem to recognise the very real difficulties many of the children had to overcome. On June 23rd 1873 the headmaster picked out Emma Hurd, William Taylor and the two Wardles for criticism:

> Arithmetic in the 1st standard much improved with the exception of Emma Hurd who will never be able to work a sum having no idea in the least of figures. In the 2nd standard William Taylor can neither read or work at his arithmetic and the more he is taught the less he knows.

This last was a harsh judgement indeed, for just a month later Reverend Marshall wrote 'Wm. Taylor, *the elder of the two deaf and dumb brothers* [authors' italics] today met with an accident having been kicked by a horse, struck in the cheek and above the eye and seems suffering much.' Small wonder that the poor boy had found school difficult!

Emma Hurd, the daughter of an agricultural labourer, was often absent even though, to the intense irritation of the headmaster, she was one of the 'Free School pupils' and therefore her parents did not even have to pay the penny a week towards her schooling that less impoverished families were charged. He fumed that 'no explanation for absences was ever given'. By 1881 she had left school and, aged sixteen, was a servant in one of the big houses in Thurlaston. One of the Wardle children seems to have been ill and not surprisingly had got behind in her lessons as she had been away from school for twelve months and returned, 'knowing nothing'. The headmaster recorded another girl, Harriett Illsen, as being 'very backward indeed in reading.' Harriett was one of the eight children of an agricultural labourer – helping at home would surely have been a bigger priority for her than learning to read. Indeed it is very doubtful whether any of the labourers and other workers in the village had a single book in their homes – except just possibly a Bible. There were no newspapers or magazines in village homes, though topical or salacious extracts from papers were sometimes read aloud in public houses by someone with a smattering of education – and there were few fliers or circulars, no labels on packets or tins. Children had little need to read and no opportunity to practise.

Absenteeism was one of the biggest difficulties the teachers had to overcome. Given that many, if not most, of their pupils were not particularly interested in learning and that the curriculum was tedious and boring, it is small wonder that the log-books are filled with attendance figures, and achievement – or lack of it – in the national curriculum. The log-books themselves make very dull reading. Just one block of entries from Mr Anscombe's log-book gives some impression of what went on every day in the classroom:

1873

May 6th: The Rev Marshall took his first class in singing.

May 23rd: Attendance irregular. Several of the elder girls ill and the nearness of the Whitsun Holidays. On Thursday there was not one child in the 4th standard. The Dictation in the 1st Class improves so slowly, the arithmetic makes better progress generally with the exception of the 4th Standard.

May 30th: Several children absent this week from different causes. The children in the 1st Standard are losing the sing-song in reading ... The Rev Marshall took the 1st class on Tuesday.

June 9th: School resumes after the Easter Vacation. Almost everything forgotten, arithmetic the best. The Rev Marshall took the infants in singing and 1st class in Scripture in the Upper Room.

June 16th: Attendance better this week. Dictation improving very much in all classes ... a quantity of new books obtained for the school. Received the Government Examination papers from Rev Marshall.

June 23rd: Attendance has improved very much, the children attending regularly ... with the exception of Emma Hurd, Wm Taylor and the two Wardles. The dictation still makes progress in all classes. Arithmetic in 1st standard much more accurate with the exception of Emma Hurd ... Average attendance for the week 43.

July 7th: Attendance small on account of the Chapel Anniversary. Tuesday Holiday, the choir taken to Alton Towers by Rev Bruxner ... reading is highly improving being less monotonous.

July 21st: Attendance still improving, reading still improving ... Rev Marshall attended the school three times during the week. Took all standards Friday in dictation separately.

July 28th: School Exam 29th 46 present. Received 9 children from Infant school only 2 out of the number not being able to put down 2 figures. Rev Marshall took the 1st class in arithmetic.

Children started in the infants' school at the age of five or six and spent a year or so learning their numbers and letters before moving up to the first standard in the main school. Many of them would never have held a crayon or a piece of chalk, nor opened a book before they started school so there was a lot to learn. Mr Anscombe's expectations were not high if he thought that seven out of nine children being able to write two figures was a success!

James Marshall recorded in his journal that the examination of the school 'passed off well. A great proportion of the children passed though numbers are smaller.' Reverend Marshall's contribution to village life was invaluable, both in the classroom, among the villagers and as manager of the school accounts. He was the person who compiled and signed the accounts for the school and club in 1875 – and took them to Leicester to have them printed – so he had to act as an accountant for the village as well as everything else:

1875.

SUMMARY OF THE

Thurlaston School and Club Accounts.

Drs. School Managers.					Crs.				
	£. s. d.	£. s. d.				£. s. d.	£. s. d.		£. s. d.
Smart's Charity :					Taylor's bill, 1874 ...	...	3 12 7½		
For Scholars ...	6 16 0				By Salaries :				
For Coal ...	1 14 0				„ Mistress ...	54 0 0			
		8 10 0			„ Moiety of Grant	16 18 0			
Rent of Room :					„ Infant Mistress	22 0 0			
Men's Club ...	0 15 0				„ Grant to ditto ...	3 0 0			
Women's Club ...	1 0 0				„ Needlework ...	7 0 0			
Co-operative Society ...	0 15 0				„ Assistants ...	14 1 0			
		2 10 0					116 19 0		
Interest from Bank ...		1 6 10			Books, Stationery, &c. ...	...	6 10 1		
Government Grant ...		59 6 4			Fuel and Lights ...	...	7 9 10½		
Subscriptions ...		59 16 0			Smart's Coal ...	...	1 14 0		
Weekly Pence :					Repairs	...	16 17 4		
Upper School ...	9 7 2½				Sundries (including printing)	...	1 10 0		
Infant School ...	10 8 0				Cleaning	...	3 6 5		
		19 15 2½			Insurance	...	0 10 6		
Night School ...		1 0 0							
Church fees given by Rector		1 4 10							
Balance, 1874 (includes Taylor's bill, 1874)		5 0 7½							
		£158 9 10					£158 9 10		

CLOTHING CLUB ACCOUNT, 1875.

			£. s. d.				£. s. d.
Contributions ...	...	...	47 13 3	Messrs. Morley and Son ...	...	13 0 10	
Bonus ...	...	...	4 11 7	Mr. Bradshaw ...	...	15 0 0	
Subscriptions :		£. s. d.		Mr. Tarry ...	...	23 18 9	
Messrs. Morley and Son	0 10 0			Accountant ...	...	1 0 0	
Mr. Bradshaw ...	0 10 0			Sundries ...	...	0 14 0	
Mr. Tarry ...	0 8 0			In Bank ...	...	11 12 3	
Contributed since October, 1875 ...		1 8 0					
		£65 5 10				£65 5 10	

SUBSCRIBERS TO THE SCHOOL FUND.

	£. s. d.		£. s. d.		£. s. d.
The Rector ...	25 0 0	Mr. Scott ...	1 1 0	Captain Whitly ...	0 10 6
R. W. Worswick, Esq.	10 0 0	Miss Fox ...	1 1 0	Odd Fellows ...	1 0 0
Mrs. Bruxner ...	1 1 0	Mr. Blastock ...	1 1 0	Mr. John Payne ...	0 10 0
M. F. Bruxner, Esq.	5 0 0	Mr. Hodgkins ...	1 1 6	Messrs. Tayler ...	0 10 0
Captain Knight ...	1 1 0	Mr. Smith's Charity	5 0 0	Men's Club ...	0 10 0
Mr. Neale, sen. ...	1 1 0	Mr. Withers ...	0 10 6	Women's Club ...	0 10 0
Mr. W. Neale ...	1 1 0	W. Everard, Esq. ..	0 10 0		£59 16 0
Mr. Mudford ...	1 1 0	Mrs. Bousett ...	0 10 0		

JAMES MARSHALL.

Samuel Clarke, Printer, Gallowtree Gate, Leicester.

Thurlaston School accounts 1875

July 1st 1875: Engaged in making up the School accounts from last July to the present July. These were audited by John Payne.

John Payne was a builder who by 1881 was employing six men, so he was probably well used to accounts. They make interesting reading. There is a separate section for the Clothing Club Accounts for the village. Clothing clubs were widespread in both urban and village societies by the mid-nineteenth century. Many labourers' wages were so low that after buying food and other domestic necessities there was nothing left to buy clothes or the cloth for making them. In many places, the gentry and clergy stepped in and started Clothing and Friendly (saving) societies to encourage workers to look after their own resources and take some pride in themselves for not having to rely totally on the parish or other charities. Many villagers in Thurlaston must have contributed as the contributions for 1875 came to over £65, and interestingly the three men in the village who sold drapery – Mr Morely, Mr Bradshaw and Mr Tarry – also contributed, though not very much. Mr Tarry, with whom the most money was spent, actually contributed the least. Money left over at the end of the year was held in a bank for the following year.

Reverend Marshall also kept the records of Smart's Charity. The original endowment of £200 was given under the will of William Smart, dated February 6th 1802. It was to be used to pay a schoolmaster to teach sixteen poor boys and girls, resident in the parish, to read and write. The investment was originally made at five percent but was later reduced to 3.5 percent, so there was a reduction in the income after 1818. After 1870 children were expected to attend school, though it was not yet a legal requirement, and somehow those families who could not afford the school fees of a penny a week per child had to be helped. In Thurlaston they were supported by Smart's Charity:

Smart's Charity
The Free Scholars admitted under this Charity

Infant School	Mixed School
M.A Evans	Albert Freason
F.W Harvey	Elizabeth Hand
Elizabeth Corbell	Ada Woodward
[unreadable]	Arthur Wallace

Lea Leggs   Sarah Vesty
Harriet Hurd   Amy Illson
Wm. Wright   Emma Cooper
Mary Garrett   Ida Corbell
(signed) George E Bruxner

The census and James Marshall's journal reveal a little about these children, and not surprisingly they all came from impoverished or disadvantaged homes. Sarah Vesty's parents were framework knitters, as was her fourteen-year-old sister – all working at home. It was a very poorly paid occupation demanding hours and hours of work for very little money. Her eight-year-old brother is listed in 1871 as a 'farmer's boy', earning a few pence a week to help his family, when he should really have been at school. F W Harvey also came from a difficult home. In September 1873 Reverend Marshall recorded that he had called on Sarah Harvey, the boy's mother, who had a very badly ulcerated leg which really needed to be treated in the infirmary, but she refused go as her husband was so 'intemperate' that she was afraid to leave the children with him. As a result it took over two months for her leg to heal. The family had an additional burden – an elderly relative, Beth Harvey, aged eighty in 1871, who was living with them and still trying to work as a framework knitter, though Reverend Marshall reported that she was in a very 'weak and poorly condition, the infection in her mouth being cancerous'. But Mr Anscombe seems to have been oblivious to the problems his pupils faced:

> August 11th: Rev Marshall taught a new song. The children have fallen off very much this last fortnight the harvesting having commenced
>
> August 18th: Numbers still less.

Harvest time was the most important time of the year. All the food for the winter, both for animals and humans, relied on it – every pair of hands, however small, was needed. James Marshall recorded that the start of the new school year in 1873 was delayed because of the harvest:

> September 22nd 1873: Mrs Warren commenced school but so few attended that she dismissed them as the small attendance could have told very decidedly in the averages.

> September 29th: School opened, but the gleaning not done so attendance consequently small.

> September 30th: The children have forgotten much, but it will soon come back to them. Attendance small.

Even families who did not work on the farms went gleaning – picking up the ears of wheat left by the reapers, to have them ground into flour for bread making. Mr Anscombe's log continued, recording what he saw as important:

> April 1874: Received a new supply of pictures on Natural history, lesson cards, including Portfolio, farm and colour etc.

> May 1st: Attendance has been small and irregular. 6 of the first class girls are so irregular in their attendance it is impossible to get them forward.

> October 23rd: Luke Maras[?] a boy of eight years old has come to the school not knowing the alphabet he not having been sent to any school before.

> November 30th 2.30pm: Mrs Turner has not marked the attendance this afternoon nor had she entered the morning attendance.

While the headmaster and Mrs Warren recorded the poor

attendance and raged about it, Reverend Marshall actually tried to do something about it:

> January 22nd 1875: Boyles, Bright, Harvey, Argyle, Mears and Chamberlain not in school again. I visited the parents in order to impress on them the duty and necessity of sending their children to school – with the implied threat of consequences if not done.

But life in the village was not without its pleasures. There were annual treats – largely paid for by Reverend Bruxner – though the organisation of them fell on Reverend Marshall and the school staff. A summer garden party to mark the end of the school year was a regular occurrence to which the more wealthy inhabitants of the village not only contributed but which they also attended:

> July 7th 1874: Final preparations for the Treat in the afternoon. The children assembled and commenced tea punctually at 4 o' clock. Many visitors were present which did not however affect the appetites of the children. After tea games were held in the 5 acre field behind Holt House to which all the children went in procession. The distribution of prizes and the ascent of two hot air balloons concluded the proceedings although I have no doubt that the receipt of a bun and bottle of ginger beer was the best conclusion as far as the children were concerned. The farmers and others were entertained to supper by Mr & Mrs Bruxner after the treat.

So wrote Reverend Marshall, and he was soon to start a new venture in the school which gave the children – and the whole village – something else to enjoy. He organised concerts and a band. James Marshall obviously loved music – he could play the harmonium, he taught the church choir and he taught music at the school, some of it as specified on the National School curriculum – beating time and learning new songs – but he introduced other things too. After being at the school only a short time the organising of the annual concert fell to him, and it was a concert in which both the villagers and the children took part:

> December 17th 1873: Intense cold and frost. Very busy all day in school preparing for the concert.

> December 18th: All arrangements for tonight's concert thoroughly completed. More of my time taken up than need be as everything is very new to me. Entertainment this evening more successful than was anticipated by many evil prophets. The room well filled and the money taken amounted to over £3. The performances were all fair – Miss Wallis being the 'star'. Duet by Mrs Warren and Clay and a reading by Mr Greenwood. Clay redeemed his character in a comic song (nigger in character). Everyone expressed themselves much pleased especially with the good order which prevailed. The children acquitted themselves well.

'Clay' was Thomas Clay, a gamekeeper; Miss Wallis was one of the two daughters of Clement Wallis, an agricultural labourer, and his wife Betty who was a framework knitter. There is no Greenwood in the census for Thurlaston so he probably came from outside the village, especially as Marshall refers to him as 'a Mr Greenwood'.

> December 22nd: Children in school making decorations for the church

> December 24th: Engaged all day in decorations for the church. Carol singers arrived at <u>2 AM</u>

> December 25th: No school today

> December 30th: School work. I called at Normanton Hall for a subscription to the school.

November 1874 again found Reverend Marshall heavily involved in the annual concert as well as working with the church choir, and the children were obviously enjoying their time with him, as he records attendance at practice sessions as 'very good'. On November 5th he recorded, 'The rector and his family went away to St Leonard's for the month.' So Marshall was again in charge of everything including church services and Sunday School:

> November 9th: Sunday morning schools. The attendance of the little children seems much better. Had the harmonium moved to a more convenient position.

> November 10th: Gave the infants a good drill in their music but cannot tell yet how far I can take them. They seem to be fond of it.

> November 12th: Practice in the evening. Illness and awful weather interrupted preparations.

And Reverend Marshall had come up with another idea to engage the children's interest:

> November 21st: Another practice tonight but not well attended. Night very rough. Began the Christmas music.

> December 3rd: Practice tonight the fullest attendance I have ever seen. The new voices are doing very well and with care will do credit to the choir.

> December 4th: Not well. Succumbed to my cold and stayed in my house, however, two practices there, one for the children, one for the whole choir.

> December 8th: To Leicester today to get the

programmes printed for the concert.

December 9th: Not at school as usual this morning, not very well ... Proofs of the programmes arrived from Leicester ... arranged decorations for Christmas.

The next few entries are lengthy but in essence they record the trouble he is having with certain parishioners who, even though the date had been set for the concert and the programmes had been printed, wanted to change the date and content to include something from their 'comic' friend. It seems to have been the last straw for Marshall and he refused their request. Of how the concert went there is no record, as the end-of-the-year entries are dominated by the awful weather and the colds, bronchitis and influenza which afflicted the villagers.

But Reverend Marshall did not give up. He had yet another idea for the children of the school – he started a pipe band for the boys, providing them with penny whistles, and he practised them for the first time on November 16th 1874. The following January he recorded, 'Practised my vagabond boys at night in the whistle band in which they make progress. Hope to make something of them.'

These brief extracts from the log-books and journals of Mr Anscombe, Mrs Warren and Reverend Marshall let us glimpse Thurmaston and its school in the early 1870s. It must have been like many other village schools up and down the country – though perhaps not all were as lucky as Thurlaston in having a curate like James Marshall. Unfortunately, he did not stay there for long so would not have known how his 'vagabond boys' turned out. In 1876, at the age of thirty-five, he got a parish of his own, Tatham Fell in Lancashire, the area in which he had grown up and where he would stay for the rest of his life. Reverend George Edward Bruxner retired the same year.

Stained glass window in the school

Endnotes

1 Volume 42, to be found at htpps//books.google.co.uk/
book?id=mE0SAAAAYAAJ.

2 Leicestershire County Record Office E/LB/33c/1, E/LB/330/1, DE
4327/6.

3 Ibid E/MB/B/330/1.

4 See the architect's plans.

5 *Report of the Royal Commission into the state of popular education* (1861)
Vol 1, p.545, Recommendation 6.

6 See Inder, Pam and Aldis, Marion, *Nine Forgotten Histories –
Staffordshire Women,* History Press, 2010.

7 Making up hosiery.

8 There was a Europe-wide smallpox epidemic in 1870-4.

'Dirty and late'

August 1882: Susan Curtis commenced duties as Mistress.

August 10th: Taught the children to sing their tables

August 11th: Broke up for "Harvest Holiday", six weeks[1]

What prompted Susan Curtis to go to Cumberland, or why she took up her duties right at the end of the summer term is unknown, but Stapleton must have come as a huge culture shock. Susan was thirty-six; she was born and brought up in Oxford where she had also taught. It seems she had no experience of country life, let alone life in the wilds of Cumberland. Maybe it was the idea of having her own home that appealed to her – the Stapleton teacher's house had been built at the same time as the school and was a solid, stone-built building, just across the playground from the school.

Susan's nearest neighbours – in fact her only neighbours – were the Rector, Thomas Fell, a bachelor some years her senior, and his servant, Jane. The Rectory stood at the end of a short, tree-lined drive on the far side of the lane that passed the school. The church was over to the right, across the glebe field, approached by a grassy path from the lane. It was along this path that many of her pupils would come to school, after a long trek across the fields and through the churchyard. Stapleton is a large parish of some fifteen square miles, but in 1881 the population was just 372. There was no village as such; the people lived in isolated farmhouses and clusters of single-storey cottages huddled in hollows in the windswept hills, and the children walked two, three, even four miles to school along paths and tracks, across streams and ditches and bogs.

Above: Stapleton church. The path to the school
lay to the right of the picture

Opposite page: Stapleton school in 2013. It has now been turned into
a two storey dwelling house – the dormer windows have been added to
bring light to the bedrooms.

Most of their parents were farmers, farm labourers or smallholders. This was – and is – sheep-rearing country – bleak and barren. The soil is mostly a thin cold clay, and the main crops are still potatoes, turnips and a few oats. There are numerous brooks and bogs and comparatively few trees, but in spring and early summer the wild flowers are spectacular – meadowsweet and harebells and buttercups, stitchwort and ragged robin, vetches and bugloss.

The parish had no real nucleus, though the church of St Mary, the Rectory, the school and the schoolhouse were clustered together in the centre. But for a shop – of sorts – you needed to go to Roweltown, a hamlet a couple of miles away, or Dam Head, two miles in the opposite direction, and the local pub was at The Crossings, down the lane and on to the 'main' road. There were no 'gentry' in the parish and few single women of Susan's age and level of education: it must have been a very lonely life for the young, town-bred schoolmistress.

The Stapleton National School was a much more utilitarian building than the school in Thurlaston. It was built in 1869. There had in fact been a school at Stapleton since the 1770s – latterly it had been held in the big room above the Rectory coach house – and there was even an endowment of £11-2s-6d a year to run it. But education was not a high priority for the people of the area, any more than it was for the families in rural Leicestershire, and though the new school had been built to house a hundred children, year after year the average attendance stood at just twenty-eight.

'October 20th 1868: The school continues rather thin, mainly owing to the potato getting,' wrote Mr Duerden, one of Susan's predecessors. He was very tolerant of his charges when they were absent because of farm work or what he usually described as 'tempestuous weather,' and you can almost sense his pride and admiration when he recorded on December 27th 1869 that 'About 16 of my boys had waded through several feet of snow to school.' They were rewarded with a week's holiday. Mr Duerden was in his twenties and comes over as a kindly, understanding man, unlike Thurlaston's Mr Anscombe. 'School in the afternoon unusually noisy,' he wrote on December 22nd 1868. 'Punished two boys, one severely – a rare occurrence.' He also sounds hurt rather than angry when he records '... a painful occurrence in the afternoon; a little girl deceptive.' (January 3rd 1869) and genuinely distressed when he writes of the funerals of two former pupils that same spring. It sounds as if the younger of them had caught a chill on his way to school. 'I was sorry to hear that his parents intimated that the children ought to be privileged to go to the fire at any time,' he wrote. There were three fires in the schoolroom but they probably made little impact because the room was so tall – and when the wind was in the wrong direction one or more of them would smoke or fail to draw properly. It rains a lot in northern Cumberland and children would often arrive at school wet and cold and have to sit in their damp clothes for a whole school day before braving the elements again on the way home – it is not surprising that they often caught chills and colds.

Mr Duerden seems to have been an effective teacher as well as a compassionate one – he records an enormous amount of map-drawing and learning new songs and poems. The inspectors' report of 1872 was especially favourable: 'The children have passed a very good examination. The character of the instruction continues good. More sets of reading books and another blackboard and easel are wanted ...' Even though the National School movement was in its infancy there was a genuine attempt to set and maintain standards in a way totally lacking in the private schools. The inspectors called annually – at Stapleton the visits were usually in April – and they tested the children on their reading, arithmetic, geography and history; looked at examples of the girls' needlework, and watched as the children performed a repertoire of songs and drill for them. It was a nerve-racking experience for both children and teachers. A week or two later the inspectors' report would arrive and, good or bad, it was carefully copied into the log-book and signed off by the rector. The children usually moved up a standard or stayed where they were on the basis of this report, and the school either secured or lost a portion of its grant – which in turn affected the teacher's salary.

Mr Duerden was succeeded by Miss Meynell who left after a matter of months and then by Miss Wrothwell, and their dislike of the school and its pupils is immediately apparent: 'November 14th 1878: Discipline is not very effective. Found it difficult to stop [the] talking and laughing', wrote Miss Wrothwell on her first day at the school and then again four days later: 'The children appear to have little idea of order. All their movements are noisy in the extreme. Home lessons badly learned and grammar this afternoon done carelessly. Examined Standard I – results moderate. Arithmetic especially weak'. On December 13th she kept the Standard I children after school for a parsing lesson – little seven- and eight-year-olds – regardless of the dangers they might face trekking home across the fields in the pitch dark. In April the following year, she punished several children for copying, which she describes as 'a fault very prevalent in the school'. She 'took the opportunity of shewing them how they broke the 8th Commandment when they looked at their neighbours' slates'. Parents took a dim view of her methods and on April 10th she wrote that 'Joseph Fenwick has taken his three children from school on account of the caning I gave Sarah last Friday for copying.' Sarah was fourteen and due to leave school at the end of term. Stapleton parents were clearly very protective of their children and quite prepared to stand up to a bullying teacher.

The last inspectors' report of Miss Wrothwell's reign was damning;

> The spelling and arithmetic of the three higher standards are inaccurate, and the reading of the first standard is poor … the sewing requires improvement. More fixing (ie. making up) should be done by the girls and when it is done it should be done tidily. The elder girls who are able to knit should be put to other forms of needlework …

Susan Curtis did not therefore have a great deal to live up to and she started off with enthusiasm. The Harvest Festival was held in the first week of the new term and children had time off to attend; she taught the girls to patch flannel, to darn stocking material and to sew samplers carefully so the stitches looked the same on both front and back. Susan seems to have specialised in needlework. In many village schools this was taught by the clergyman's wife or daughters, but Mr Fell was a bachelor and no other local lady stepped forward to help. In fact, the parish was remarkably short of women who might have had time to help – so it fell to Susan to teach the girls 'fixing loose pleats into a band', cutting out nightdresses and all the other skills the curriculum required them to learn:

> October 13th: All are going on fairly well. They require a good deal of help in arithmetic, needlework and spelling.

> October 20th: I am better pleased with the whole school this week.

New reading books arrived at the end of the month and all seemed to be going well, but on November 3rd she had to punish eight children for being late. This she described as unusual 'except in the case of the three Tweddles with whom I have to be very strict.'

The Tweddles lived at Dam Head and their parents, Henry and Annie, ran a small grocery and general stores; they had a farm and also acted as the local carriers. They had a large family – George Alfred, Stanley, John and Mary Ann who had all left school, and thirteen-year-old Henry, nine-year-old Frederick, and seven-year-old Peter who were the bane of Susan Curtis's life. The youngest Tweddle child, Elizabeth Jane, was just three when Susan arrived in Stapleton, and not yet in school.

On December 5th Susan wrote: 'The Tweddles are most annoying in attendance and behaviour' and she complained to the parents. There was a slight improvement in early January but she reported 'I still cannot get work from Henry.' After a few days they reverted to type and she was so exasperated by the dirty state in which they arrived at school that 'January 19th: The Mistress had the Tweddles washed and their hair dressed by two elder lads. They have come each day since cleaner.' Susan quite often wrote of herself in the third person as 'the Mistress'. It is quite possible that the boys' mother sent them off each morning looking reasonably clean and neat –

*Dam Head where the Tweddles lived. The name over the door is
'G.A. Tweddle' – George Alfred, the boys' eldest brother who took
over the business in the 1890s*

but three active boys, chasing each other along the muddy
lanes, pushing and teasing each other, could probably get
themselves in a pretty dirty state well before they arrived at
school. A month later things had deteriorated again and this
time the Rector spoke to the boys – with absolutely no effect.
The Tweddles' bad behaviour, lateness, absences and dirty
clothes would continue to annoy Susan throughout her time
at Stapleton.

But as the months passed she had other things to worry
about – the dreaded annual inspection was fast approaching.
More new reading books arrived, this time for Standard IV,
and new history books for Standard III, together with a ream
of foolscap for the older children to write on. She moved
several children up a standard and reported happily that they
all seemed to be getting on well: 'April 13th: They certainly
seem to be understanding their new rules (arithmetic) fairly'.
She taught them a series of new songs to sing for the inspectors

– 'Soon as Ruddy Morning', 'Stay Little Blackbird', 'March Away', 'The Minstrel Boy', 'A Sailor Song', 'The Violet', 'The Daisy' and 'Hurrah, Hurrah for England'. The parents understood the importance of the school making a reasonable show for the inspectors and in the few weeks leading up to the big day attendance always improved. On March 1st Susan had the fullest attendance of her career at Stapleton with '42 on the books, 37 present, 2 sick, 1 has left for the winter' – leaving just two pupils unaccounted for.

Children leaving 'for the winter' were not unusual – parents of little ones who lived far from the school did not want them setting out and returning home in the dark and it was not unusual for the doctor to provide sick notes to that effect. But some parents were incorrigible. On April 1st she recorded that John Irving had attended for just one day that year – but her ire was still reserved for 'the boys Tweddle – still late, dirty, idle ...' 'They are the only children who, I am happy to say, give me trouble'

The report, when it came in May 1883, was mixed. 'The order is good,' it said, 'but the attainments have fallen off seriously ...' though the inspectors acknowledged that the change of teacher partway through the year had been disruptive. They also criticised the singing, which must have been disappointing – however tongue-tied the children were when strangers asked them questions they could usually be relied upon to sing. For a few weeks in May the Rector tried to work with the children to improve the singing as the report had suggested. He spent a lot of time at the school; he taught scripture, helped with music, subscribed to children's magazines which he donated to the school and from time to time filled in for Susan if she was off sick.

Sickness was an ongoing problem. Because of the arduous journeys they had to make, parents often kept their children at home with relatively minor ailments, but the children in school always seemed to have coughs. 'The coughing in school is very disturbing', Susan wrote on 4th May and it was a theme she often returned to. Then there were the usual epidemics of childhood ailments – in the winter of 1885, for example, there was a measles epidemic. For a fortnight in January the school was closed because so many children were ill or kept home to avoid infection, and when it re-opened 'the snowy slippy weather prevented the children returning.' The summer of 1891 saw an epidemic of mumps and in August she reported that 'sickness and hay keep the children away.'

But for the first few years of her time at Stapleton, Susan remained optimistic. On October 5th 1883, a few days into the new term, she recorded that the children 'take an interest in their work and seem to be happy' though she still 'spoke to the Tweddles about being late and not so neat as they might be.' She began to give object lessons – a National School favourite – her first was on chalk; its source, properties, uses, how it was manufactured into sticks and so on; and her second – no doubt in an attempt to engage her pupils by talking about a subject they knew well – was on potatoes. She also began to develop an increasingly close relationship with the attendance officers who, since education became compulsory in 1880, had the unenviable task of persuading reluctant parents to send their children to school. On November 9th she wrote that: 'The Attendance Officer brought forms to be filled in quarterly for children paid for by the Guardians'. Most families paid a penny a week for each child they had in school – though large families with four or more children in school at any one time only had to pay for three of them. Pupils from very poor homes had their fees paid by the parish – after 1880 inability to pay was no longer an acceptable excuse for keeping school-age children at home.

Susan kept a regular record of new books as they arrived and of improvements to the school building. In May 1883 she started using *Llossie* [?] lesson books and said that the children were 'very pleased with them'. Later the school acquired Queen Prince's books for Standards I and II and *Star* and *Royal Readers* for Standard I and later still some 'Zoological cards' were bought for the infants, which proved extremely popular. Stapleton had few benefactors, but in April 1885 a Miss E Jones presented each of the girls with a needlework book.

Work was done to improve the children's desks and they were 'grooved' – presumably to provide a hollow for pens and pencils to rest in. However, they were still too large for the infants, as the inspectors' report for 1891 pointed out. At the start of the new school year in 1886 Susan reported that 'the room has been well cleaned and the windows painted. It has so brightened it; the children will be delighted.' But not all the improvements pleased her so much – in April 1887 a new fireplace was fitted while school was in session. The work took a week and distracted the children abominably. The fires were a constant problem – in July three new grates had to be installed. The school seems to have had a thorough clean each February and November, and presumably someone was responsible for lighting fires and sweeping the building in between, but who carried out these tasks is not recorded – perhaps it was Jane, the Rector's servant.

However, despite the various improvements, we can see Susan becoming progressively more disenchanted with Stapleton. On March 21st 1884, a new boy started school and Susan records: 'admitted Joseph Forester, he is past six years old and knows nothing whatever.' This would become her standard way of recording the arrival of most new children:

> May 12th 1884: Joseph Ewart admitted, six years and seven months of age and has no idea of anything … it is a pity they cannot be brought in before that age.

> May 1st 1885: Admitted Mary Ann Johnston, nearly seven, she has no idea of reading or writing, letters or figures.

Children could start school at any time after their fourth birthday but few Stapleton parents were willing to let their children go before the age of six, and many, like Mary Ann and the two Josephs, were nearly seven. In April 1887 Susan wrote: 'One or two new ones not entered. They [the parents] dally on with the same plausible excuses until the summer is about over, then they say they shan't send them until next spring. I have lost a great deal through that sort of thing these last five years, nothing seems able to be done.'

The children came from homes where there were no books and their parents seldom needed to write anything down – small wonder that they did not know how to hold a book, recognise their letters and numbers or even count. Indeed, their parents probably still used the old Cumbrian system of counting – yan, tan, tethera, pethera, pimp, hethera, lethera, hovera, dovera, dick – but this would have made no sense at all to Susan Curtis. Education was her bread and butter – her salary quite literally depended on the school getting a good report – and the children doing well mattered much more to her than it did to their families.

In the towns the certificates children received for passing the various Standards were beginning to have some meaning. In rural Cumberland, however, most children's careers were mapped out for them at birth – boys would work on the family farm or take the tenancy of one nearby, labourers' children would work alongside their fathers for farmers who had known their families for generations. Girls would stay at home helping in the house and on the farm till they married, and a few of the more adventurous would go into service. That was how it had been for generations and the possession of a new-fangled school-leaver's certificate would make little difference. Parents were happy enough for their children to learn to read and write, but their real education came when they were kept off school to help at home.

School attendance was thus as heavily bound up with the farming year as it was in Thurlaston, though the pattern was rather different. When the harvest was late, the children would not come back to school till after it was gathered in – hence the school broke up in early August and did not restart until towards the end of September. In November, the potato crop was harvested and children would again be absent digging potatoes. In May the new crop would be planted and extra help was needed, then there was hay to be cut, requiring as many pairs of hands as could be found to pile the hay in stooks, turn it and get it safely under cover during one of Cumberland's occasional dry weeks. Then there was peat-cutting, another early summer job – done then so that the peat would have time to dry out before it was needed for fuel. Susan reported on May 23rd 1874 that several children in the upper school were 'working at the peats and potatoes'. In November there was Term Week, the time when tenancies were reviewed and labourers' contract renewed or terminated, so each year several families would up sticks and move to new properties in Stapleton itself or in other parishes in the district, causing yet more disruption to their children's education.

Bad weather was an even bigger problem than it was further south in Leicestershire. Cumberland is wet, windy and cold and snow can last from November through to March. Children did not have proper waterproof clothing and came to school draped in potato sacks. On their feet Cumbrian boys and girls alike wore clumsy leather clogs, tightly laced at the ankle, and worn over thick, hand-knitted woollen stockings. They were indestructible, those clogs, with wooden soles and metal tips at the toe and heel – the boys could make them strike sparks off the stones in the playground – but woe betide you if they accidentally kicked you or stood on your foot! Pam Inder attended Stapleton School in the 1940s and many children still wore these clogs – it would be several years before they were replaced by wellingtons.

At the end of November 1886 Susan had to give the children a week's holiday because of the snow – it was an exceptionally bad winter. On January 7th 1887 only twelve out of fifty-two children made it to school and on February 11th only fourteen attended. Needless to say, the Tweddles were the worst offenders and the Attendance Officer was still being uncooperative. Susan was submitting, week after week, lists of children not attending school but nothing was done. 'It appears he is powerless,' she wrote on July 3rd 1885.

The Attendance Officer was not, in fact, powerless – in extreme cases he could take parents to court where they would be fined – but the officer assigned to Stapleton seems to have been unwilling to do this. On April 7th 1886 she wrote in even stronger terms 'Compulsion appears to be a terrible farce, parents have such loopholes.' Old habits died hard and it would be some years before parents fully accepted that it was now illegal to keep children out of school. Susan felt she had little control:

> July 18th 1889: Punished John Watson for lying – one stripe on each hand, and Isabelle Potts for rude behaviour – one stripe. She is being kept at home for it, children are withheld if I only speak to them of their fault. I cannot cure their lying habit.

A few days later she complained about the Attendance Officer again. 'I am weary of sending the names of absentees – children and parents are master, in fact anyone but the teacher rules.'

Some parents found alternative ways of educating their children – school was school and they had no way of judging the quality of what was on offer. On November 6th 1885, Susan had reported disapprovingly that: 'I am sorry to hear that three little children are being taught by a woman in the place, two are of school age and should, of course, be here, it is thought too far to send them, there are still two others past six not attending anywhere.'

Families could always find other, more exciting things to do than going to school – there were annual sports days at the Crossings Pub, for example, which many children attended despite being expressly forbidden to do so.

The Crossings pub. This shows how bleak and isolated the area is

These fell in Whit Week, which was also the time when labourers were hired and families might have to move house. Brampton livestock fairs took place in June and September with a consequent drop in school attendance, and there were occasional treats like the annual July picnic which left the children too exhausted and over-stimulated to work. In July 1886 Susan warned the children that they must not take time off to go to the election – none of them were old enough to vote and it was no concern of theirs. They took little notice. 'The slightest excuse keeps them,' she wrote wearily. Whenever something new and interesting was on offer, people took advantage of it – life in Stapleton offered few distractions. In March 1888, for example, there was a magic-lantern show at the school one evening. 'I see that even delicate children can, at half-past seven, in the snow, come to school to see a 'magic lantern',' Susan reported.

Not surprisingly, erratic attendance had its effect. On January 12th 1885 she 're-admitted' eleven-year-old John Watson. He had left Stapleton School in December 1883 – it is not clear why, but perhaps his parents had left the district temporarily. It does not sound as if John had had any sort of education in the meantime – Susan wrote that he still read like an infant and his spelling and arithmetic were poor to non-existent. Children would reappear after many months of unexplained absence. In October 1885, for example, George Tweddle (a relative of the troublesome boys at Dam Head) returned to school after several months away and Susan noted that he had only been to school six times since the examination in early April. Several others had had a very poor attendance record in the same period – Ellen Johnson, Mary Hannah Little and Frances Heslop among them. Such children 'will terribly keep the school back as well as not having time to put up their own work,' Susan complained. On May 27th 1889, after the examination, she wrote 'Mrs Little of Old Town keeps her children away as she always has done, the only mystery is that Thomas passed …' Thomas was twelve and it is not clear whether he had passed Standard III, IV or V – but whichever it was it was a triumph.

Susan did what she could to mitigate the effects of all these absences. On April 29th 1887 she 'marked six children rather than send them home … the slightest inclemency of weather is taken advantage of' and she admitted that she didn't bother to register those children who only attended for a few days before being removed. The Tweddles remained her bêtes noirs. Henry seems to have left school in 1884 but as he had not been seen for months his leaving went unremarked; however Frederick's and Peter's irregular attendance and bad behaviour continue to crop up at regular intervals throughout the log-book. Sometime around 1885 Elizabeth Jane joined her big brothers at school, and though there is no evidence that she was as naughty as they were, she was late or absent equally often. Susan must have despaired when, in February 1888, she got a note from the school doctor allowing Elizabeth Tweddle and Jane Little, another regular absentee, to stay away from school while the bad weather lasted.

Elizabeth returned eventually, but by July 1888 she had again been absent for a full seven weeks: 'she has been sent to Newcastle but does not go to any school,' wrote Susan. Elizabeth's elder brother, Stanley, and his wife were provision dealers in Newcastle and had several children. No doubt Elizabeth had gone to help her sister-in-law. In October 1891 she was again absent for a long stretch, this time at home at Dam Head, 'nursing the baby' – her niece, Fanny, daughter of her eldest brother, George Alfred. The child's mother was delicate and died when Fanny was still tiny.

All this disruption showed up in the school's reports. Year after year the school was criticised because the children achieved so little, and in 1886 the school lost a tenth of its grant because of 'faulty instruction in arithmetic and writing'. Susan wrote philosophically: 'I feared the long trying winter and measles would act against us, we must try again to see what next year will do.' But the reports continued to be lukewarm. The instruction was never more than 'fair' and the inspectors seem to have gone out of their way to nit-pick – in 1889, for example, they complained that 'drill was feebly executed'. But the worst report of all came in 1891 when the inspectors warned that if there was no improvement the following year they would be forced to issue an official warning 'under Article 86(1)'.

By then Susan had had enough. She had been unwell for some time – 'unequal' as she called it. On December 16th 1891 she wrote that it had been a very trying day. Her sister had died earlier in the month and Mr Fell, the Rector, had taken school for her while she went home for the funeral. She obviously did not want to ask him again so 'The Mistress dragged through' although at one point she had a fit of coughing and 'had to go outside to be sick, then come in and go on with her work as she is the single teacher and does not like troubling the Rector'. Of course, Mr Fell read and signed the log-book, so he was well aware that she was playing the martyr for his benefit.

On November 27th 1891 she wrote that 'the three Armstrongs from Longrigg have been absent for fourteen weeks straight off. How is it possible they will do well on Examination Day?' She continued to prepare the children for the inspection, teaching the infants and Standard I to recite 'What does Little Birdie Say?' and 'Love your Brother'. Standards II and III learnt 'The Inchcape Rock' and Standards IV, V and VI were to recite 'The Armada'. The whole school were to sing 'Men of Harlech', 'Rule Britannia', 'Hearts of Oak', 'Music in the Morning' and 'Just in Time'.

But Susan was not going to be there. She left Stapleton School at the end of March and was replaced by John Thomas Bailey, a married man whose wife would help the girls with their needlework. The report when it came, was the worst ever, beginning 'I must report the school inefficient' and ending with a threat to remove the grant entirely. But somehow, the school survived.

And what of the Tweddle brothers who had caused Susan so much grief? At least two of them were still alive in the 1940s. They had gone into the family businesses – Henry stayed at Dam Head and worked with his eldest brother, George Alfred, who took over the family firm in the 1890s. Henry was a carter, delivering goods to people all over the parish. Frederick and Peter went to Newcastle to work for several years in their brother Stanley's provisions shop while Stanley's wife had babies and brought them up. Stanley had sons, so there was no chance of either Frederick or Peter inheriting the Newcastle shop, but they both stayed there until they were in

The Tweddles' delivery van, early 20th century. The name on the side is 'S.J. Tweddle' – Sarah Jane, George Alfred's daughter, who took over the business in the 1920s

their forties. They both married late: Frederick and his wife emigrated to America where they ran a boarding house in Los Angeles for many years, and Peter moved to Carlisle, set up his own shop and had six children. Henry does not seem to have married and the last record of him is in the workhouse hospital in 1911. The boys' erratic schooling had done them no harm whatsoever. Susan Curtis would have been mortified.

Endnote

1   The Stapleton School log books on which this chapter is based are in Carlisle Archives SSR1/133/1.

'I got to Oxford'

'I got to Oxford.' So wrote John Sneyd on May 19th 1817. For the sons of the wealthy, education could continue into early adulthood. John was a gentleman, the second of William Sneyd's four surviving sons, and as such he was not expected to inherit his father's estate, Ashcombe Park. A 'suitable' opening for younger sons was to go into the church, and for that he needed a degree. Happily for us, John – like most of his family – was an inveterate diary keeper and because of this we can share with him his life at Brasenose College in the early part of the nineteenth century[1], just as we shared his grandson's schooldays in Chapter One.

The Sneyd diaries in Keele University Library Special Collections.
There are over 200 diaries kept by five family members

A university education was only for the wealthy and well connected. Who you were, who you knew and how much money you had were really the only qualifications you needed to gain a place – not how intelligent you were. There were scholarships – but again, the most important factor was who you knew to put your name forward for one. There was no written examination for entry to a degree course at Oxford prior to 1914. A young man applying to a college would have taken an oral examination in Greek, Latin and basic arithmetic, and perhaps geography – nothing much else. And it was, of course, only men. When young John Sneyd went 'up' to Oxford in 1817 no-one considered that women might one day go to university – and it would be another sixty years before the first women's colleges at Oxford were founded.

Unlike his elder brother William, who had gone to Rugby, John Sneyd had not been sent away to endure the rigours of life in a public school, because he suffered from epilepsy:

> August 7th 1816: ...William, Ralph [his brothers]
> and I went to the races and afterwards a play where
> I was taken ill of an epileptic fit. I was obliged to be
> bled and taken to Dr Northern's where I slept.

> August 8th: I stayed in my room all day and took
> Calomel ... Adam sat up with me all night.

Calomel, consisting mainly of mercuric oxide, was a widely used medicine, especially for fevers, until the early twentieth century. Its side effects were severe and could be lethal if it was taken for too long or in too great a quantity. It could cause abdominal pain, bloody diarrhoea, decreased urine output which could stop completely, extreme difficulty in breathing, mouth sores, throat swelling that could cause the throat to close, and vomiting. In very large doses it also caused people to lose their teeth and hair.

But since he would need a degree to enter the church, John was educated, and then coached for his oral entrance exam to Oxford, by Reverend William Carlisle who lived in nearby Belmont Hall, one of several grand houses on the Ashcombe estate.

*Ashcombe Park near Leek in North Staffordshire,
the Sneyd family seat*

Like many vicars, he supplemented his income by running a small school in his home. John boarded there, sharing lessons and tutorial sessions with Carlisle's own sons and a few other boys who were boarding, and coming home at holiday times to share French, drawing and dancing lessons with his sister. Drawings of his which still survive in Keele Special Collections show him to have had considerable talent. His older brother had gone to Brasenose College – so of course John would go there as well.

*John Sneyd
aged about 17*

Being taught by Reverend Carlisle seems not to have been too demanding. Lessons were interspersed with gardening, hunting and fishing – and sometimes he cooked the prey they caught on an open fire:

> April 10th and 11th 1816: I got some raspberries and strawberries out of the old garden. I roasted a wood pigeon in my bedroom.

The Sneyds had been innovative gardeners for many years: Basford Hall – another fine house on the Ashcombe Estate had an ice house, the remains of which can still be seen. Belmont, where John was, had an extensive heated garden designed by his grandfather – hence John's ability to pick raspberries and strawberries in April. The pipework leading to the heated beds and early greenhouses can also still be seen. He was a keen gardener himself, planting salad stuffs – spinach, mustard and cress, radishes and flowers in his garden at Belmont – and it was with some pride that he recorded eating them.

Belmont Hall, home of the Reverend Carlisle where John was educated

Learning social skills was as important as learning Greek and Latin: together with Mr Carlisle's children, John bought a tea-set and some tea and sugar, then, going to a cave in the hills near Belmont, they cleared it and built a stone table:

April 1st 1815: Fanny, William Carlisle and my brother William and I drank tea off the table at Gog.

Nowadays we might find it bizarre that a nineteen-year-old was playing with a tea-set in a cave – but John was honing the skills he would put to very good use when he got to Oxford. There were other examples: 'November 18th 1815: I had a fire in my room. John, Bob, Ted Carlisle and Burton and I had coffee in my room.'

John's mother sent him some wallpaper to paper his room at Belmont – she was preparing him for Oxford in her own way. And the young men were inventive as well. By opening the ammunition used in their hunting guns, they managed to get enough gunpowder together to fire the old cannon which stood in the grounds of Belmont. John wrote: 'July 15th 1815: William and I fired the cannon five times because Bonaparte was taken.' Together they built a swing in the woods and a wheelbarrow. They bathed in local pools and walked for miles on the hills. But John was growing up. On July 28th 1816 he recorded in his diary, 'My Father gave me a pair of razors. I began to shave.'

In May the following year he went up to Oxford. As for many young people now it was his first time away from home and his immediate family and he revelled in the freedom that his college rooms gave him, even though they were shared with his brother. In the time-honoured way he mismanaged his money, threw himself into new societies and activities, made new friends, came in late, got drunk – and only applied himself to study when it became absolutely necessary. The brothers had a suite comprising a bedroom and sitting room and John went to the trouble, and expense, of stamping his personality on it. He had it re-painted and carpeted, and bought tableware – a china tea-set and glasses. A pair of plated silver candlesticks – bought cheaply at an auction for the equivalent of £10[2] – added a further touch of class.

He bought prints to hang on the walls and had them framed, his choice showing a leaning towards prints of royalty – they included Princess Charlotte of Wales, Prince Leopold and the Empress Maria Louisa. His accounts show that he spent over £165 on them.

Royal crest over a doorway at Brasenose College. This would have appealed to John Sneyd – he was an ardent royalist

But that did not satisfy him. Sometime later he spent a further £300 on more pictures from 'Mr Taylor'. But he also bought useful things: a writing desk, a toasting fork, a hammer and some nails, a 'turning tool', a looking glass, coal and faggots, drawing paper, a palette and a box of paints, soap, candles, a tea kettle and kettle holder, and a hairbrush, and later at Talboy's – a bookshop – he bought a bookcase and books for a staggering £650. His mother, who held the family purse-strings as their father was also hopeless with money – he had lost extremely large sums in very unwise purchases of stocks and shares in mining companies that failed completely – insisted that he kept full and accurate accounts, which he had to show her. It is from the detailed accounts that he was obliged to keep that we learn as much about his activities as we do from the actual entries in his diaries.

Unlike some Oxford colleges, Brasenose does not seem, at that time, to have been a hot-bed of academic excellence: under the tenure of Principal Edward Hartopp Cradock, Brasenose's academic record waned greatly, with much of its success focused on sports – at which it excelled – most notably in cricket and rowing. It is not surprising, therefore, that John's diaries are dominated by rowing and by supper and breakfast parties. Not all colleges were like that. Some had very high expectations of their students. Corpus Christi was one. William Phelps, a student there who later became Archbishop Phelps, wrote in a letter home, 'I rise at seven. When I am more settled I hope to rise earlier...' He went on to describe his day in detail; it started at 10am with lectures in either Greek or Latin, then smaller classes after that for more Greek, logic and mathematics. Classes took up the whole day with short breaks for meals and attendance in chapel – then he had preparation late into the night for the next day.

Brasenose College from an early 19th century engraving

Although John Sneyd made many new friends, some of whom were to be lifelong, there was little or no opportunity for him to make new female friends – though opportunities for illicit relationships were, of course, available: 'Was attacked by two whores but soon got shut of them in C.C.', he wrote.

Since universities were entirely male preserves, as was the 'school' he had attended, the only young women he knew were female relatives or the daughters of his parents' close friends. In the Brasenose years the only ones mentioned in his diary are his cousins Catherine and Penelope. Catherine was a great favourite with many of his friends and he obviously had a very soft spot for her too, but it was Penelope whom he married on graduation and who was to bear him thirteen children. His father was especially fond of this niece, the only child of his sister Mary Anne. Penelope had frequently stayed at Ashcombe Park and William Sneyd was also the trustee of a fund of over a million pounds that was to come to her on her marriage. The law at that time stated that when a woman married, all her money and property became her husband's – given the Sneyds' precarious financial state William Sneyd would surely have been pleased to see his son marry her, and maybe he had even indicated as much.

The diary that John kept at Oxford is far from complete. He left many days blank and sometimes complete weeks and months are missing. The entries themselves are short and factual and rarely record his feelings about anything. There are practically no records of current or national events. But although sparse, it is one of the first, almost complete, undergraduate diaries ever to have been found that describes Oxford at the beginning of the nineteenth century. It even precedes the first records of the Boating Club.

However, since he was required by his parents to keep a very detailed cash account, short entries like 'I gave a wine party' have a great deal more colour and life when supplemented by an account of how much he had spent on wine-glasses, crockery, plated silver candlesticks and other tableware. And some idea of his personal appearance can be imagined by seeing what he bought to wear and how much he spent on his hair. Silk stockings, a gold seal and knee buckles are not exactly necessary items – unless you are intent on making a certain kind of impression and mixing with a certain class of people – and that was definitely part of young Mr Sneyd's agenda.

1817

May 19th: My Mother, Mary, and I got to Oxford.

May 20th: Went to the Vice Chancellor and got entered. I dined in Hall and slept in my rooms.

On that same day he paid the Vice Chancellor's fees of about £150 and 'caution money' – the deposit the college held as insurance against any damage caused by the undergraduate – of over £1,100.

May 21st: We went to a party to breakfast. I went to Chapel. Was lectured in Homer.

May 22nd: Went shopping and bought a good many books. I skipped my Sophocles lecture. My mother gave me a present of £500 and £100 to buy small clothes [underclothes].

He spent about £84 on that first book-buying trip. Many of the books are as you would expect – Homer's *The Iliad* and *The Odyssey*, Watt's *Logic*, Shakespeare and Milton, but *A Treatise on Self-knowledge* gives some insight to another aspect of his character. John Sneyd was ambitious and anxious for any information that might help him succeed in life. However, the book does not seem to have helped him greatly – had he been more self-aware and self-critical he would have avoided a great many problems in later life!

May 24th: Roland, Unwin and I went down the river in a skiff. I drank tea at E's rooms.

May 25th: William gave a wine party. I went walking with Butler.

Brasenose College, 20th century

May 26th: Went down the river with R. Unwin. I had a row.

May 27th: Had a row on the river. Went to Cholmondley's rooms to drink.

'Cholmondley' was Hugh Cholmondley of Cholmondley Castle – seat of the Marquis of Cholmondley since the twelfth century. John Sneyd obviously felt there was some kudos in having him as a friend – though in fact Hugh Cholmondley would soon be expelled from Oxford in disgrace.

May 30th: Was lectured in Homer.

May 31st: William and I went to a wine party of Mr White's of University College.

June 1st: William and I breakfasted with Wickstead. I drank tea with Unwin and went to a wine party at Mabberley's.

June 3rd: ... there was a very good boat race down the river. The Commoners beat The Scholars and The Gentlemen.

June 5th: I breakfasted with Green of Christ Church and went for the first time to a Public Lecture on Sophocles but was not called for.

'Not called for' means not required to answer questions.

'Hall's Boathouse Tavern' from a drawing by Musgrove of 1817. Musgrove was a Brasenose man so it is quite likely that the boat in the foreground is the Brasenose boat

June 6th: Gave a breakfast.

June 13th: Mabberley and Lewis received their tickets for their responses, commonly called Little Goes. Went down the river with Roland Unwin.

'Little Goes' or 'Responsions' was the first of the three examinations required for an academic degree at Oxford. It was nicknamed the 'Little Go' and was generally taken by students prior to or shortly after entry to the university, the idea being that without standardised qualifications from school examinations the university had to verify for itself the quality of the students that colleges were accepting. The examination consisted of comparatively simple questions on Latin, ancient Greek, and mathematics. It was abolished in 1960. John Henry Newman wrote to his father on May 29th 1818: 'I go up for my Little Go tomorrow,' and records in his journal for the following day that he had 'passed Responsions'. Little Goes were followed by other examinations called 'Collections' and 'Schools'.

> June 18th: Went to the Commemoration and
> Concert. Went to a Wine party in Charles' rooms.

The 'Commemoration' was the equivalent of a Founder's Day. Honorary Degrees and prizes for poetry were awarded, followed by a concert.

> June 19th: I went up for my collections. I went on a
> skiff [this cost him £4] with Thomson a duck hunting
> and fell in the lock but was pulled out with only a
> wetting.

> June 20th: Thomson passed his Little Go. I went out
> in the morning in a skiff and bathed in the Isis. I took
> another in the afternoon duck hunting.

There are no further entries for 1817. His diary starts again in January 1818.

> January 17th: We got to Oxford before breakfast. My
> brother Ralph was entered at Brasenose.

> January 18th: Ralph left Oxford at 8 am this
> morning.

January 19th: Breakfasted with Bouverie. Saw Louis Sneyd at All Souls.

Ralph was his younger brother. There was only three years between the three eldest Sneyd boys – William was born in 1797, John in 1798 and Ralph in 1799. 'Bouverie' was probably the son of William Pleydell-Bouverie, 3rd Earl of Radnor. John Sneyd was always anxious to chalk up his connections with the aristocracy.

> January 20th: Breakfasted with William. Barton, Leigh, Musgrove and William drank wine with me, the first party I ever invited to wine.

> January 21st: Breakfasted with Penny. Lectures commenced today. The First Book of Herodotus.

> January 22nd: I gave a breakfast. I attended a logic lecture in the Hall.

> January 26th: Betty Moreley's [sic] Day. The Scouts dined in Miss Mones Room, the principal etc dined in the Buttery, we dined in the Hall.

Betty Morley was a benefactor who died in 1515 and left money to the college for Fellowships. An extravagant dinner was – and still is – held every year in her memory.

> January 27th: Went to a wine party at Barston's the Commoner. William gave breakfast.

> January 29th: Went to wine at Bouverie's.

> February 2nd: Morral, Clarke, Perrin, Leigh, and Milemay came to wine. William and I drank tea with Leigh. Parkin came to Oxford. My breakfast.

February 6th: Parkin, John Pairs, and Perrin came to breakfast with our club in our rooms. William's breakfast. Logic Lecture – Herodotus.

February 7th: I went skating for the first time. [The skates cost him £6] Took a theme to Hall, the first I ever gave to a tutor at Oxford. Musgrove was elected a member of our breakfast club, he gave us breakfast. I dined at the principals.

February 12th: William and I and many many more went to Abingdon to see Hugh Cholmondley's horse run against Barnet's The former won. I was introduced to E.C Ogle.

February 13th: My breakfast. Sir Charles Lockhart, Hill, Leigh, Maberly, Barston, Bouverie and Giredot came to wine.

February 14th: I and Barton rowed to Sandford.

February 19th: Low sent my bill for Battles.

'Battles' was the undergraduate term for board and lodgings – John Sneyd paid about £680 a term. The £20 note he was to receive on February 27th was the equivalent of about £1,000 in 2015 money and was probably to pay his Battles bill.

February 23rd: Buller and I took a two oared boat to Sandford. I gave breakfast.

February 24th: I rode to Chipping Norton.

February 27th: I received a £20 note from my father.

March 2nd: I went to wine with Barton.

March 3rd: Leigh, Bouverie, Graves and Clive came to wine with us.

March 4th: I attended Logic and Herodotus lectures. Went a sailing. Roland Unwin was expelled from Exeter.

March 5th: William went up for Collections. He left Oxford at about 12 o'clock last night to go home.

March 7th: I gave breakfast to our club.

March 10th: I breakfasted with Roland Unwin. My father and Mother, Miss Morton and Mary came to Oxford and took me to London.

And that was the end of his first term. A few days before he returned to Oxford for the start of the summer term he wrote:

March 30th: I attended an auction
A Pair of plated candlesticks – 5s [about £12]
A china tea-set – £1 [about £48]
A pair of silver salt spoons – 10s [about £24]
A tea board – 12s [about £30]

This entry is especially interesting. Although green, or Chinese, tea had been drunk since the seventeenth century, Indian tea was not grown until the late 1830s. But drinking green tea was the 'in' thing to do in early nineteenth-century Britain. Tea was not cheap – tea caddies in large houses had locks on them and ordinary people did not drink tea at that time. John Sneyd was equipping himself to cut a figure of gentility and fashion. His 'tea board' would have been a wooden tray – probably elaborately decorated or japanned. His tea with William and Leigh in February was therefore a significant event for him. He had 'arrived' in Oxford and the goods bought at the auction would help to secure his place amongst the elite set.

Brasenose College. The rooms seen here are very similar to the one the Sneyd brothers shared

The term followed much the same pattern as before; parties of all kinds, rowing, and avoiding too much work. He was more concerned with building contacts: new names appear fairly frequently, as does card-playing – which was to occupy a great deal of time and lose him a great deal of money.

> April 4th: I got to Oxford at about 4 o'clock. William and Clement Kynnersley [a cousin] arrived a short time after from Northampton.

> April 5th: We breakfasted with Bouverie. Clem and I went to Iffley in a skiff.

> April 10th: William, Clement and I went to wine with Cholmondley and he made me a present of Latin Theme.

April 11th: C.J.S.Kynnersley was entered as a gentleman commoner.

April 16th: I supped in Hall for the first time.

April 18th: I breakfasted with Bouverie. I withdrew from the breakfast club of which I had been a member ever since I resided in Oxford. Buchan asked me to wine.

April 20th: William and I breakfasted by ourselves. I went to Mr Dawson, my private tutor, for the first time.

April 21st: I did not go to my private lecture.

April 23rd: I was set an imposition by Mr Cardwell for not going to his lecture.

April 28th: I went to Iffley in a skiff.

May 2nd: William and I dined at little Barton's and drank tea and played cards at Vassall's.

May 4th: I attended a Botanical lecture and two lectures with my private tutor.

May 6th: I went to lectures as on Monday.

May 7th; Hugh Cholmondley was expelled.

May 8th: I went to the same lectures as on Monday. I drank tea and played cards at Vassalls.

Saturday May 9th: We had a public lecture.

May 10th: Unwin breakfasted with us. Lockhart, Vassall, Johnnes, Unwin, Leigh, Morral and Starkie took wine in our rooms.

May 14th: Sillifant and Unwin took tea in our rooms and played at cards.

The diary pages for the remainder of May and June are largely blank. What entries there are record yet more wine and tea parties, rowing and playing cards. His accounts, strangely, record no expenses for wine – though quite a considerable amount must have been consumed, and he did not only spend money on himself and books, he often gave money to an old beggar woman and a little street boy – about £2.50 at a time – and subscribed £30 to a fund for music on the river. What particular game of cards he played we do not know – but it was a gambling game and he was not very good at it. He won about £15 in the term – but lost £170!

On June 5th he was taken ill – perhaps another epileptic fit. He gives no detail of his illness but left Oxford on June 23rd to go to Leamington with other members of his family and friends. It was the year of the General Election and he had an entertaining time seeing the new Member of Parliament being 'chaired', bathing in hot spring water, and learning to dance quadrilles. At the end of July he returned to Ashcombe.

1818
October 17th: Ralph and I got to Oxford.

October 21st: Began the 5th book of Herodotus.

Book Five of Herodotus' lengthy and detailed history of the Greek people (written around 400 BC) begins: 'The Persians left behind by King Darius in Europe, who had Megabazus for their general, reduced, before any other Hellespontine state, the people of Perinthus, who had no mind to become subjects of the king'. If John Sneyd was reading this in Greek it must have been very taxing – and probably exceedingly tedious.

October 23rd: Barston, Johnnes, Ticker and Morris took wine with us. Ralph and I dined with Pool of St Mary Hall.

October 24th: Barston, Johnnes, Ticker and Morris took wine with us. We all went to Ticker's rooms for supper.

October 25th: Ralph and I wined in Phoenix Common Room.

The Phoenix was part of Brasenose College and the oldest dining room in Oxford, founded in 1786 – it was private, very expensive and very prestigious. Members had to adhere to a strict code of dress when dining, consisting of a claret-coloured coat with a velvet collar, and buttons of a pattern to be determined by the secretary. A white waistcoat was also to be worn with buttons of the same pattern. Whether John Sneyd actually dined there – or simply took wine before dinner and therefore did not have to have the regulation dress – is not clear. The dining club is still in use to this day, though the name and atmosphere have changed dramatically. It was called the Hell Fire Club at one time and is now the Bullingdon Club, to which the likes of David Cameron and Boris Johnson once belonged.

October 31st: I sat the Schools.[3]

November 11th: Kynnersley, Ralph and I breakfasted with Mr Lowe.

November 12th: Ralph went a shooting with Price of Corpus Christie [sic] and killed a hare, a partridge and 3 pigeons.

November 13th: We had meat from Gadney [a butcher – the bill was £12-50p) for breakfast.

November 18th: The old Queen died.

This was Queen Charlotte, wife of George III. She was seventy-four and died of pneumonia at Kew Gardens, sitting upright as she could not breathe lying down, attended by her two eldest sons – George, the Prince Regent and Frederick, Duke of York – together with two of her daughters, Princess Augusta and Mary, Duchess of Gloucester. The Queen was a patroness of the arts and an amateur botanist who helped expand Kew Gardens. George III and Charlotte had fifteen children, thirteen of whom survived to adulthood. George's bouts of physical illness and insanity, which became permanent in later life, resulted in their eldest son being appointed Prince Regent in 1810. John Sneyd was an ardent royalist.

The rest of the entries for November are very thin indeed, but the accounts reveal that John was still playing cards and losing every time, entered a lottery for a horse – and lost – and had his room repainted, which cost him nearly £140.

> December 4th: I was examined by Mr Lowe in
> Homer. I did not attend Cardwell's lecture. I wrote to
> my Father for money.

He needed nearly £600 to pay for his 'Battles' for that term.

> December 9th: Unwin passed his great Go
> Examination. Clement, Ralph and I dined with Creek
> of Corpus.

> December 10th: Clement went home.

> December 11th: I passed my Collections.

1819
> January 15th: Ralph and I left home, called at
> Huntley and dined at Loxley. We took Clement
> Kynnersley with us as far as Birmingham where we
> slept. [Huntley and Loxley are in Staffordshire and

were the homes of family members]

January 16th: We left Birmingham and got to Oxford and took tea with Aunt Marsden.

His Aunt Marsden was his father's younger sister. She and her daughter, John's cousin Catherine, had moved to Grafton House near Oxford.

January 17th: Parkin, Cave and Vassal breakfasted with us. Clement, Ralph and I drank tea and dined with my aunt.

January 18th: Ralph took a ride with Catherine.

January 20th: I commenced lectures with Mr Lowe and Dawson. We drank tea at Grafton House.

January 21st: Clement took a ride with Catherine.

January 26th: E Buller, Fielding and Cave came to wine with us. I took a long ride with Catherine.

All the cousins seem to have been taking long unchaperoned rides with Catherine. Perhaps the reason for her mother's move to Oxford was to find Catherine a husband. The rest of January is a repetition of breakfast, wine and dinner parties – and not much else.

February 4th: I went to a music meeting.

February 5th: I wined with Starkie, took tea at Grafton House and wrote to my father.

February 8th: Smith and I took a Tandem down to Bicester and back.

February10th: I received a letter from Henry (another brother) and wrote to Penelope.

February 11th: My Aunt, Catherine, Ralph and I went to see Blenheim. Clem. and I breakfasted with Mr Lowe.

February 12th: Smith, Vassall, Stapleton, Barton and I took 3 tandems 8 miles beyond Whitney.

February18th: William arrived at Oxford.

February 19th: William and Catherine went a riding.

February 23rd: J.Buller, Pool, Dugdale, J. Adams, my brothers, Kynnersley, Mr and Mrs Grosvenor and myself took tea at Grafton.

March 1st: My Aunt, Catherine, Ralph, Clement and I went to a concert to hear Miss Stevens.

'Miss Stevens' was a well-known opera singer whose performances had glowing reviews. John's ticket cost him about £17.50.

March 6th: Received a letter from my Father.

March 8th: I wined with Barton.

March 9th: Ralph and I wined with Unwin.

March 15th: My Aunt, Catherine, Ralph and I went to a Ball given by Mrs White.

March 16th: I wrote to my Mother. Received a letter from x.

This is a very significant entry. The letter was from his cousin Penelope, the first one he had had, and for some reason he is concealing her identity.

Penelope Holley, John's first cousin, who he married in 1821

March 18th: Stapleton, Parkin, Johnnes, and I took a four oar down to Sandford. Had tea at Grafton House.

March 19th: Smith, Johnnes, Bouverie, Girandot, Stapleton, Parkin and Kynnersley breakfasted with me.

March 23rd: Went up for collections

March 24th: Took a ride with Catherine.

March 30th: I rode to Abingdon on one of Mr Vassall's horses. Wrote to x.

April 1st: My Aunt, Catherine, Ralph and I went down to Iffley in a two oared boat.

April 2nd: Ralph and I were sent away from Oxford by the Vice-Chancellor for knocking in at half past two.

April 3rd: Vassall, Ralph and I left Oxford and got to Woodstock to dinner.

April 4th: We read prayers and took a ride afterwards.

April 6th: Dawson and Penny dined with us.

April 7th: Vassall, Ralph and I left Woodstock and rode to Oxford where we got lodgings. [His expenses at Woodstock were just over £190]

April 9th: I breakfasted with Penny and wrote to my father. I dined at Dickenson's. My Aunt, Catherine, and Ralph left Oxford for Cheltenham.

April 10th: I had my dinner from Dickenson's and dined in my lodging.

April 11th: I had 2 mutton chops for my dinner.

Things were changing for John. He was still not allowed to use his rooms at Brasenose due to having come in in the early hours of the morning on April 2nd, so he could not dine in Hall. He was having to pay for lodgings and buy his food in the town. Pressure was obviously being put on him to give up so much reckless socialising and get down to some work – whether from his father or the university or both he does not record, but the rest of that term was given to unadulterated study.

> April 12th: I read some Virgil.

> April 14th: I breakfasted with Penny. I finished the Georgics of Virgil.

The Georgics, a poem in four books, was published in about 29 BC and was Virgil's second major work, following his Eclogues and preceding the Aeneid. The name comes from the Greek word γεωργικά, geōrgika, meaning 'things agricultural' and although the subject of the poem is agriculture, it is far from being an example of peaceful rural poetry: it is a work characterised by tensions in both theme and purpose.

> April 15th: I read the first 2 books of Homer. Sylvia [his horse] slept at Seckhams.

> April 16th: I read the 3rd and 4th books of Homer. I had a Guirkin [sic] of pork for dinner.

This was probably a cheap meal consisting of belly of pork and a crunchy gherkin – the recipe can be found to this day.

> April 18th: I read The Acts of the Apostles and a Chapter of St Paul's Epistle to the Romans.

> April 19th: I read the 8th book of Homer.

> April 20th: I read the 9th and 10th books of Homer. Got a letter from Ralph.

> April 21st: I read the 11th part of Homer. Received a letter from my Father.

April 22nd: I finished Homer. Read some Greek Grammar and wrote some questions on Logic.

April 23rd: I finished my logic.

April 24th: Left my Lodgings. Arrived at B.N.C [Brasenose College] Ralph arrived from Cheltenham and Clement from home.

April 29th: Went to my private tutor for this first time this term.

April 30th: Played at cricket in the morning and went down to Sandford in the evening in a four oared boat.

Most of May, and all of June are almost completely blank. Such entries as there are record only boating and drinking wine. Study seems to have been at an end. But the furious revision in April had worked and on June 26th John Sneyd recorded with some pride: 'Ralph and I passed our Little Go.' Ralph was younger than John and had been at Oxford for less time. Perhaps his more rigorous schooling at Rugby had prepared him better. John's diary starts again in October. Presumably he had spent the summer at home at Ashcombe and it would seem that his cousin Penelope had also been there. Over the next three months the diary has many missing entries.

1819
October 15th: Charles Parkin came here (to Ashcombe). We killed 12 rabbits, 3 hares, 3 partridges, and a woodcock.

October 16th: Parkin, Ralph and I got to Birmingham where we slept.

October 17th: We three got to Oxford at about 5

o'clock. Johnnes, Vassall, Blackwell, Worsely and Parkin dined with us.

October 18th: Breakfasted with Vassal and dined with Johnnes.

October 20th: Began the 5th Book of Herodotus again.

October 21st: Wrote to my Mother.

October 26th: Took a ride with Vassall. Breakfasted with young Parkin.

November 8th: Wrote to my Mother and Henry

November 22nd: The following eight men: Vassall, Johnnes, Cave, Worsley, Parkin, Blackwell, my brother and myself forming a club, entered into an agreement to give wine and supper parties alternately once a week, but as this term would now be so soon at an end it was agreed we should meet twice a week till the vacation. I being the senior man in the club the suppers are to be given in my room

For the first time John Sneyd reveals something of his true self. In later life he became a very dominant, and some would say arrogant, man who was always organising people and events, often with disastrous results.[4] It was not in his nature merely to be a member – he had to be in charge. His accounts show that each member of what they dubbed the 'Octo Club' was paying a subscription of about £90 a term for their wine and supper parties. He does not indicate who was the treasurer.

December 1st: Wined with Cave and supped with Vassal.

December 4th: The Oyster Club was held in Cave's rooms.

December 7th: The Oyster Club was held in our rooms. [The subscription for this was about £45]

December 9th: Took up for Collections half of Luke, 4 books of Caesar and 5th book of Herodotus.

There are no further entries for this year and many of his accounts are missing as well. There are also very many missing entries in January and February 1820. Wining and dining still featured with great importance – the highlight being a wild goose for dinner on January 23rd – but John was doing more academic work as well.

January 19th: Breakfasted with Penny. Began the georgics of Virgil with Lowe, (a tutor) read some Roman History and one of Porteus's lectures.[5]

January 20th: Read a chapter of Herodotus and one of Porteus's lectures. Wined with Ellice and dined with Parkin.

January 21st: Read some Georgics of Virgil, some Herodotus and Roman History.

January 24th: Began the 6th Book of Herodotus with Mr Hall and read some Virgil with Mr Lowe.

January 27th: I gave the Octo wine, Ellice gave the supper.

January 30th: Put on mourning for the Duke of Kent.

The only work recorded in February are two brief readings of St John's Gospel – though there is much wining, dining and rowing, and he recorded his weight as eleven-and-a-half stone. But then on February 11th there is a most significant entry:

> Wrote a valentine to my dear P...e. Walked with Kate [Catherine], had a sentimental conversation and kissed her eyelids at parting.

This would seem to be his farewell to Catherine as she is not mentioned again in his diary.

During March many new names appear – and he was making a note of them – though many of the old favourites are there as well. On March 9th he remarked that 'The Members for the City of Oxford were chaired.' John rarely mentioned events outside his university life at Oxford – this was an exception and perhaps we see in it the first glimpse of his interest in politics. A decade later he would become heavily involved in canvassing for David Watts Russell of Ilam who was standing for Parliament in the first election after the Reform Bill. Russell was not elected.

> March 11th: Went down to Sandford in a 6 oar. Wined with Cave, and had Colleridge, Bowen, Rigby, Perkins, Maddock, Penny and Lewis with the 8 to sup in or rooms.

> March 12th: Wined with Cave. Was invited to the Phoenix but did not go.

> March 13th: Breakfasted with Pearce. Wined with Worsley of Alban Hall.

> March 17th: I was invited to a Blow Out party at Corpus but did not go. [Blow-out was Oxford slang for a grand feast]

> March 20th: Passed my collections.

He spent part of the Easter break in London with some of his Oxford friends, going to plays and exhibitions and visiting friends and relatives but then illness struck again – this time it was Penelope who rushed to be at his side.

> April 6th: I got to Oxford about 6 o'clock and slept at the Mitre.

> April 7th: I dined at Dickensons. Parkin, Bulteel and Neilson took tea with me.

> April 8th; I received a package from my Mother containing 8 India handkerchiefs and a £10 note, a letter from herself and 2 others. I likewise received a letter from Ralph by post.

The £10 note was worth about £490 in 2015 money. The eight handkerchiefs his mother sent would have cost over £100. John had also received nearly £4,000 from his father in March. Keeping young Mr Sneyd in the manner to which he wished to become accustomed was an expensive business.

> April 9th: I wrote to my Mother.

> April 10th: I received a letter from Penelope.

> April 11th: Wrote to my father and Pen.

The rest of April and the whole of May and June are one long party: rowing and rowing competitions between the Oxford Colleges, bathing, cricket and, of course, much wining and dining. The following entries are typical:

> May 9th: I wrote to Penelope. Went to Sandford in our 8 oar and raced the first Brasenose up to the Barge from Iffley.

May 10th: The 2nd Brasenose boat went out of the lock before Jesus and gained 2 lengths in the race to the Barge. I had some beer afterwards at Penny's lodging.

May 11th: About 30 Brasenose men and myself went to Nuneaton in three 8 oared boats.

May 17th: Dobson breakfasted with me. The first Brasenose raced the Jesus with 6 oars and won.

May 21st: Gave a dress wine party of about 16 men. Wrote to Penelope.

May 22nd: Bathed with Cave. Fixed to row down to Eton with 5 other men but changed my mind.

May 27th: Was bumped by the Jesus boat. Wined with Vassall. Got drunk. Brasenose Cricketers beat the Ballingtons.

But in June there was one discordant entry:

June 8th: Bungled over my Collections.

It did not, however, seem to affect what he did for the rest of that term:

June 15th: Lunched with Gilbert, dined with Bulteel at Sadlers. Helped to row 5 ladies and 2 gentlemen to Iffley and back again....Went to a Ball given by Mr Gilbert.

June 17th: Ralph, Bulteel and Bowen left Oxford for the long vacation. Received a letter from my Mother.

Some time in 1820 a memorable incident happened

The Brasenose College rowing jersey, c.1840 from a booklet
with illustrations of the jerseys worn by the rowers
of various colleges

which many believe gave Deer Park in Brasenose its name. The *Gentleman's Magazine* printed an account of a stag hunt in which the quarry was hunted from Blenheim Park to Oxford, where it 'proceeded up the High Street, as far as Brasenose College, when ... the stag took refuge in the Chapel during divine service, where it was killed 'sans ceremonie' by the eager hounds.' John Sneyd does not record the event – but he must have known of it.

Brasenose College Chapel

The term of pleasure was over. He had failed an examination and decided, along with several other students, to stay on in Oxford and get down to some serious work. Where April, May and June had been almost unadulterated hedonism, July and August were to be spent in monk-like application to scholarship. Perhaps the letter from his mother was the reason for this. In the last few days of June and the first of July he allowed himself some small pleasures, but after that the workload was punishing and his diary entries give a very clear record of the syllabus he had to follow and the way in which he was expected to work. The entire emphasis was on learning and memory and being able to scan Latin and Greek texts. Original thought was not called for, nor was any kind of creativity.

July 2nd: Dined with Hall. Read 6 chapters of St John's Gospel.

July 3rd: Read a little Caesar with Hall and 14 pages of Herodotus by myself. Wined with Nelson.

July 4th: Breakfasted on bread and milk. Received 2 letters, 1 from Penelope and 1 from my Mother. Read some Caesar and 14 pages of Herodotus. Wrote to my Mother.

July 5th: Read some Caesar and 14 pages of Herodotus. Dined with Neilson.

July 6th: Dined with Mr Hall. Read some Caesar and 14 pages of Herodotus.

July 7th: Finished the First Book of Herodotus read some Caesar. Dined at Dickensons.

July 8th: Was examined in the First Book of Herodotus by Mr Hall. Finished the First Book Caesar and read Ruth, Esther, The Song of Solomon, Ecclesiastes and some of Bishop Lincoln's Theology.

July 9th: Wrote to Penelope.

July 10th: Read 14 pages of Herodotus, 4 chapters of John, some divinity and a little Caesar.

July 11th: Read 14 pages of Herodotus, 4 chapters of John, some Caesar and a few leaves of Tolman's Theology.

The whole of the rest of the month follows this rigid pattern as he ploughed through the whole six books of Herodotus, five *Eclogues* of Virgil, the 21st chapter of St John in Greek, the *Georgics, Polyhymnia* (the Greek Muse of Sacred Poetry), St Matthew in Greek, the Gallic wars, Johnson's *Theology* and so on and on. On July 19th he records that he took a very long walk and, 'got wet through' and on the following day he wrote in Greek that his horse, Sylvia, had a line attached to her collar. Penelope wrote frequently. On July 22nd he was examined by Mr Hall on *Polyhymnia*. For the rest of the month, the whole of August and the start of September the relentless reading goes on. Very occasionally there were outings: to a street fair, to visit friends and once to the races, but they are isolated events. Letters from his mother and Penelope and his brother seemed to sustain him, but it is not altogether surprising that on September 11th he wrote that he 'was not very well.' By then he was on the 12th Book of Homer, had read eleven essays on Ancient Greece in that week alone, as well as the ever-present Caesar, Malachias, Edras and the Apocryphal chapters of Esther. He must have been almost at the end of his tether for on September 12th he went out and 'shot a fish'!

Presumably feeling better after this outburst he applied himself again to his studies, reading the whole of the Bible and yet more Caesar and Homer, but then on September 23rd he 'lionized two of Gilbert's friends around Oxford and rode next day to Blenheim and got beastly drunk.' The next day he wrote to his mother that he was 'very unwell'. He put himself back on track and throughout this period it is possible to sense that though the work was dreary and repetitive in the extreme he knew he had played hard in the summer term and was now getting a great deal of satisfaction out of his own self-discipline. By the end of the month his tutor, Mr Hall, who was examining him, was also taking him out occasionally and inviting him to dine. At the beginning of October, term started. His friends returned to Oxford and he faced serious examinations.

October 16th: Was examined in two books of Homer.

October 17th: Was examined in Five Books of the eclogues of Virgil.

Then we have a gap. For whatever reason, probably just because he was totally engrossed in studying, he wrote nothing else in his diary until December 4th – when there was cause for celebration.

December 4th: Passed my examination.

December 5th: Took my degree. Dined at High Table and wined in the Common Room. Gave breakfast at Dickenson's, [Dickenson's bill for the term came to a whopping £1,000] was made a member of The Common Room. Wrote to my Father and Pen.

He had succeeded. His mother was delighted and sent him a gold watch, which he took to be engraved with a crest, and he set off for a few days in London where he met Penelope. The fare cost him £85 and he spent about £120 whilst he was in London. They spent two happy days going to exhibitions and to see the panorama of the Battle of Waterloo, a superb representation of the battle in a rotunda at the foot of Lion Hill. The very realistic circular panoramic mural (110 metres long by 12 metres high) showed Marshal Ney's first charge against the Allied infantry. Penelope gave him a gold ring.

From January 1821 to the end of April, John stayed at Ashcombe, spending a great deal of time with Penelope and following the usual pursuits of young country gentleman – hunting, shooting, riding, going to balls and assisting in the running of the estate. It was a happy and relaxed time. In May he returned to Oxford and it was to be a term of pleasure. To gain his MA he had to spend a residential term. He had to attend Divinity Lectures – but other than that it was all boating, cricket and dining. The river sports were slightly soured at the end of term by a confrontation between Brasenose and Jesus when the Jesus flag was destroyed. With Herodotus and Caesar behind him, John could now read for pleasure. He recorded finishing *The Black Dwarf* and *Old Mortality*, both by Sir Walter Scott, for which he paid about £2.50 a copy.

> June 5th: Began 'The Favourite of Nature' – a novel.

> June 6th: Maddock asked me to wine with him but I excused myself. Read most of the second volume of 'The Favourite of Nature'.

> June 8th: Finished 'The Favourite of Nature'. Was never more affected with a book than with it.

With attendance at one more Divinity lecture on June 23rd, the academic work of the term was completed – the rest was given over to sport and pleasure – though it seems to have been a very wet summer which somewhat spoilt things. On his last morning John records, 'I gave a chaw this morning' – possibly a tobacco chewing party, though that is the first mention of such a thing. He began to prepare to leave Oxford and go home. He sold a lot of books back to Talboys for about £350 and then on June 28th sent most of his other goods and the books he wanted to keep back to Ashcombe by canal, which was then the easiest and cheapest way of transporting heavy and bulky items. He settled his bills, his brother Ralph returned to Ashcombe, and with the £60 he still had left, John set off to row to London with friends – a final extravagant row of about 108 miles followed by outings in London.

> July 4th: Puxley, Bulteel, Stephen, Dixon, Boughton, Slade, Taggitt and I took our 8 oar boat to Reading. We left Oxford between 2 and 3.

> July 5th: We left Slade at Reading to ride to Eton and the rest of the crew rowed there.
> Penny, Tysson and Wilson met us there. We all dined together.

July 6th: We rowed from Eton to Westminster. We all dined at Richmond where we waited for some time for the return of the tide.

July 7th: Slade and I went to the Haymarket Theatre.

July 8th: Slade and I dined at Rosslyn House and rode in the Park. Saw Westminster school.

July 9th: Penny, Wilson, Puxley, Slade, Bulteel, and I dined at St George's Café in Coventry Street. We got a capital dinner and then went to Covent Garden Theatre.

July 10th: Left London at 2 o'clock.

His Oxford days were over. The following January John Sneyd married his cousin Penelope, took up the curacy of Odstone in Leicestershire and started on his long and difficult life which was to bring some early success but later deep sorrow. The lavish and uncontrolled spending, so evident in his Oxford diaries, was to continue into adulthood. He borrowed recklessly, invested unwisely, and by the end of 1832 he owed nearly £360,000 to eighteen people – many of whom were his own tenants. Only the support of loyal friends, and a lengthy sojourn abroad out of his creditors' reach, saved him from the humiliation of bankruptcy.

He was a difficult and self-opinionated man, alienating many people – including members of his own family – throughout his life. He died in 1871 aged seventy-four: his eldest son, John William, refused to attend his funeral. They had quarrelled irrevocably back in the 1840s over John Sneyd's obsession with copper mining and his mismanagement of the family finances. John Sneyd could not accept criticism, least of all from his son, and John William was disinherited of the family estate. Consequently John Sneyd never knew his grandson, Ralph De Tunstall Sneyd – little 'Ralphy' – who was the subject of the first chapter in this book.

The Reverend John Sneyd c.1830

Endnotes

1 Diaries of John Sneyd, 1817-1821, Keele University Library Special Collections.

2 From this point on all the figures for money are quoted at an approximation of 2015 values to give a clearer idea of just how much John Sneyd was spending.

3 Examinations held in the Bodleian Library.

4 See Inder, Pam and Aldis, Marion, *Thirty Pieces of Silver. John's Sneyd's Diary 1815 – 1871,* Churnet Valley Books, 1998.

5 *Sermons and lectures on The New Testament* by Bishop Beilby Porteus, published and printed in the early nineteenth century. They have frequently been re-printed and can still be bought online.

Conclusion

This book has dealt with the experiences of individuals in particular schools at specific times. As such, it would be a mistake to base too many generalisations on these findings. Not only did schools change over time – then, as now, a new head teacher could alter the ethos and atmosphere of a school within a matter of weeks – but not all children reacted to their surroundings in the same way. Not all Mrs Priest's pupils were traumatised for life like Frederick Hibgame, for example. Mary Mann and her brother Willie were pupils at the same school, with the same teachers, but seem to have suffered no lasting ill effects – though admittedly they were not boarders and were not there for as long. But such differences do not negate the value of examining individual experiences, and some general themes do emerge.

To modern readers it is astonishing how much freedom quite young children were allowed in the nineteenth century. Children like Ralph Sneyd or the boarders at Brookfield wandered the fields and woods, swam in rivers and skated on frozen lakes with minimal supervision. Young Charles Longsdon and others like him travelled alone across the country on coaches and trains. Accidents must have occurred from time to time, but most children seem to have learnt to behave responsibly and to look after each other.

Despite teaching methods that may seem to modern eyes uninspiring at best and unbelievably tedious at worst, nearly all the children in this book became literate adults and many were imbued with a lifelong love of learning. In the nineteenth century teachers did not believe children needed to be stimulated or entertained: they perhaps believed that for children to do boring tasks without question or complaint was a useful skill in its own right. And despite what might seem to have been a very limited school curriculum, there is no doubt that the nineteenth century produced more than its fair share of scientists, engineers, poets, artists, writers and original thinkers.

Many writers on education have fixated upon the cruelty perpetrated on children in nineteenth-century schools, but while undoubtedly many children were beaten and punished, this does not feature in the children's – or teachers' – accounts to any extent. It is probably understandable that children would not record their own punishments in diaries kept for their parents to read – but one might have supposed the punishments meted out to others would have merited a comment if only to highlight the diarist's own good behaviour. It might be that punishment was so commonplace as not to be considered worth recording – or that draconian punishments were less universal than we have been led to suppose. Certainly it is revealing that parents of National School children were quite prepared to remove them from school – and risk a fine for so doing – as a protest against what they saw as unfair punishment.

It is also worth noting that the quality of education to which the National and Board schools aspired, especially after 1870, was impressive. The concepts of national standards, external monitoring, and teachers who had been trained to teach, were quite innovative – and they are concepts that inform educational practice to this day. Practice may not have matched theory – but that does not lessen the breadth of the ambition. It is probably not much of an exaggeration to say that many of us – writers and readers – are literate and numerate as a direct result of Forster's Education Act of 1870.

And finally, the apparent mismatch between education and achievement in later life is worthy of comment. Gerald Upcher, Emma Longsdon and John Sneyd followed the career paths mapped out for them, but Ronnie Love/Fred Hibgame, despite being mystified and terrified by his teachers, went on to become a historian and antiquarian and wrote a book on the history of Norwich. Ralph De Tunstall Sneyd's spelling was idiosyncratic at best – but he became a published poet. Sarah Jane Perry trained to earn her living at a craft that was in decline even before she was born; nonetheless she ended life as a woman of independent means. The Tweddle boys missed more school than they attended, yet two of them went on to run their own businesses. Perhaps the achievements of our nineteenth-century forbears should give us pause for thought when considering today's education system.

Further Reading

Baker, E, *A Victorian Schoolboy in London. The Diary of Ernest Baker*, The Geoffrye Museum, London, 1989

Barnard, H C, *Were Those the Days? Victorian Education*, Pergamon Press, Oxford, 1970

Chandos, John, *Boys Together – English Public Schools 1800 – 1864*, Yale University Press, 2007

Creighton, Ellen R C (ed), *Ellen Buxton's Journal 1860 – 1864*, Geoffrey Bles. London, 1967

Hardy, Sheila M, *The Diary of a Suffolk Farmer's Wife 1854 – 1869*, Palgrave Macmillan, Basingstoke, 1992

Horn, Pamela, *The Victorian Country Child*, Sutton, Stroud, 1997

Horn, Pamela, *The Victorian Town Child*, Sutton, Stroud, 1999

Horn, Pamela, *The Victorian and Edwardian School Child*, Amberley, Stroud, 2010

Hughes, Mary Vivien, *A London Child of the 1870s*, Persephone, London, 2005

Hughes, Mary Vivien, *A London Girl of the 1880s*, Oxford Paperbacks, 1978

Hughes, Thomas, *Tom Brown's Schooldays*, first published 1857

Inder, Pam and Aldis, Marion, *John Sneyd's Diary 1815-1871*, *Thirty Pieces of Silver*, Churnet Valley Books, Leek, 1998

Inder, Pam and Aldis, Marion, *Finding Susanna*, Churnet Valley Books, Leek, 2002

Inder, Pam and Aldis, Marion, *Finding Ralphy*, Churnet Valley Books, Leek, 2005

Inder, Pam and Aldis, Marion, *Nine Forgotten Histories, Staffordshire Women*, History Press, Stroud, 2010

Lacey, C A, *Barbara Leigh Smith Bodichon and the Langham Place Group*, Womens' Source Library, Routledge, London, 2010

Mann, Mary E, *Memories of Ronald Love*, Methuen, London, 1907

Mann, Mary E, *Bound Together*, Mills and Boon, London, 1910

Anne Marsh Caldwell, *Two Old Mens' Tales*, Saunders and Otley, 1834 – and numerous other titles

Naden, Constance C W, *The Complete Poetical Works of Constance Naden*, Nabu Press, Charleston SC, 2012

Pocock, John Thomas, *The Diary of a London Schoolboy 1826-1830*, Camden History Society, London, 1980

Raverat, Gwen, *Period Piece – A Cambridge Childhood*, Faber and Faber, London, 1952

Reed, D W, *The Friends' School Wigton*, WOSA, Wigton, 1954

Trevelyan, Raleigh, *The Diary of Raleigh Trevelyan, Schoolboy, April 1813 – July 1814*, Wigan Archives Service, 2011

Yallop, H J, *A History of the Honiton Lace Industry*, University of Exeter Press, 1992

INDEX

NB: 'Ordinary' school subjects such as reading, Latin, arithmetic and music are not separately indexed as they appear in almost every chapter. The names of school/university friends which are not given in full in the original source appear in inverted commas in this index